PIPE FITTINGS

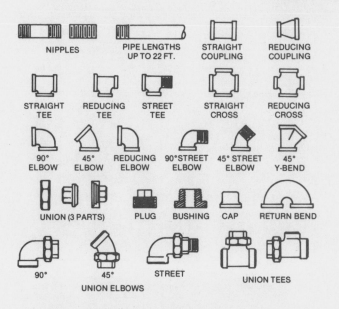
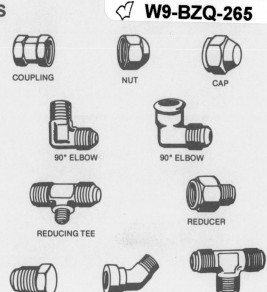

Here are the common steel pipe fittings. Nipples are simply short lengths of pipe threaded on both ends. Reducing fittings join two different sizes of pipe.

Compression fittings of the flared-tube type are the easiest for the novice to handle when working with copper tubing.

STANDARD STEEL PIPE
(All Dimensions in Inches)

Nominal Size	Outside Diameter	Inside Diameter	Nominal Size	Outside Diameter	Inside Diameter
1/8	0.405	0.269	1	1.315	1.049
1/4	0.540	0.364	1 1/4	1.660	1.380
3/8	0.675	0.493	1 1/2	1.900	1.610
1/2	0.840	0.622	2	2.375	2.067
3/4	1.050	0.824	2 1/2	2.875	2.469

SQUARE MEASURE
144 sq in = 1 sq ft
9 sq ft = 1 sq yd
272.25 sq ft = 1 sq rod
160 sq rods = 1 acre

VOLUME MEASURE
1728 cu in = 1 cu ft
27 cu ft = 1 cu yd

MEASURES OF CAPACITY
1 cup = 8 fl oz
2 cups = 1 pint
2 pints = 1 quart
4 quarts = 1 gallon
2 gallons = 1 peck
4 pecks = 1 bushel

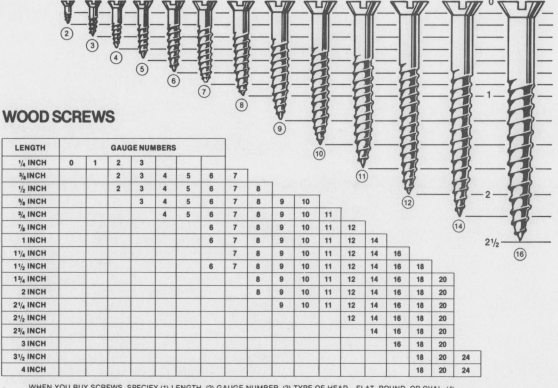

WOOD SCREWS

LENGTH	GAUGE NUMBERS														
	0	1	2	3	4	5	6	7	8	9	10	11	12	14	16	18	20	24
1/4 INCH	0	1	2	3											
3/8 INCH			2	3	4	5	6	7							
1/2 INCH			2	3	4	5	6	7	8						
5/8 INCH				3	4	5	6	7	8	9	10				
3/4 INCH					4	5	6	7	8	9	10	11			
7/8 INCH							6	7	8	9	10	11	12		
1 INCH							6	7	8	9	10	11	12	14	
1 1/4 INCH								7	8	9	10	11	12	14	16
1 1/2 INCH							6	7	8	9	10	11	12	14	16	18
1 3/4 INCH									8	9	10	11	12	14	16	18	20
2 INCH									8	9	10	11	12	14	16	18	20
2 1/4 INCH										9	10	11	12	14	16	18	20
2 1/2 INCH													12	14	16	18	20
2 3/4 INCH														14	16	18	20
3 INCH															16	18	20
3 1/2 INCH																18	20	24
4 INCH																18	20	24

WHEN YOU BUY SCREWS, SPECIFY (1) LENGTH, (2) GAUGE NUMBER, (3) TYPE OF HEAD—FLAT, ROUND, OR OVAL, (4) MATERIAL—STEEL, BRASS, BRONZE, ETC., (5) FINISH—BRIGHT, STEEL BLUED, CADMIUM, NICKEL, OR CHROMIUM PLATED.

GUIDE TO CAR CARE

Books in the series, or with the imprint, of the *Popular
Mechanics Do-It-Yourself Encyclopedia* are published in
close cooperation with the editorial staff of POPULAR
MECHANICS:

Editor-in-Chief: Joe Oldham
Managing Editor: Bill Hartford
Special Features Editor: Sheldon M. Gallager
Automotive Editor: Wade A. Hoyt, SAE
Home and Shop Editor: Steve Willson
Electronics Editor: Stephen A. Booth
Boating, Outdoors and Travel Editor: Timothy H. Cole
Science Editor: Dennis Eskow

The information in *Guide To Car Care* is based on material
originally published in POPULAR MECHANICS Magazine

do-it-yourself
GUIDE TO
CAR CARE

Edited by PAUL STENQUIST

HEARST BOOKS NEW YORK

The information published herein is based on material published in POPULAR MECHANICS Magazine. © 1982, 1983, 1984, 1985 by The Hearst Corporation

Coordinating Editor and Writer: Paul Stenquist
POPULAR MECHANICS Writers: Paul Stenquist, Mort Schultz, Brad Sears, and Pete Warren

Production Coordinator: Janet Kulesh
Book Design: A. Christopher Simon
Copyeditor: Wendy Fisher
Editorial Assistant: Cynthia W. Lockhart
Illustrations: Hank Iken, Ed Lipinski, George Retseck, Fred Wolfe, and Russel Von Sauer

Although every effort has been made to ensure the accuracy and completeness of the information in this book, Hearst Books and POPULAR MECHANICS make no guarantees, stated or implied, nor will they be liable in the event of misinterpretation or human error made by the reader, or for any typographical errors that may appear.

ISBN 0-87851-090-7
Library of Congress   85-80892
10 9 8 7 6 5 4 3 2 1
PRINTED IN THE UNITED STATES OF AMERICA

Contents

Introduction

PAUL STENQUIST

■ HELPING READERS TAKE BETTER care of their automobiles is one of the things *Popular Mechanics* does best. Every month except May, PM automotive writers focus their attention on one particular vehicle system and explain, in graphic detail, how a home mechanic can repair, trouble-shoot or service it. Called "Saturday Mechanic," the special sections include the very latest information. For May the same group of experts creates an extensive "Car Care Guide" that includes a variety of information designed to help simplify the very difficult job of keeping your auto in tip-top shape.

Over the years numerous driveway mechanics have saved PM car care articles in a box or binder so they could use them as a general reference source for solving automobile service problems. They've discovered that the information is much more detailed than that in the typical home mechanic automotive service guide and is an ideal supplement to the sometimes cursory instructions found in a car owner's manual. Because the PM articles were prepared one at a time, they treat each subject in depth.

It was only reasonable that some of the best Saturday Mechanic and Car Care Guide pieces be featured in a single book. Organized according to general subject area, the collection will prove a tremendously valuable ally for any weekend warrior who struggles with the problems of vehicle maintenance and repair.

The first part, "The Popular Mechanics Plan for Automobile Maintenance," is a step-by-step guide to preventive maintenance, an outline for taking care of your car. Most of the maintenance procedures that are outlined in this section are covered in greater detail in subsequent sections of the book.

Part II, "Outside Your Engine," includes articles that can help you solve nasty driveability and starting problems that are caused by the failure of external components like carburetors, emission control parts and sparkplugs.

Part III, "Inside Your Engine," explains the diagnosis and repair of cooling system and power train components.

Part IV, "Automobile Electricity and Electronics," includes features that deal with the service, diagnosis and repair of charging systems, starting systems, electronic ignitions and batteries.

Part V, "Drivetrain and Chassis," deals with a wide range of chassis and drivetrain subjects, including automatic transmission maintenance, power steering service, ball joint replacement and much more.

Part VI, "Comfort and Appearance," includes information that will enable you to care for the exterior of your car and better understand your car's air-conditioning system.

This book is a collection of previously published magazine articles and was designed to cover every aspect of every car. It is not intended to serve as a replacement for your repair manual. Its ideal use is in combination with a manual. With its extensive background information and detailed how-to procedures, it can help you develop strategies for dealing with your car on a week-by-week basis.

Part I:

THE POPULAR MECHANICS PLAN FOR AUTOMOBILE MAINTENANCE

New or old, any car will live longer with tender loving care

■ FOR MOST SATURDAY MECHANICS, a large part of the joy of owning a car lies in getting their hands dirty. If you really want to develop an intimate relationship with a machine, there is no better way than to crawl under it and over it, to take it apart and put it back together, to clean it and polish it.

But the benefits of doing it yourself are more than spiritual. If you live with a car long enough, you'll eventually come to know it so well that even the most insignificant faults will immediately be recognizable, and you'll be able to anticipate the need for repairs before serious problems develop.

The key to establishing this kind of relationship

with your car is a systematic approach to maintenance and repair. In the following pages, you'll find outlined a plan for car care that will help whip any car into shape and keep it there.

A helping hand

Before you even think about diving under that prized hunk of iron, you should equip yourself with as much information as possible. Ideally, you should obtain a copy of the vehicle manufacturer's service manual for your car.

If you can't obtain the factory book for your car, general service manuals, which cover most domestic makes, are available for early-model cars. Motor Publications (555 West 57th St., New York, N.Y.

10019) publishes the *Motor Auto Repair Manual.* Published every year, it covers the previous six years. For older cars, Motor publishes "Vintage" editions.

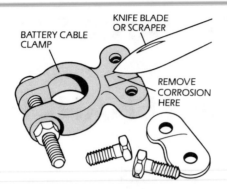

1 Battery cable terminals must be kept corrosion free to ensure reliable starting.

Battery

A battery checkup is a good place to begin the maintenance procedure. This check should be repeated at 15,000-mile intervals or when a problem arises. The battery cleanup part of the procedure should be performed every time you change oil.

Begin by removing the battery terminals, negative cable first. Then, use a small brush to clean all parts of the battery and terminals with a paste made from baking soda and water. Remove corroded metal inside the terminals and from the battery posts using a small knife or a battery-post cleaning tool. A three-cornered bearing knife works better than a flat-bladed knife.

If the terminals are attached to the cable by means of screw clamps, disassemble each clamp and clean it and the bare cable end with the paste and brush (Fig. 1). Scrape any corrosion from the terminal. This type of terminal is particularly subject to corrosion and must be cleaned at regular intervals. Your best bet is to replace a cable that has a screw-on terminal with one that has a conventional molded terminal.

If your battery is of the standard type—as opposed to a maintenance-free battery—remove the caps and check the electrolyte level. If it's not up to the indicated FULL level, add distilled water. If you add water when the temperature is below freezing, you must drive the car for at least 20 minutes.

Check the other ends of the cables—where the negative attaches to ground and where the positive connects to the relay or starter motor. Make sure that all connections are tight and free of corrosion. If not, disconnect the cable end. Clean it, and the post or

bolt it was attached to, with the paste and brush.

Reconnect all cables, starting with the ends that are not attached to the battery. Then connect the positive cable to the battery *before* connecting the negative.

Hydrometer checks

If your battery is equipped with filler caps, you can determine its state of charge by checking the specific gravity of the electrolyte solution with a battery hydrometer. The hydrometer reading must be corrected for temperature. If readings vary by more than .05, the battery should be replaced. See the instructions for your hydrometer.

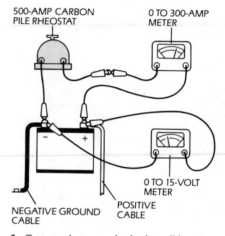

2 To test a battery under load conditions, an adjustable carbon pile can be used.

Many maintenance-free batteries have a built-in hydrometer that indicates approximate state of charge by changing color. In most cases a green eye indicates fully charged, a dark eye indicates a discharged condition, and a clear or white eye indicates that the battery is bad and cannot be charged.

If you don't have a hydrometer, you can get a general idea of battery charge level by measuring voltage. With the engine off, the battery should store at least 13.5 volts. If you've just charged the battery, turn the lights on for 15 seconds before measuring voltage.

If your hydrometer check or voltage test indicates that the battery is not fully charged, connect a trickle charger for several hours or until you get a fully charged indication. Some maintenance-free batteries that have been almost fully discharged have to be charged with a high-amperage service station type charger for a long period of time. If any battery won't eventually come to full charge, it's defective and must be replaced.

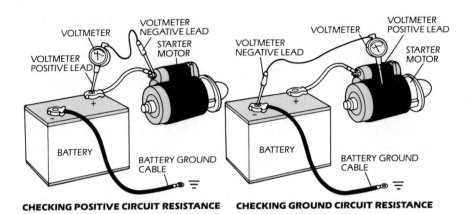

3 If the battery passes a cranking capacity test, but the engine still cranks slowly, check both the positive and negative starter motor circuits for excessive resistance.

CHECKING POSITIVE CIRCUIT RESISTANCE   CHECKING GROUND CIRCUIT RESISTANCE

If your voltage check or hydrometer reading indicates that the battery is charged, it should be load tested to determine its cranking capability. Ideally, you should use an adjustable carbon pile to load the battery while you take a voltage reading (Fig. 2). The amount of load that a specific battery should be able to handle can be found in the service manual. In most cases, it will be between 150 and 270 amps.

If you don't have a carbon pile, load the battery by cranking the engine with the coil wire removed and attached to ground. On GM cars with HEI ignition, disconnect the wire that is attached to the distributor's BAT terminal. The battery should be able to provide 9.6 volts while cranking the engine for at least 15 seconds at 70° F. At 30° F. you should measure at least 9.1 volts, at 0°, 8.5 volts.

If the battery is not able to maintain voltage under load but appears to be fully charged when the load test begins, it's worn out and must be replaced. Batteries are not supposed to last forever. Four years is about the limit for most.

Resistance tests

If you find that your battery does produce enough voltage during the cranking test but the engine still doesn't turn fast enough to start, check for excessive circuit resistance (Fig. 3). To check positive-circuit resistance, connect a voltmeter's lead to the positive battery post and its negative lead to the relay terminal or to the starter motor's positive terminal (the big one). The meter should read less than 0.5-volt. Check ground circuit resistance by connecting the negative voltmeter lead to the negative battery post and positive lead to the starter housing. Voltage should be less than 0.2-volt. If either voltage check exceeds maximum, there is too much resistance in that circuit, probably due to a bad cable. Replace suspect cables and check connections again.

If the resistance test does not reveal a problem, either the starter motor or the solenoid/relay is

defective. If both prove to be okay, the engine is suffering from an internal problem that makes it hard to turn. Should the battery take a charge and pass the load test but discharge while driving, there's trouble in the charging system. Further testing will determine whether the alternator, regulator or wiring is to blame. Consult a manual for troubleshooting procedures.

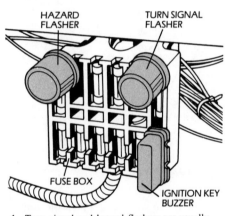

4 Turn signal and hazard flashers are usually mounted under the dash, in fuse box.

Lights and accessories

Once you've determined that the starting circuit functions as it should, check the brakelights, taillights, turn signals, headlights and other electric accessories to make sure they operate. It's a good idea to check operation of all lights every time you change oil. Check other electric accessories as problems arise.

If you find that a single bulb is out, remove it and check the filament visually, with a test light or with an ohmmeter. Clean the bulb contacts before installing a new one. Should that fail to solve the problem, check for voltage at the light socket connector and ground. If it's lacking, trace the wire, checking for voltage at various points with a test light needle probe by piercing the insulation.

Maybe the taillights and brake lights work but turn signals don't. Try replacing the flasher unit. In most cars, it's a small metal can that can be found under the dashboard or in the area of the fuse box (Fig. 4).

In cases where all brake lights, taillights or turn signals are out, check the fuses. If just the brake lights are out, replace the brake light switch. On most later model cars, it's a mechanical switch near the brake pedal. Earlier models have a hydraulic switch at the end of the master cylinder.

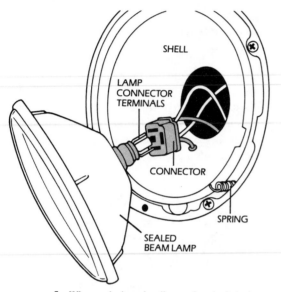

5   When replacing a headlamp, clean both the lamp and connector terminals.

Headlight problems

If one headlight is inoperative, replace the unit, clean the connector and tighten (Fig. 5). If lights are dim, check the connection between the headlight mount and body ground.

When both headlights are out or flash on and off, check for a loose connection at the dimmer switch and the headlight switch. You say that doesn't help? Check for voltage at the dimmer switch with a test lamp. If the test lamp lights only on the switch side (hot wire side) of the dimmer, replace the dimmer switch. Should the test lamp fail to light on the hot side of the dimmer switch, check wiring from the headlight switch to dimmer with a test lamp. In the event that there's still no voltage, check the hot wire terminal on the headlight switch for voltage. If the test lamp does not light, repair the wire from the battery to the switch. There may be a fusible link in this wire that is the source of the problem.

If you find that voltage is available on the hot wire side of the headlight switch but not on the output side (with the switch turned on), replace the headlight switch.

In cases where the headlights flicker after a few minutes of operation, there is probably a short to ground in the circuit between the battery and the headlight switch. The flickering may be accompanied by a clicking noise from the headlight switch. Repair any shorts in the wire from the battery to the light switch and check the lights again. If they still flicker, the circuit breaker in the headlight switch has been damaged by the short and the switch must be replaced.

Troubleshoot other failed electric components in a similar manner. After checking fuses, test for voltage at the component. If no voltage is available, trace back along the wire with your test light until you locate the source of the trouble (either an open circuit or a defective switch). If voltage is available at the component, the problem, of course, is in the device itself.

Engine cleanup

To make it easier to service your car, clean up the engine compartment. Buy two cans of aerosol-spray engine cleaner, available through most auto parts stores. If possible, take the car to a self-service car wash with high-pressure hot water wands, or use your garden hose attached to a hot water tap.

Cover the alternator, distributor cap and coil with plastic bags, securing them with string. Remove air cleaner and cover the carburetor in a similar fashion. Following the directions on the can, spray the cleaner liberally all over the engine and engine compartment, avoiding electronic or electric components. Allow it to soak in a few minutes, then hose it off. If the engine is not clean, repeat the procedure using a

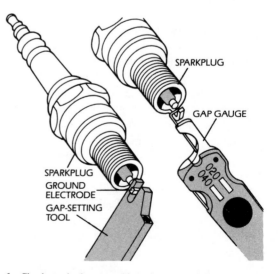

6   Check spark plug gap with a wire gauge. Adjust by bending the ground electrode.

small brush to work the cleaner into particularly dirty spots. Don't allow the cleaner to come into contact with your skin.

If the engine won't start when you've finished, clean any moisture from distributor and coil wire cables, then spray them with a water-displacing lubricant.

Engine tuneup

The complete powerplant maintenance procedure should be performed when you first purchase a car and at regular intervals thereafter. For cars with contact breaker (points) ignition, plan on doing this service at 10,000-mile intervals. For cars with high-energy electronic systems, perform the service at 15,000- to 20,000-mile intervals.

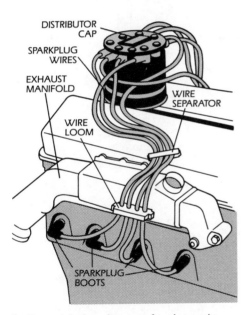

7 Keep spark plug wires away from hot manifolds with wire looms and separators.

Some enthusiasts replace all high-wear items when they first purchase their classics. This strategy will give you a baseline for future reference—you'll know just how old these components are. Maintenance items include air filter, PCV valve, sparkplugs, fuel filter, distributor cap and rotor, ignition cables, and, in cars with contact breaker ignition, points and condenser.

Begin the maintenance tuneup by removing all of the sparkplugs. Carefully note the condition of the old plugs. Depending on type of fuel used and model year of the car, their color can range from white to gray to light brown. However, it should be clear that all of them were operating. None should be markedly darker than the others and all of them should be dry.

Compression testing

If some of the plugs look wet and oily, you should perform a compression test. Before you can test compression, you have to arrange some means of holding the throttle and the choke open. Then, disconnect the negative wire from the coil and cover its terminal end with a piece of electrical tape. On GM HEI systems, disconnect the wire from the BAT terminal of the distributor.

With a compression gauge held firmly in place or threaded into the No. 1 sparkplug hole, crank the engine five revolutions or until the gauge goes no higher. Write down the compression reading and move on to the next cylinder, cranking the engine the same number of revolutions. Continue until all cylinders have been tested, and compare your readings. All should be within 75 percent of your strongest cylinder and each should at least reach the minimum pressure found in the spec table of your repair manual. If readings are not up to spec, further diagnosis will be necessary to determine the cause.

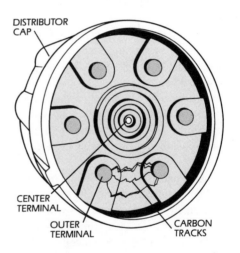

8 Replace the distributor cap if any signs of carbon tracking are found inside.

If your car has high-energy electronic ignition and if the plugs look okay and are no more than 15,000 miles old, you may want to clean and regap them. Check for rounding of the sharp edges on both inner and ground electrodes. If they look good and are all nearly the same color, clean them with a wire brush and a sharp awl or knitting needle. Use the awl to clean any deposits from around the insulator. Take care not to break the ceramic insulator body. On cars with contact breaker ignition, sparkplugs should be replaced at 10,000-mile intervals regardless of condition.

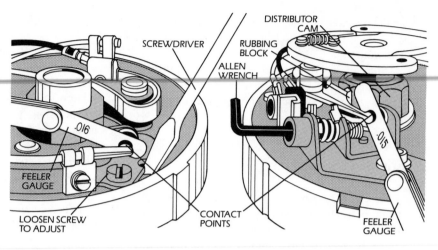

9 Set contact point gap with a feeler gauge after positioning the rubbing block on the high point of the distributor cam. Adjust with a screwdriver or Allen wrench.

Replacing the plugs

Before installing the plugs, check the gap with a wire sparkplug gauge (Fig. 6). Use the gap tool to bend the electrode if the gap is not to specs. Don't try to close the gap by hammering the electrode. You could crack the insulator.

Reinstall the plugs, starting each one by hand to make sure it doesn't cross thread. If possible, tighten them to 20 ft.-lb. with a torque wrench. In any case, don't overtighten them. If you can't reach the sparkplug hole easily, try slipping a length of rubber hose over the terminal end of the plug. This will act as an extension handle.

Inspect the plug wires for checking, cracks, burns, brittleness or other visible damage. Clean any corrosion from the terminals. The boots must fit securely on both the plugs and the cap. Replace the set if any are damaged.

Install new wires one at a time as the old ones are removed. Take care to use all looms and separators. This can be extremely important in cases where the exhaust manifolds are close to the plugs (Fig. 7). Premium grade hypalon-type or silicone rubber jacketed plug wires—such as those used on high-energy ignition applications—offer far better heat and current-leakage protection than conventional wires.

Checking the cap and rotor

Once the wires are installed, remove the distributor cap and clean the inside with a dry rag. Look for cracks, fractures or any evidence of carbon tracking (Fig. 8). Carbon tracks are lines running from one outer terminal to another or from one terminal to the center terminal. If tracking or physical damage is noted, replace the cap. If the cap looks okay, clean

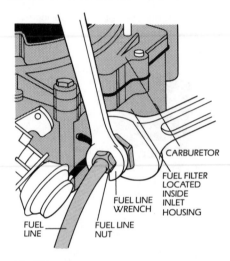

10 When disconnecting a fuel line for service, use two wrenches to prevent damage.

all corrosion from the terminals. If it cannot be scraped from the terminals with a small knife, replace the cap.

Remove the rotor and examine it. It should be replaced if it is cracked, chipped or carbon tracked. Clean corrosion from the tip with a knife. If the rotor is to the point where it cannot be cleaned easily, it should be replaced.

On cars with electronic ignition, the distributor service ends here, assuming of course that there has been no ignition-related performance problem. If an ignition problem is affecting engine operation, diagnostic procedures must be performed. This differs from car to car, and in some cases substitution testing with known good parts is part of the procedure. Therefore, you may want to let a dealer or large independent service facility handle such problems. They're also equipped with an oscilloscope, which can confirm the presence of an ignition fault.

Replacing the points

If your car has a contact breaker ignition system, replace the points and condenser. Begin by rotating the engine until the rubbing block of the points is on the high point of the distributor cam. Disconnect the distributor's primary wire and the condenser wire from the points before removing the points and condenser. Don't drop the screws or you may have to spend hours recovering them. On many cars, the screws that hold the points need only be loosened for removal.

Install the new points and condenser and attach both wires to the points. With the rubbing block of the contact set touching a high point of the distributor cam, adjust the point gap to specification using a feeler gauge (Fig. 9).

Lubricate the distributor cam with a small amount of cam lubricant or white lithium grease. A very small amount is enough. Don't overdo it. If the distributor is equipped with a lubricating wick that touches the cam, don't attempt to oil it. Replace it instead. Reinstall the distributor rotor and cap. If you have a dwell meter, start the engine and check point dwell. Readjust if necessary.

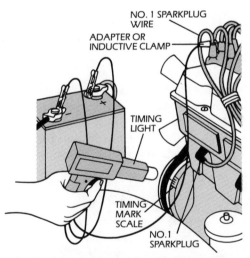

NO. 1 SPARKPLUG WIRE
ADAPTER OR INDUCTIVE CLAMP
TIMING LIGHT
TIMING MARK SCALE
NO.1 SPARKPLUG

11 Check spark advance setting with a timing light wired to number one plug.

Choke adjustment

Remove the air cleaner and check the filter. If it appears dirty, replace it.

Replace the fuel filter. On most cars, it's in the fuel line or behind the inlet fitting on the carburetor (Fig. 10).

Clean the choke mechanism and carb linkage with carburetor cleaner. Then, start the engine and ob-

serve the operation of the choke. If the engine is cold, the choke should snap closed and the throttle should come to rest on the fast-idle cam when you open and close the throttle. If it doesn't, adjust the choke and fast idle according to manufacturer's specs. As the engine warms, the choke should gradually open and when you rev the warm engine, the idle speed should drop. If the choke system doesn't permit the cold engine to run without hesitation or stumbling, adjustment is necessary.

Checking the timing

Warm the engine and check ignition timing with a timing light (Fig. 11). On late-model cars, you'll find specs and general instructions on the vehicle information label under the hood.

Once you've checked initial spark advance, check vacuum advance by accelerating the engine to 1,500 rpm. Then, while holding it at this speed, connect the vacuum advance line to the distributor. Timing should advance. If not, replace the vacuum diaphragm unit.

Disconnect the vacuum advance line and check centrifugal advance by accelerating the engine to 3,500 rpm while watching the timing marks with your light. Timing should advance. If it doesn't, remove the distributor cap and check the centrifugal weights for binding on applications where weights are located directly under the rotor (Fig. 12). Where weights are not located under the rotor, the distributor will have to be removed and disassembled to service the centrifugal advance mechanism. The latest engines have no vacuum or centrifugal advance, as a computer controls engine timing.

PCV valves

Replace the PCV valve and the PCV filter every 30,000 miles. Check and clean them every 15,000 miles. To check the PCV valve, remove it from the intake manifold or rocker cover and start the engine. Check for vacuum at the end of the valve with your thumb (Fig. 13). If you feel nothing, the valve or hose is clogged. Replace any hoses that don't look good. If vacuum is present and the hoses look okay, shut off the engine and remove the valve. Shake it. You should hear the needle rattle inside. If it doesn't rattle, the valve must be replaced.

Before you call your maintenance tuneup complete, you should check the condition and connections of all vacuum hoses. If they're cracked or brittle, replace them. A vacuum leak will make the best tuned engine idle roughly.

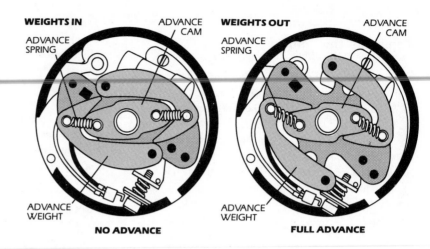

WEIGHTS IN   ADVANCE CAM   WEIGHTS OUT   ADVANCE CAM

ADVANCE SPRING   ADVANCE SPRING

ADVANCE WEIGHT   ADVANCE WEIGHT

NO ADVANCE   FULL ADVANCE

12 If a check of centrifugal advance shows that timing isn't advancing as the engine is accelerated, check for binding or sticking of the distributor advance weights.

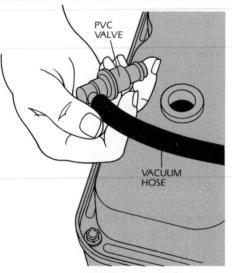

PVC VALVE

VACUUM HOSE

13 With engine running, check PCV system by feeling for vacuum at valve end.

Lube service

If you want to prolong the life of the engine and suspension parts, you should change your oil and lube your chassis at 3,000-mile intervals. While some manufacturers recommend far longer oil-change intervals, most mechanics will tell you that the best thing you can do to make your engine last a long time, particularly with an older car, is to change the oil frequently.

Warm the engine completely before changing the oil. Drive the car for at least 20 minutes. Idling it in the driveway won't make it warm enough. Once the engine is warm, shut it off and raise the car on jackstands or ramps. To do the job correctly, the car must be level. This means you'll have to lift the front and rear. Getting the car up in the air will also allow you to inspect the chassis components and other undercar parts.

Place a drain pan that is large enough to hold all the oil under the car. Use a socket wrench or box wrench to remove the drain plug. If the plug has a square hole in its center, use the square drive of a ratchet to loosen it. Allow the warm oil to drain completely.

While the oil is draining, remove the filter. If your drain pan doesn't extend to the area of the filter, use another pan to catch the filter spillage or wait until the oil has drained. Don't shortchange the drain time, though. Make sure the oil has stopped dripping from the plug hole.

Oil filter removal

Use a filter wrench to loosen the canister-type filters that are found on nearly all late-model vehicles (Fig. 14). Make sure the old gasket comes off with the filter. Clean the filter mounting area and partially fill the new filter with some of the oil that will be

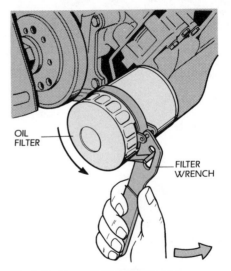

OIL FILTER

FILTER WRENCH

14 A band-type oil filter wrench grips securely to make removal clean and simple.

used to fill the crankcase. Lube the filter gasket with the clean oil as well (Fig. 15). Install the filter, tightening it according to the directions printed on it.

Cars that are more than 20 years old may have a cartridge-style oil filter, contained within a metal can. The can is held onto the mount by means of a bolt through its center. Remove the filter by loosening the bolt. Dump the old cartridge into your drain pan, and clean the can thoroughly with solvent and a brush. Install the new filter element in the can and lube the gasket with engine oil. Make sure that the old gasket has been removed, and reinstall the filter can.

Once you're sure that the oil has drained completely, reinstall the drain plug. Tighten it with moderation. Use a wrench no longer than 10 in. and *don't* make it as tight as you possibly can.

Choosing an oil

Check your owner's manual to determine proper refill oil if your car is relatively new or under warranty. Carmakers recommend SF grade oils for the latest gasoline engines and SF/CC or SF/CD oils for the latest diesels. Some, most notably General Motors, prohibit use of certain viscosities. For older high-mileage cars, use an SF 10W40 multigrade oil in winter and an SF 20W50 in summer. If your car has a new engine, use SF 5W30 in winter and SF 10W40 in summer.

Fill the crankcase with the correct amount of oil and run it for a few minutes, checking the leaks from the filter or drain plug. Shut it off and check oil level on the dipstick.

Chassis lubrication

Lubricate all steering and suspension joints with water-resistant EP chassis lube (Fig. 16). If the

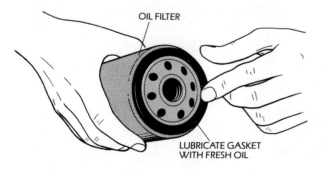

15   Before installing a new oil filter, lubricate the gasket with fresh engine oil.

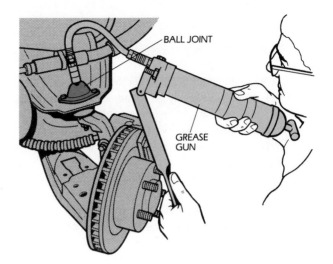

16   Snap the coupling of the grease gun onto the grease fitting and pump grease in until the dust boot begins to swell or until grease is forced out the bottom of the joint.

chassis parts are not equipped with grease fittings, you may be able to install them in some components by removing the screw-in plug (Fig. 17). If a part doesn't seem to be taking any grease, wiggle it a bit. Continue pumping in grease until the dust cover of the suspension joints swells.

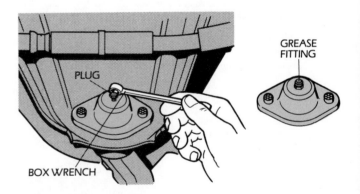

17   On some vehicles, chassis joints may be fitted with plugs rather than grease fittings. Remove the plugs with a box wrench and thread grease fittings into place.

Check the level of differential lube and manual transmission lube. Differential lube and transmission lube levels usually are checked by removing a plug from the side of the unit. Most cars use hypoid-type lube in the rear end. Some cars that are equipped with limited-slip–type rear ends require special lubricants. For most rear-drive cars, the lube that is used in the rear end is also used in the manual transmission. Check your shop manual or owner's manual. Manual transaxles in front-drive cars generally are lubed with automatic transmission fluid.

Automatic transmission service

Check the fluid level in automatic transmissions after driving for about 10 minutes. Idle the engine and leave the trans lever in the PARK position. If the fluid level is low, make sure you use the recommended type of automatic transmission fluid for your brand of car.

Change the automatic trans fluid and filter at 30,000-mile intervals. If your trans pan is not equipped with a drain plug, remove all bolts except one and allow the fluid to drain from a corner of the pan.

Lube other moving parts under the car, like gearshift linkages and parking brake mechanisms, with a few drops of engine oil. Use a small squirt can.

Open the hood and lube the accelerator linkage and hood hinge mechanism with engine oil. Clean the hood latch mechanism and apply a light coating of lithium grease.

Use engine oil to lube the trunk lock and hinge mechanisms. Lightly coat the door latch mechanisms with lithium grease. If the hinges squeak, apply a few drops of the engine oil.

Check the level of the power steering fluid, and top it off if necessary (Fig. 18). Most older power steering pumps take automatic trans fluid. Some newer units require special power steering fluid.

Check the brake fluid level in one or both master cylinder reservoirs. Use only DOT 3 fluid to top it off. Make sure that the can of fluid you use is fresh and tightly sealed.

Undercar inspection

Every time you have your car up on jackstands for an oil change, you should perform at least a basic undercar inspection. Check all exhaust system components for possible leaks or deterioration. Make sure all the hangers are intact and in good condition.

Look for areas where the undercoating has fallen off. Remove any dirt, sand off any rust and recoat the area with aerosol can undercoating, which is available at auto parts stores.

Check all rubber bushings and dust boots for obvious deterioration. Pay particular attention to those bushings found at each end of front or rear sway bars, as well as those that hold the center of the sway bar to the frame. The bushings used on front and rear control arms are also potential problem areas (Fig. 19). If bushings have shrunk or shredded, handling will suffer and in many cases the component will produce a lot of noise.

Check engine and transmission mounts for looseness or cracking of rubber parts. A broken engine mount that allows the engine to rise up from its proper location can be more than an annoyance. In some cases it can make the throttle stick open.

18   Power steering fluid level is read on a dipstick, usually attached to the fluid reservoir cap. Clean the surrounding area to keep dirt from entering and ruining the pump.

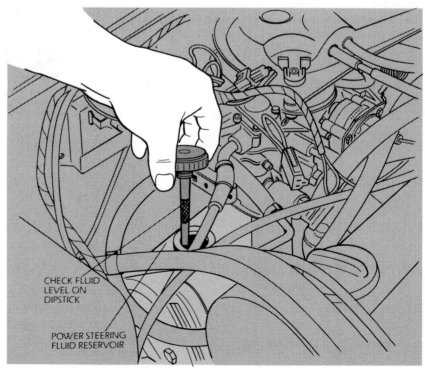

CHECK FLUID
LEVEL ON
DIPSTICK

POWER STEERING
FLUID RESERVOIR

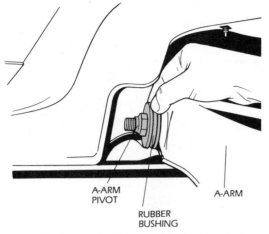

19 Inspect all rubber suspension bushings for drying, cracking or shredding.

Inspecting ball joints

Every 15,000 miles your undercar inspection should include a check of steering and suspension components. Begin by checking ball joint condition. Cars with upper and lower control arms have both loaded and unloaded ball joints. Most mechanics check the condition of the loaded joints only. If these are okay, the unloaded joints should be okay as well. Of course, if the loaded joints have been replaced,

they could be in better shape than their weak sisters.

The loaded ball joint is the one that carries the spring. If the spring is mounted on the upper control arm, then the upper joint is the loaded joint. If the spring is on the lower control arm, the lower joint is the loaded joint. To check a loaded ball joint for looseness, the load must be relieved (Fig. 20).

On cars where the coil spring is mounted on the lower control arm, relieve the load by placing a jack under the control arm as close to the joint as possible. On vehicles where the spring is mounted on the upper control arm, a block of wood should be wedged between the control arm and the frame, and the car should be lifted at the crossmember until the wheels just leave the ground. Jackstands must then be located on the frame to support the car.

Check axial (up and down) movement of either type of joint by inserting a pry bar between the bottom of the tire and the floor, then lifting the wheel. The joint should allow the wheel no more than 0.05-in. free movement. You can measure axial movement precisely by mounting a dial indicator so its stem rests against the bottom surface of the wheel's knuckle. The stem must be parallel to the imaginary line that runs through the center of both joints. However, most mechanics forego the dial indicator. If there's a noticeable amount of axial movement, it's probably well in excess of 0.05-inch.

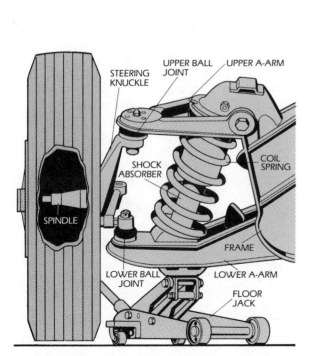

20 Check for play in loaded lower ball joints by jacking up the lower A-arm, placing the jack as close to the joint as possible.

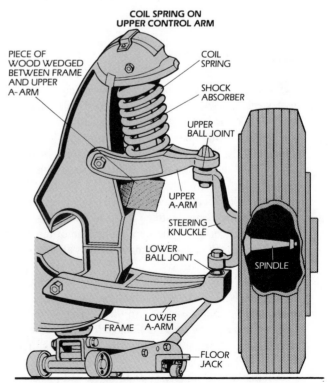

Relieve the weight from loaded upper ball joints with a wedge between A-arm and frame, then jacking car up at crossmember.

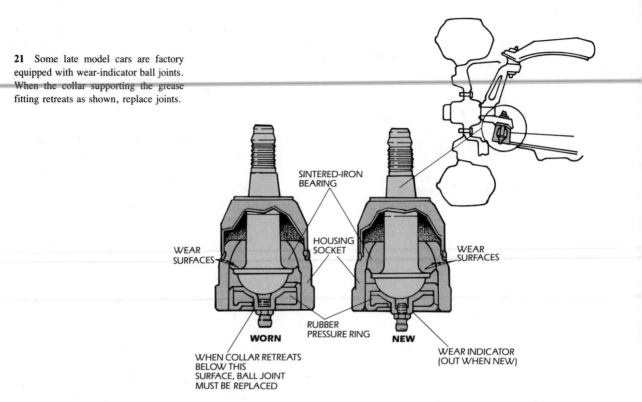

21 Some late model cars are factory equipped with wear-indicator ball joints. When the collar supporting the grease fitting retreats as shown, replace joints.

SINTERED-IRON
BEARING

HOUSING
SOCKET

WEAR
SURFACES

WEAR
SURFACES

RUBBER
PRESSURE RING

WORN   **NEW**

WHEN COLLAR RETREATS
BELOW THIS
SURFACE, BALL JOINT
MUST BE REPLACED

WEAR INDICATOR
(OUT WHEN NEW)

If you're not sure about how much axial movement the joint allows, check radial movement by pushing the bottom or top of the tire in and out (depending on which joint is the load carrier). More than ¼-in. of movement at the far edge of the tire is excessive.

Wear-indicator joints

Some cars produced after 1973 were equipped with wear-indicator ball joints as standard equipment (Fig. 21). Wear-indicator joints have a collar around the grease fitting that protrudes from the lower surface of the joint. As the joint wears, this collar sinks below the surface of the joint, indicating that replacement is necessary.

There are no specific recommended procedures for checking tie-rod ends, Pitman arm and idler arm—the parts that constitute the steering linkage of most cars (Fig. 22). But a little common sense is all that's required.

One good way to check these parts is to block the front wheels, completely prohibiting their movement, and have an assistant turn the steering wheel while you watch the steering linkage for movement at each joint. If a joint is sloppy, the component or rod end must be replaced.

Another way is simply to grab the tie rod pieces and shake them as hard as you can (Fig. 23). The idler arm and Pitman arm should show little or no

vertical movement, while the tie rod ends should not show unrestricted looseness. A torn dust boot on a tie rod end or other joint is reason for replacement.

On front-wheel-drive cars, check all CV joint dust boots for visible damage. Generally, unless a torn boot is discovered immediately, the joint will have to be replaced along the boot, since CV joints that are not protected from dirt deteriorate rapidly.

Shock absorbers and springs

Because they can cause a vehicle to handle erratically, worn springs and shocks can be as dangerous as they are uncomfortable.

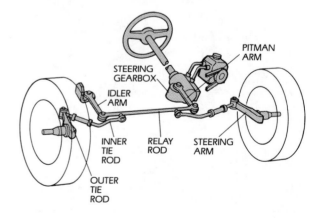

STEERING
GEARBOX

PITMAN
ARM

IDLER
ARM

INNER
TIE
ROD

RELAY
ROD

STEERING
ARM

OUTER
TIE
ROD

22 When checking steering joints, idler arm and Pitman arm should have no play at all.

To check spring condition, you have to determine if the car's body and frame are as high above the rear axle and front spindles as they're supposed to be. To do this, you must measure ride height. Measurements are taken at each end of the car. The exact method varies, but usually you have to measure from a spot on the rear axle to a snubber or other component on the frame and from a point on the front spindle to a specific location on the frame or unibody. These measurements are compared to manufacturer's specs to see if they fall in the acceptable range. If not, coil springs must be replaced and leaf springs must be replaced or rearced. Once ride height has been corrected, wheel alignment must be checked.

Shock absorber condition is best determined by the way your car behaves on the road. If it bounces every time you hit a bump or dips and sways as you corner, it needs new shocks.

Cooling system service

Some motorists who take very good care of the rest of their car ignore the cooling system completely—except perhaps for a yearly check of antifreeze protection level. This is unfortunate because the radiator and various other cooling system components will deteriorate rapidly if coolant is not renewed at regular intervals. Furthermore, if the system is not flushed periodically, cooling capacity will be lost as passages clog with contaminants.

Most manufacturers recommend yearly inspection and pressure testing, accompanied by a backflush and refill every two years. However, for the do-it-yourselfer who doesn't have access to backflushing equipment, a yearly drain, flush and refill is a good idea.

Before draining coolant, check the condition of all belts and hoses. Look for cracking, swelling and oil or grease damage to hoses. Pay particular attention to the area just behind the clamp. Sometimes the clamp will dig its way into the hose. Black flecks in the coolant are an indication of internal hose deterioration. Tests indicate that most hoses last no longer than three or four years, so regular replacement is a good idea regardless of the outside appearance.

The same is true of most conventional V-belts. It's difficult to judge belt condition on the basis of appearance. Of course, any belts that are cracked, glazed or shredded must be replaced, even if they are less than four years old.

When replacing belts, it's best to tension them using a gauge that is designed for this purpose. However, a little push with your thumb in the center

of the belt's longest span is better than no tension check at all. If you can deflect the belt more than 1 in while applying moderate pressure, it's too loose.

Flushing the system

Once you've examined all the belts and hoses, remove the radiator cap, run the engine until it's hot, and drain the coolant by opening the petcocks in the radiator and engine block. If you can't loosen the petcock valves, drain the engine and radiator by removing the lower radiator hose.

You can flush most of the dirt from the system by alternately filling it, running the engine until the thermostat opens, and draining it. Continue in this manner until the water runs clear. Make sure the heater is turned on. You can probably do a better job

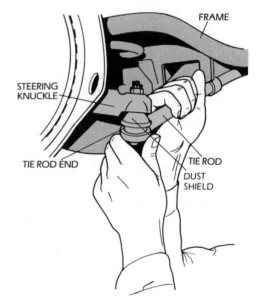

23 Tie rod ends should move some when wiggled, but not have excess freeplay.

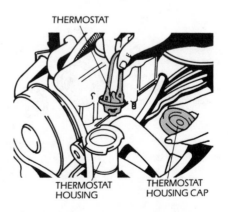

24 Some GM Fours locate the thermostat under a radiator-cap type housing cover.

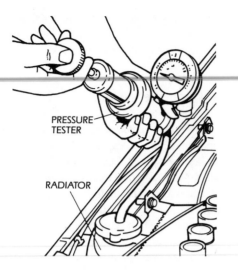

25 Check for cooling system leaks by pumping it up with a system pressure tester.

if you install a flushing tee in your upper heater hose. This device is available at auto parts stores, and it allows you to connect a garden hose to your cooling system. With the hose connected to the tee, run water through the system until it flows clear.

If your heater has not been performing as well as it should or if your car has been running hot, you should check the condition of your thermostat. It is most often found under the housing attached to the upper radiator hose. To remove the thermostat, loosen the two bolts on the base of the housing. Some newer models locate thermostats in a housing sealed by a cover that looks just like a radiator cap (Fig. 24).

To test the thermostat, hang a thermometer in a pan of water and place it on the stove. Suspend the thermostat in the water. Heat the water, noting the temperature at which the thermostat begins to open. If the thermostat does not open at the temperature stamped on its body, it is defective and must be replaced.

Pressure testing

If you have a pressure tester, you should check the system for leaks once it has been flushed completely. To do this, fill the system with water, make sure the heater is turned on, and attach the pressure tester to the filler neck of the radiator (Fig. 25). Pump up the system to the pressure specified in your service manual. If the system won't hold pressure, there is a leak. Carefully check all connections, the radiator, heater control valve and thermostat housing.

If you can't readily find the source of a pressure leak, use a flashlight and mirror to check the water pump's vent hole and seal. To check engine block core plugs for leakage, support the car on jackstands and take a look at the various plugs in the side of the block.

If your pressure test shows that there are no leaks, refill the system with enough antifreeze to provide at least a 50 percent antifreeze/water solution. Do not allow the concentration of antifreeze to exceed 70 percent, as freeze protection deteriorates above this level. Make sure you fill the recovery tank, if your car is so equipped, to the COLD FULL level.

If your car has an aluminum radiator or aluminum engine parts, you must use an antifreeze that's formulated for use in engines with aluminum components.

Before reinstalling the radiator cap, check it with your pressure tester to make sure it will maintain pressure at the specified level. If you don't have a pressure tester, examine the cap seals for any signs of damage or excessive wear. Replace the cap if the seals don't look good.

Wheel bearings and tires

The front wheel bearings of rear-drive cars and the rear wheel bearings of front-drive cars should be

26 Wheel bearings should be inspected and repacked whenever brakes are serviced. The grease cap on the hub can be removed with a large pair of adjustable pliers.

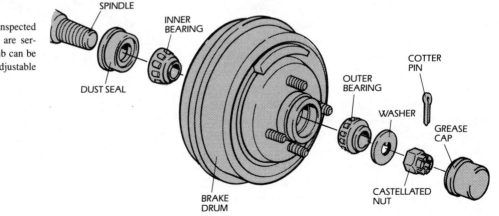

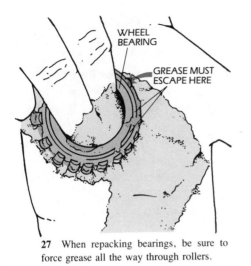

27 When repacking bearings, be sure to force grease all the way through rollers.

checked whenever brake drums or brake rotors are removed for brake inspection (Fig. 26). Brakes should be inspected every 15,000 miles or whenever trouble is suspected.

Clean the bearings in kerosene or solvent, and examine them and the bearing races, which can be found within the hub, for signs of pitting or other surface damage. Some minor discoloration is normal. If the bearings are okay, repack them with a high-temperature multipurpose EP grease.

To repack, place a substantial amount of grease in the palm of one hand, cup your hand and push the side of the bearing cage into your palm with your other hand (Fig. 27). Make sure you force the grease past the rollers. Continue until grease begins to ooze out of the top of the cage. Rotate the cage, pushing each uncoated area into the grease. Make sure all rollers are covered completely.

Reinstall the bearings along with a new grease seal. Tighten the hub nut to about 20 ft.-lb. while rotating the wheel. Back the nut off to release the load on the bearing and then bring it back up to finger tight. Position the hub nut lock or the castle nut slot so that it aligns with the hole in the spindle and install the cotter pin. When you're finished, there should be less than a noticeable amount of end play (about 0.001 to 0.003 in.), and the wheel should spin freely.

Tire check

Check tire pressures every time you check oil, which means at every other gas fillup. It's a good idea to keep your own tire pressure gauge in the glove box, as you may find a wide discrepancy from one service station gauge to the next.

Keep an eye on your tires for excessive tread wear or unusual wear patterns (Fig. 28). Excessive tread wear has occurred when less than 1/16-in. of tread-groove depth remains.

Most tires have tread wear indicators that become visible when tread wear exceeds normal limits. Molded into the bottom of the tread grooves, these indicators appear as 1/2-in.-wide bands across the tire tread.

Unusual wear indicates incorrect inflation or wheel alignment problems. On bias-ply tires, wear that occurs only on both outer edges of the tread is a sign of underinflation. Wear that occurs only in the center of the tread is a sign of overinflation.

This doesn't apply to radials though, since their stiff tread construction tends to retain its shape over a wide range of inflation pressures. Excessive camber, a wheel alignment adjustment, causes one side of the tread to wear more than the other side. Incorrect wheel toe-in or toe-out causes the edges of the tread to feather. Cupping, scalloping or bald spots are generally due to unbalanced tire and wheel assemblies and/or failure to rotate tires.

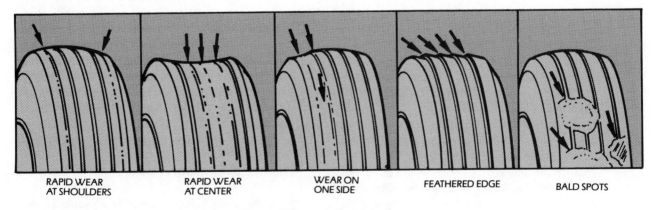

RAPID WEAR AT SHOULDERS   RAPID WEAR AT CENTER   WEAR ON ONE SIDE   FEATHERED EDGE   BALD SPOTS

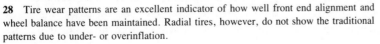

28 Tire wear patterns are an excellent indicator of how well front end alignment and wheel balance have been maintained. Radial tires, however, do not show the traditional patterns due to under- or overinflation.

Rotating tires

Tires should be rotated every 10,000 miles, following a conventional cross rotation plan (Fig. 29). When a spare is included in the rotation, the left front goes in the trunk, the spare goes on the right rear. The right rear goes to the right front, the right front goes to the left rear, and the left rear goes to the left front.

When reinstalling wheels, tighten the lug nuts with a torque wrench as illustrated here (Fig. 30). You'll find a spec for wheel torque in your service manual. Torque each one to half of the recommended figure the first time around, then bring each to full torque. If you can't find a spec in your service manual, torque $1/2$-in. wheel lug nuts to 85 ft.-lb., torque $7/16$-in. lug nuts to 70 ft.-lb.

TORQUE WRENCH

30   For correct seating, install and torque wheel nuts in the order shown above.

FRONT OF CAR

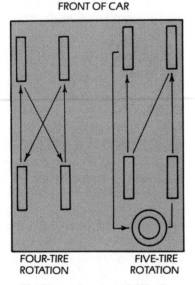

FOUR-TIRE   FIVE-TIRE
ROTATION   ROTATION

29   Tire rotation every 10,000 miles will prevent abnormal tire wear patterns.

Brake system inspection

Check your brakes at intervals of approximately 15,000 miles, unless prior experience indicates that less frequent inspection will suffice. Begin by looking for hydraulic fluid leaks at the master cylinder, calipers, wheel cylinders and at every junction or valve in the hydraulic system. If you find hydraulic system problems, you may want to seek professional help. At the very least, you should be equipped with a complete service manual and any required tools before attempting to rebuild or replace calipers, wheel cylinders or a master cylinder. In fact, because

the safe operation of a car's brakes depends on the hydraulic system, even advanced do-it-yourselfers often leave hydraulic component rebuilding to professional mechanics.

If the hydraulic system checks out okay, inspect disc brake pads and drum brake shoes to make sure that the lining has not worn to the point where replacement is necessary.

If you know for sure that your disc pads are of the bonded type, rather than of the riveted type, you might be able to inspect the lining thickness through an inspection hole provided for this purpose in the top of many calipers (Fig. 31). If the pads are bonded, the thinnest section of the friction material should be at least as thick as the pad backing plate.

If you don't know whether the pads are bonded or riveted, you'll have to remove the caliper to check pad thickness. In most cases, the job is not very difficult. Exceptions would include some rear wheel disc brakes that incorporate parking brake mechanisms.

Once the caliper has been lifted off the rotor, check the friction material. If it's of a nonmetallic type, the pads must have more than $1/16$-in. of material above the rivets (Fig. 32). Semimetallic friction material should be at least $1/32$-in. above the rivets.

While you're at it, check the rotors for excessive discoloration or any heat cracking. If the rotors are damaged, they'll have to be machined or replaced and the pads will have to be replaced. If everything looks okay and there's plenty of friction material on the pads, you can go ahead and bolt it all back together.

Drum brake inspections

To check the linings of drum brake vehicles, the drums must be removed. In most cases, the shoes will have to be retracted before the drums will come

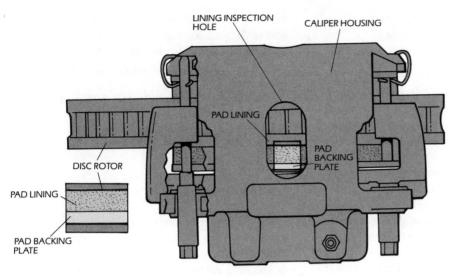

LINING INSPECTION HOLE

CALIPER HOUSING

PAD LINING

PAD BACKING PLATE

DISC ROTOR

PAD LINING

PAD BACKING PLATE

31 When bonded-type brake pads are used, check wear by comparing thickness of lining to that of backing plate by looking through the caliper inspection hole.

off. To retract the shoes on most vehicles with self-adjusting brakes, locate the adjusting slots, which are either in the backing plate (most likely) or in the drum. The slots should be filled with rubber insert plugs. On cars with slots in the backing plate, reach into the slot with a very small screwdriver and lift the self-adjusting lever away from the star wheel. Insert a brake adjusting tool in the slot alongside the screwdriver. Engage the brake adjusting tool in the star wheel and turn it to back off the adjustment. Often, you'll have to move the brake-tool handle upward to retract the shoes.

If the slots are in the drums, use a hook to hold the adjusting lever away from the star wheel for most applications. Insert the brake tool next to the hook to turn the star wheel.

Once the shoes have been retracted, cover your mouth and nose with a breather mask like those sold in automotive paint stores, and remove the drum. Inspect the friction material and drums for visible damage. If the drums are scored, they'll have to be remachined. If they are heat cracked or discolored, they'll have to be replaced.

Check the lining for excessive wear. Bonded linings should be replaced when they have $1/16$-in. or less of friction material. Replace riveted linings when they wear to within $1/32$-in. of the rivets.

Keep it shiny

The best thing you can do to protect the painted exterior of your car is to wash it on a regular basis. This will remove the industrial pollutants, bird droppings and other substances that can eat their way through the paint.

The best choice for washing a car is one of the carwash soaps sold in auto parts stores. With respect

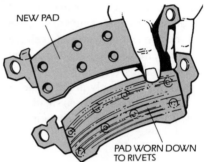

NEW PAD

PAD WORN DOWN TO RIVETS

32 Riveted brake pads must be replaced when lining wears to $1/16$ in. above rivets.

to other soap products, there is widespread disagreement on what's okay and what's not. If you can't see your way to spending a little extra for carwash soap, use a mild solution of any other commercial detergent.

Don't wash your car in full sunlight. You could end up spotting it permanently. Have the garden hose standing by, ready to rinse off. Begin by washing the roof, using a sponge or soft cloth, and work your way down the car so that dirt from one area won't be rinsed onto parts already washed.

After a thorough rinsing, dry the car with a chamois. Soak the chamois in water and wring it out before using it. Continue wringing out the chamois as it becomes saturated.

Once you've finished washing, check the painted surface for bug or tar spots. Solvents to remove these substances are available through auto parts stores.

If the surface appears lightly scratched or spotted after washing and a solvent treatment, you should polish it with a light polishing compound before waxing. If it is extremely oxidized or faded, machine compounding may be necessary. Apply fine polishing compound to small areas using a damp cloth or rubbing pad. Rub only until the scratches or blemishes disappear. If you overdo it or rub extensively on an edge, you'll end up with a bare spot.

Final wax and polish

When it comes to application of a final wax and polish, you have a number of options. The newest polymers, offered in both basic configuration and rather expensive kit form, provide the longest lasting protection. However, many retailers contend that polymers can't produce the lustrous sheen a conventional wax and silicone product can. In general, the more wax a product contains, the brighter the shine. A high concentration of silicone, on the other hand, offers longer lasting protection.

Most products that offer a combination of wax and silicone also contain some abrasive for the removal of very minor scratches or stains. Sometimes these are offered in two-component systems, one being a cleaner, the other a wax. Some of the one-component polishes do not contain abrasives.

When applying a wax, work only in the shade or on a cloudy day. Apply the product to one small area at a time. Most wax manufacturers recommend working in areas of about 2 sq. ft. at a time. When you've finished waxing, wash the car with lukewarm water and a soft rag to remove polish residue. Polish caught in crevices can attract moisture, which leads to rusting.

Use wheel polish to clean and shine custom steel or aluminum wheels. A vinyl dressing will clean and protect plastic exterior and interior parts.

Carpet cleaning

To clean interior carpeting, vacuum the interior thoroughly, then scrub with carpet shampoo. You can use the same shampoo that you use in the house or purchase carpet shampoo through an auto parts store. The handiest type for use in cars comes in a brush-applicator bottle. Instructions usually tell you to apply the shampoo, scrub until foam disappears, allow to dry and then vacuum up the residue. The final vacuuming is an important step. If you don't do it, the dirty residue will be left at the bottom of the carpet piles. Vacuuming on a regular basis will help keep the carpets clean between shampoo treatments.

Part II:

OUTSIDE YOUR ENGINE

Silencing Spark Knock

PAUL STENQUIST

■ THE RATTLE AND CLATTER of spark knock is a nearly unmistakable sound. It's easily distinguished from mechanical noises because it isn't rhythmic like a ticking lifter or noisy bearing. "Marbles in the hubcaps" is a fairly good description, but the sound obviously comes from the engine.

However you describe it, the sound of spark knock is so distinctive that it's simple to recognize—but it can be a lot more difficult to eliminate.

And it's quite necessary that you work to cure a spark-knock problem just as soon as it becomes apparent, since it's a great deal more damaging than it sounds. The death rattle of spark knock is the result of excessively high combustion pressure pounding the pistons.

The term "spark knock" isn't a very good one, because the condition is not always related to spark or spark timing. Sometimes it's called "detonation," but spark knock can occur without detonation taking place (as you'll see in a moment). At any rate, it's a serious problem and shouldn't be ignored.

Spark knock is usually the result of detonation. This occurs when a second flame front is ignited in the combustion chamber some time after normal ignition has occurred. This means that the air/fuel mixture is burning on both sides of the chamber, creating tremendous heat and pressure between the two flame fronts. At some point this heat and pressure cause the remaining gases to explode violently—usually when the piston is close to top dead center (TDC). This violent explosion pounds the top of the piston, opening up the ring lands, damaging rings and hammering connecting rod bearings.

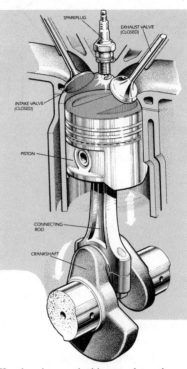

In normal combustion, spark ignites the mixture, which burns evenly across chamber.

Hot deposits or compression ignition of low-octane gas may start another flame front.

When the two flame fronts collide, high pressures and temperatures are generated.

Knock, ping, preignition or detonation—whatever you call it—can damage pistons, rings and connecting-rod bearings.

Preignition

Detonation can sometimes result from a condition called preignition. This occurs when a hot, glowing spot on the sparkplug or in the combustion chamber causes the mixture to ignite before the spark occurs. Because the chamber heat builds up too soon, the compression squeeze may cause more of the mixture to ignite in another part of the chamber, causing detonation. Or the normal spark ignition may start a second flame front, again causing detonation.

The high cylinder pressures that result from preignition can cause a spark-knock noise even if detonation doesn't occur. This is particularly true if the preignition takes place well before the piston reaches TDC. The premature combustion creates a situation where the piston slams into a veritable wall of high pressure.

However you define spark knock, the result is the same: engine damage. And although some domestic

2. Simple EGR valve is operated by vacuum from the carburetor. At engine speeds of 2,000 rpm, you should be able to feel the vacuum in the hose and see the valve movement.

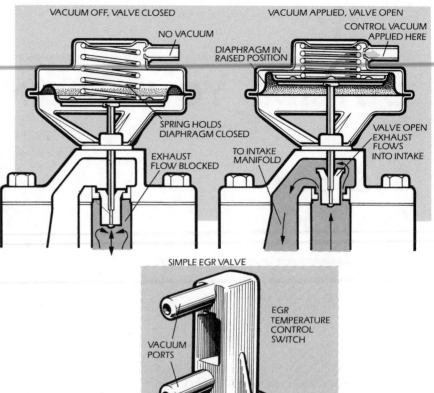

VACUUM OFF, VALVE CLOSED

VACUUM APPLIED, VALVE OPEN

NO VACUUM

CONTROL VACUUM APPLIED HERE

DIAPHRAGM IN RAISED POSITION

SPRING HOLDS DIAPHRAGM CLOSED

VALVE OPEN EXHAUST FLOWS INTO INTAKE

EXHAUST FLOW BLOCKED

TO INTAKE MANIFOLD

CENTRIFUGAL ADVANCE WEIGHTS

ROTOR ATTACHMENT HOLES

IGNITION CONTROL MODULE

1. Check distributor advance weights for sticking caused by corrosion, lack of lubrication, or weak return springs.

SIMPLE EGR VALVE

EGR TEMPERATURE CONTROL SWITCH

VACUUM PORTS

COOLANT TEMPERATURE SENSOR

3. Temperature control switch in some systems should block flow of vacuum to EGR valve only when engine coolant is cool.

carmakers called spark knock "the sound of economy and efficiency" when they couldn't eliminate it from their engines, it's a serious problem.

Fortunately, a completely clear understanding of the causes is not necessary in effecting a cure. Spark knock is undeniably the result of either preignition or excessive chamber heat, and steps can be taken to eliminate both.

Begin by checking your sparkplugs to make sure they're the correct heat range. An excessively hot plug can cause preignition. Use a plug recommended by the manufacturer, but check an up-to-date listing to make sure the recommendation has not changed. Switching to a colder plug might help cure preignition, but may cause other driveability problems. Usually, if the correct plug runs hot enough to cause preignition, something else is not working properly and the resulting plug heat is a symptom, not a cause.

Once you're sure the correct heat range sparkplug is installed, check ignition timing. If timing is too far advanced, heat and pressure will build up too soon and detonation will result. You should be able to run as much spark advance as the manufacturer specifies, but don't exceed the factory recommendation.

Retarding the spark from the maker's specs may eliminate knock, but this should be done only when all else fails. Retarding the ignition too far could cause valve damage, loss of power, increased fuel consumption and high emissions.

If you find that ignition timing is okay, check the centrifugal advance weights for corrosion and binding if the engine is so equipped. These spring-loaded weights are located inside the distributor, usually underneath the rotor (Fig. 1).

Overheated engine

If ignition timing is *not* the source of your problem, it may be due to overheating. If you haven't serviced your cooling system once a year, do a thorough flush and a pressure test. Then refill the system with a 70 percent solution of new antifreeze.

If your car has a temperature gauge, check fully warmed engine temperature and compare it to manufacturer's specs. If there's no gauge, you can install

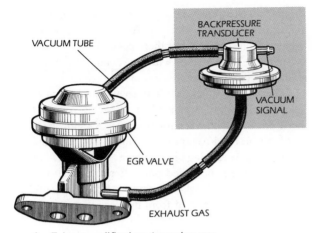

4. Exhaust modifications (removing catalyst, installing free-flow muffler) can affect EGR on cars with backpressure transducers.

one. Simply replace the coolant warning light probe with the temp-gauge probe and mount the gauge under your dash.

If engine operating temperature exceeds manufacturer's specs, it must be lowered. The cause could be a defective or incorrect thermostat, slipping fan belt, bad water pump, collapsing hose, defective fan clutch or cooling system blockage.

When you suspect overheating problems, begin by checking the fan belt. If the sides are glazed or the belt is more than four years old, replace it. Make sure the belt (old or new) is properly tensioned. Have a mechanic adjust it with a belt tension gauge if possible.

A thermostat can be tested by suspending it in a pan of water with a thermometer. Heat the pan on the stove and note where the thermostat opens.

Bad water pumps and collapsed hoses can sometimes be diagnosed by watching the coolant flow through the open neck of the radiator. Once the thermostat is open, coolant should move vigorously through the radiator.

A fan clutch is a bit tougher to diagnose, but you can get a general idea of its condition by watching the fan spin when you shut off the engine. If the engine is cold, the fan should continue to spin; with a hot engine, the engaged clutch should stop the fan when you turn off the ignition.

Severe blockage in the engine sometimes is indicated by a pounding sound that comes from the affected area. Radiator blockage can sometimes be detected by checking for cool spots on the radiator core while the engine is running. Fan position and grillwork often make this impossible. The best way to check a radiator is to have it removed, flow-tested and cleaned.

A power backflush with chemical cleaners may eliminate blockage without removing the radiator. Most garages are equipped for this, but make sure a shop has a power backflush machine before you sign for the work.

Defective EGR system

If you determine that neither engine operating temperature nor ignition timing is the cause of the spark-knock problem, it may be the result of a defective exhaust gas recirculation (EGR) system. EGR failure is probably the single most common cause of spark knock.

The EGR device routes a predetermined amount of exhaust gas back to the intake system to help lower combustion chamber temperature (Fig. 2). The reduced temperature lowers NOx emissions and prevents spark-knock problems. In the early days of emission controls, EGR systems were basically add-on devices. If the valve was removed and the air/fuel mixture adjusted to compensate, engine performance sometimes could be improved. This led some people to believe that disabling an EGR system would

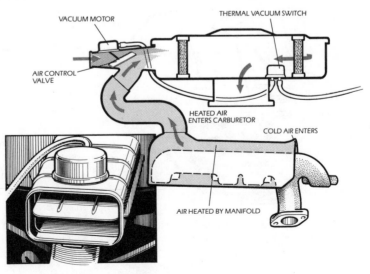

5. Intake hot-air system can cause spark knock if the control valve sticks closed. The valve should open as engine warms up.

always improve performance, but nothing could be further from the truth. Engines of the last seven years or so are calibrated around the EGR system. Removing or disabling it is usually a disaster, but some people still do it. They usually get a spark knock, and then must retard ignition timing to stop it. Performance and fuel economy end up worse than before the tinkering began.

Today's informed power plant mechanic makes EGR testing part of every tune-up or engine diagnosis. He makes sure that (1) the EGR control vacuum is present and at spec; (2) the EGR valve opens when control vacuum is supplied; (3) a flow of exhaust gas actually passes through the EGR valve when it opens.

Procedures for these steps vary greatly from engine to engine, depending on the type of EGR control used. The manufacturer's service manual for your car should include complete directions. Some general auto repair manuals, particularly the professional editions, include this information. Do-it-yourself manuals frequently gloss over or ignore this important diagnosis.

The simplest EGR valves use a vacuum signal—taken from just above the carburetor throttle plates—to open the valve. Called ported vacuum, this signal is not present at idle. A temperature control switch in the vacuum line prevents exhaust gas from being recirculated until the engine warms up (Fig. 3).

To check this EGR system, make sure that control vacuum is present when the engine is warm and running about 2,000 rpm. To verify valve opening and exhaust flow, apply vacuum to the EGR valve with a hand vacuum pump while the engine idles. The EGR flow should cause the engine to stumble, or even stall. If there is no change in performance, the valve is defective or the exhaust flow is blocked. Feel the underside of the valve diaphragm while vacuum is

applied (wear gloves if the engine is warm). If it doesn't move, the valve is defective. If the valve appears to be opening but there is no change in idle when the valve is opened with the vacuum pump, the exhaust recirculation passages are plugged.

Other EGR valves won't open when vacuum is applied. They are regulated in respect to exhaust back-pressure and vacuum (Fig. 4). Specific tests vary. Some Ford backpressure valves can be tested quite easily by revving the engine in NEUTRAL. Other Ford valves can be tested only after the exhaust is restricted with a socket. Some GM backpressure valves must be removed from the car for testing.

Various EGR systems

Backpressure EGR systems used on a majority of late-model Ford and GM vehicles are sensitive to changes. Some won't open if the catalytic converter is removed or burned out. Others may be affected if the muffler is replaced with one that does not meet original equipment backpressure specs. Today's cars rely on the interaction of many different systems. Tampering with emission-control components can be bad news.

There are many other systems: Some computerized vehicles use a solenoid in the EGR vacuum line for control. The computer can eliminate EGR by switching the solenoid. Others use a more sophisticated dithering solenoid to modulate EGR flow. Sometimes they are used with backpressure valves.

Some Fords and Chryslers make use of a venturi-vacuum signal to trigger EGR. This signal is strengthened by a vacuum amplifier, since it is too weak to move the diaphragm of the EGR valve on its own.

Many Chrysler products use an EGR timer that prevents EGR flow for a specific amount of time after the engine has been started. Chrysler products with the Mitsubishi 2.6-liter four-cylinder have a complex, three-stage EGR system. Unless your car obviously has a simple ported vacuum EGR, you'll need a factory service manual for troubleshooting directions.

Vacuum leak

If you determine that your EGR system, spark timing and engine temperature are okay, spark knock may be caused by a vacuum leak. This is usually accompanied by a lean misfire.

Tiny vacuum leaks are tough to pinpoint. Try applying carb cleaner to gaskets and vacuum hose

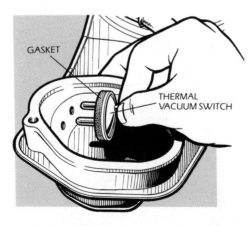

GASKET

THERMAL VACUUM SWITCH

6. Switch inside air-cleaner housing should shut off vacuum supply to vacuum motor as intake air warms. If not, replace switch.

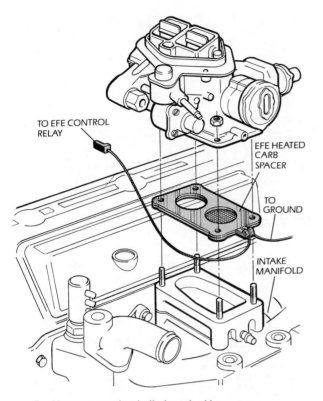

7. New cars use electrically heated grid to warm cold intake air. System must shut off when engine warms up.

connections while the engine is idling. If idle speed increases perceptibly when the solvent is applied, you've found a vacuum leak.

A mechanic with an emissions analyzer can find leaks by closing off lines with a hose pliers while watching for a drop in emissions.

An excessively lean fuel mixture can also cause spark knock, usually accompanied by hesitation, surge or misfire. Again, an emissions analyzer helps pinpoint problems.

Excessive preheating of air or the intake manifold can also cause detonation because the incoming mixture is too near the flash point. This can occur if either the intake hot-air system or the early fuel evaporation (EFE) system fails.

The intake hot-air system draws air from a stove surrounding the exhaust manifold (Fig. 5). On most cars it's controlled by a vacuum motor. Vacuum supply for the motor is turned on and off by a thermal switch in the air cleaner (Fig. 6). When the intake air is cold the motor closes a door in the air cleaner, forcing the carburetor to draw its supply from the stove. As intake air warms, the switch should shut off the supply of control vacuum, and the door should return to the heat-off position.

If the door remains in the heat-on position, check for vacuum at the vacuum motor when the engine is warm. If you find vacuum, the thermal switch is de-

fective. If you don't have vacuum, the door is stuck.

EFE or manifold heat systems supply heat at the base of the intake manifold to aid in fuel vaporization when the engine is cold. Most use exhaust heat to warm the manifold. Some late models use an electrically heated grid under the carb (Fig. 7). If either system fails to shut off the heat as the engine warms, spark knock can result.

Carbon accumulation

Carbon accumulation in the combustion chambers can cause detonation, due to the resulting increase in compression ratio, or preignition because of hot spots in the carbon.

GM sells a top-engine cleaner/solvent that will remove carbon from combustion chambers and pistons.

If you have eliminated all possible mechanical solutions to a spark-knock problem, a change in fuel is in order. Premium unleaded gasolines provide considerably more antiknock protection than regular grades. Octane boosting additives may be equally effective.

In extreme cases where both mechanical solutions and fuel-switching fail, a thicker head gasket can be installed on the engine—a far better solution than retarding the spark because it won't cause other damage. This is, of course, expensive and difficult. The thick gasket may cause some loss of power and fuel efficiency, because it lowers the compression ratio. But the engine may end up being more efficient if it was constantly detonating.

The death rattle of spark knock is a warning. Don't ignore it or you'll be looking for your piston rings in the bottom of your oil pan.

Solving Cold Start Problems

PAUL STENQUIST; ILLUSTRATIONS BY FRED WOLFE

■ AUTOMOBILES AND EXTREME COLD don't go well together. As the temperature drops, the

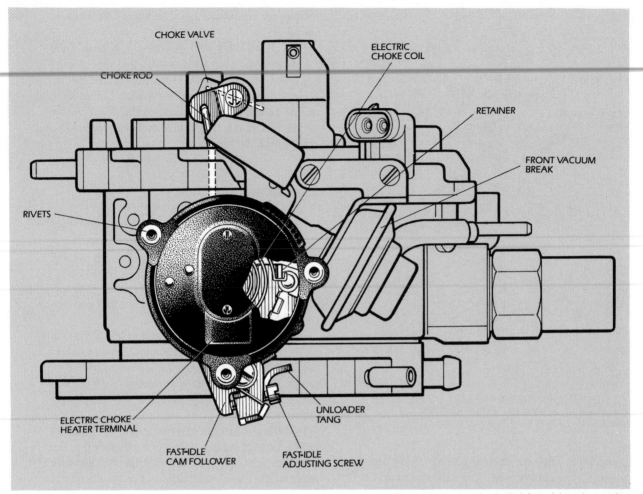

CHOKE VALVE

CHOKE ROD

ELECTRIC
CHOKE COIL

RETAINER

FRONT VACUUM
BREAK

RIVETS

ELECTRIC CHOKE
HEATER TERMINAL

UNLOADER
TANG

FAST-IDLE
CAM FOLLOWER

FAST-IDLE
ADJUSTING SCREW

Proper choke operation is vital for quick engine starting in cold weather. Late-model carburetors typically use an electrically heated thermostatic coil to snap the choke plate shut when the engine is cold and bring it to the open position as the engine warms up.

crankcase oil thickens, making the engine very hard to turn. The battery loses some of its energy. And the fuel puddles, rather than vaporizes.

Today's cars are equipped to overcome these difficulties, but only when everything is as it should be. The lubricant must be of the correct viscosity, the battery must be capable of holding a full charge, the engine must be in a good state of tune and the choke system (or fuel-injection control system) must be functioning properly.

But even if all these variables check out okay, you might have trouble starting your car if you don't use the prescribed starting technique. Mechanics in cold-weather cities feel that the principal cause of cold-weather no-starts is driver error.

Starting technique

If you don't use the proper cold-weather starting method on the first try, it will probably be too late on your second try because the battery quickly loses charge in low temperature and the plugs will be drenched with unvaporized gas. Most carbureted cars must be cold-started in the idle position after slowly pressing the accelerator to the floor one, two or three times. Most fuel-injected cars are cold-started in the idle position without depressing the accelerator. But techniques vary for both types. Read your owner's manual.

If the correct starting technique won't fire the engine, you should look for the cause of the problem (rather than trying to alter your technique to compensate). Both cranking speed and cold-start adjustments are critical.

Cranking speed is affected by both battery charge and oil viscosity. If your oil is too thick, even a fully charged battery won't start your car. Most manufacturers now recommend 5W-30 motor oil for winter use. In some cases, a 10W-40 oil may be too heavy to allow adequate cranking speed. A straight 30- or 40-weight oil is definitely too heavy. Check your owner's manual for a specific cold-weather recommendation. Many vehicle manufacturers list recommended engine oil on the basis of the coldest temperature expected.

A fully charged battery is essential when cold weather greatly increases the cranking system's burden. However, even a fully charged battery can't deliver voltage to the starter motor and ignition coil if an accumulation of crud has increased battery cable resistance.

A quick glance at your battery posts should tell you if corrosion is a problem. If the posts and terminals are covered with a powdery white or yellow substance, remove the terminals (negative first) and clean them and the battery with a small brush and a paste made from baking soda and water. If this treatment doesn't get them down to shiny metal, scrape the inside of the cable terminals and the outside of the battery posts with a small knife or a battery terminal cleaning brush. If the terminals are the type that bolt onto the cables, remove them and

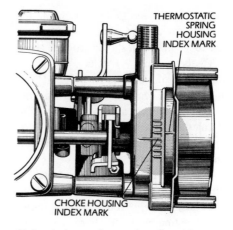

Choke closing tension can be adjusted by aligning the index marks to factory spec.

clean the connection area, or better yet, replace the cables with a set that have terminals molded to the ends of the cables.

Hydrometer "eye"

Check the charge level of most maintenance-free batteries by examining the hydrometer "eye." Normally, a dark eye means a drained battery, green is okay, clear or yellow indicates a defective battery.

For the battery to start your car, it must be able to

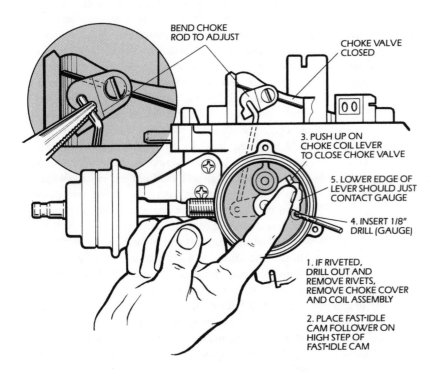

On carbs with fixed spring housings, the position of the choke valve lever must be gauged with an ⅛-in. drill. The setting is corrected by slightly bending linkage rod.

produce at least 9.6 volts for 15 seconds while the engine is cranking (at a temperature of 70° F. or above). At zero to 18° below, it should produce about 8.5 volts, at 30° above zero, 9.1 volts.

Your battery will, of course, discharge if you crank your engine for 20 seconds or so in zero-degree weather. But it should be capable of providing enough juice for the 15-second first chance. If it won't, further battery/charging system troubleshooting and repair are called for.

If, on the other hand, the battery seems to take a charge and checks out okay with a hydrometer but the engine still cranks slowly, you may have starter motor or internal engine problems. Further diagnosis—checking starter amperage draw, or torque required to turn the engine—will be necessary.

If *you* discharged the battery by cranking the engine for a considerable time, you should remove it (negative cable first), take it to a warm place and hook it up to a battery charger. Be careful when handling a battery. If you allow it to come in contact with your clothing, the acid will burn big holes in the fabric. Use old rags or a battery carrying strap to keep it well away from you. Discard any rags that have come into contact with the battery.

A 6- or 10-amp trickle charger will do a good job of charging batteries that have not been drained completely. A battery that still holds some charge may reach full charge in a few hours, but one that is almost fully discharged may require as much as 24 hours.

To determine when full charge has been reached, check a conventional battery with a hydrometer. To determine when a maintenance-free battery is fully charged, check its hydrometer eye as described above. Some fully discharged maintenance-free batteries have to be charged for a long time with a high-amperage service station-type charger. Don't attempt to charge a maintenance-free battery that has a clear or yellow hydrometer eye.

Jump-starting can also help to get you going in a pinch. But it's less effective than a recharge, as your battery will be left in a partly discharged condition if you don't drive the car for a few hours before shutting if off.

Finding the cause

While your battery is recharging, you'll have to try to figure out why the car didn't start on your first attempt. If your engine cranked at an adequately fast pace and wouldn't fire in 15 seconds or so, you probably have a cold-start (choke) system malfunction, a tuneup-related problem (like sparkplugs,

distributor cap, cables, filters) or a fuel line freeze-up.

Eliminate the possibility of fuel line freeze-up right away on carbureted cars. Remove your air cleaner or its top cover and climb up somewhere where you can see into the carb. Shine a flashlight directly into the carburetor barrels. Then hold the choke open (if it's already open you have a choke problem) and open the throttle.

You should see fuel squirt out of the accelerator pump nozzles when you open the throttle. If you don't, the fuel line is probably frozen. To thaw, let it sit for half a day or so in a warm place.

You can probably avoid fuel line freeze-up by using a fuel deicer. However, if your tank contains a lot of water (the cause of fuel line freeze), you may have to have it drained.

Choke adjustment

While you're checking to see if fuel is available, pay attention to the operation of the choke plate or valve. Once you've determined that the accelerator pump nozzles squirt fuel, release the choke plate while holding the throttle open. The choke should snap to a closed or nearly closed position.

If it doesn't move smartly into position, the choke linkage may be jammed with crud and corrosion. Try cleaning the external linkage parts with carb cleaner and a small solvent brush.

If the choke valve won't snap closed after cleaning the linkage, the malfunction must be corrected. It could be a simple misadjustment, but it's also possible that the thermostatic coil, which closes and opens the choke valve on most cars, is worn out.

On most cars the thermostatic coil is inside a housing attached to the side of the carburetor (see lead illustration). On early-model cars, the housing is secured by three screws, but on late models it's held by rivets in order to prevent tampering. To tamper (which you are allowed to do if you have to fix your choke), simply drill out the rivets. When reinstalling the housing, use self-tapping screws to retain it. These, with their special washers, can be purchased at an auto parts store.

The thermostatic coil within the housing holds the choke plate closed when the engine is cold. As the engine warms, the coil is heated and tension is released. Heat is usually provided by exhaust, an electric heater or both.

On some GM and Chrysler products the thermostatic coil is located in a heat stove that mounts on the manifold and is connected to the choke plate with a linkage rod.

On cars with a carb-mounted thermostatic coil, choke adjustment usually is accomplished by turning the housing until a specified mark aligns with a pointer on the carb. However, on most late-model GM cars, the cover is installed in a specific position. Adjustment is accomplished by gauging the position of the choke valve lever with a drill bit or plug gauge. The adjustment is corrected by bending a linkage rod until the lever is in the correct position.

On most cars with intake manifold-mounted thermostatic coils, adjustment is made by bending the rod that joins the well to the choke plate lever.

In either case, a service manual is required. You'll find directions and specifications for most models in professional editions of general repair manuals. These books are available in most libraries. Of course, the complete factory service manual for your vehicle is the best source of information. It's available through your dealer's parts department. No serious Saturday Mechanic should be without the factory service manual for his or her car.

While a correct choke adjustment alone may be enough to get it started, the vehicle won't operate properly when cold if you don't make the other choke system adjustments. On most cars, these include choke vacuum break adjustment, fast-idle setting and a fast-idle/choke relation adjustment.

To complete some of these adjustments on 1978 and later GM cars, you'll need a choke valve angle gauge. This is available at auto parts stores.

For most procedures, the gauge is mounted on the choke plate by means of its magnetic base. The choke plate is then closed, and the tool's scale is rotated until 0 is opposite the gauge's pointer. The bubble level on the gauge is then adjusted until the bubble is centered. The scale is rotated to the angle specified for the particular procedure, after linkage rods or other components have been positioned according to the instructions. Check the position of the bubble. If it's off-center, an adjustment must be made. For most carbs, this is accomplished by bending a linkage rod.

Many cars equipped with Holley-type carburetors use a vacuum break device to open the choke slightly after startup. If this is incorrectly set, there will be an over-rich condition while the car warms up, and driveability will suffer. On Ford products, the adjustment is checked by gauging the amount the choke opens when vacuum is applied to the diaphragm, and it can be reset to the shop manual specification with an adjustment screw on the diaphragm. Cars using remote-mounted vacuum breaks generally require slight bending of an adjustment rod to bring the choke plate angle back to spec.

Resetting the fast-idle speed is also required when

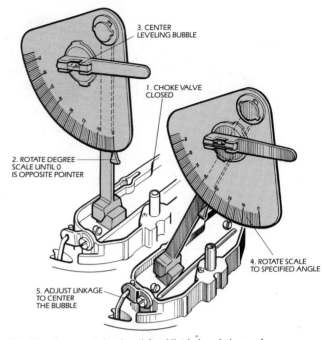

To adjust the vacuum break and fast-idle/choke relation angles on late-model GM carbs, use a choke-valve angle gauge as shown above. Auto parts stores carry the gauge.

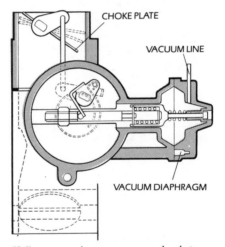

Holley-type carbs use a vacuum break to open the choke slightly after car's startup.

any choke adjustment has been changed. On most carburetors, the fast-idle screw rests on a stepped fast-idle cam. Position the screw on the proper step as called for in the shop manual. Turn the screw left or right as required to match the rpm level called for by the maker.

Other problems

If you found that choke and choke-system adjustments were okay, the cause of the cold no-start has not been determined. Although internal damage or

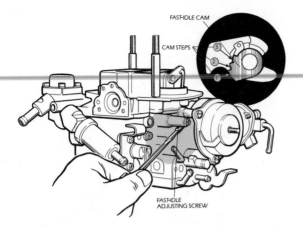

The fast-idle speed must be rechecked after any choke adjustment. Set the fast-idle screw on the proper step of the fast-idle cam, as is called for in the service manual.

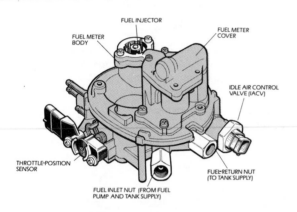

Electronic fuel-injection systems have no conventional choke, but they do use built-in electronic controls to provide a richer mixture for cold-weather starting.

other serious problems could be the cause, it may be the engine is simply in need of normal maintenance.

Check the sparkplugs. If the electrodes have eroded or have been fouled, the voltage available under cold-cranking conditions may not be enough to fire them. Clean and gap them if slightly worn or replace them.

If the plugs are wet with fuel, you probably flooded the engine trying to start it. This may be the case if your choke was misadjusted or stuck open. Dry the plugs completely. You'll have to get them into a warm place or spray them with plug cleaning solvent. Then, gap and reinstall them.

Other problems that might contribute to a no-start include a bad distributor cap, leaking ignition cables or coil tower, a defective coil and other types of ignition failure.

Check ''Troubleshooting Electronic Ignitions'' on electronic ignition maintenance and diagnosis for more on ignition problems.

Fuel-injected cars

Most late-model, fuel-injected cars have a cold-start system that is integrated with the engine's electronic control system. If cold no-start is a problem, the self-diagnostic trouble codes have to be checked in the vehicle service manual.

Some manufacturers provide additional checklists that should be consulted when a problem is evident but no trouble code has been set. For example, on cars with TBI, GM specifies 15 different items that should be checked when hard starting is experienced and no trouble codes are set. These include checking the fuel pump relay, throttle-position sensor, coolant-temperature sensor and fuel pump check valve.

Imported cars equipped with Bosch L-Jetronic and K-Jetronic fuel injection systems have cold-start valves that provide extra fuel for initial startup. If this valve doesn't function properly, you won't be able to start the engine when the temperature drops.

In general, K-Jetronic cold-start valves are tested by removing the valve, holding it over a container and attaching a current supply to the valve to see if it sprays. (Obviously, this can be dangerous. Don't attempt this test without a factory service manual.)

L-Jetronic cold-start valves are usually tested by hooking a special fuel system pressure gauge into the fuel-supply line. The valve is then activated, and the technician watches to see if pressure drops at the prescribed rate.

Of course, the cold-start valve isn't the only Bosch injection component that can cause a cold no-start problem. Fourteen items are listed as possible causes. A service manual is needed for most Bosch injection problems.

Solving Hot Start Problems

PAUL STENQUIST

■ IT'S A HOT DAY in the middle of August. You park your car for 30 minutes or so while you do a bit of shopping. When you leave the store you discover that the car, which started easily on the coldest mornings last winter, won't start.

Hot starting problems are a very common source of driver distress. And, because they sometimes "go away" when the engine has cooled completely, they can be very difficult to diagnose.

Hot start problems can be divided into two separate categories: those that cause the engine to crank so slowly that it won't fire and those that make the engine hard to start but don't affect cranking speed. In the following sections both types of problems will be discussed, as will likely causes and solutions for each.

Hot start, slow crank

Hot engine cranking problems are very common. When you turn the key to the START position, the engine sounds like it's turning one revolution at a time with a pause between each. The engine may suddenly begin to crank faster, or it may just continue cranking laboriously until the battery is dead.

If it occurs only once, this type of starting problem may be due to nothing more than a discharged battery or an inoperative charging system. But for our purposes, only those cases that recur continuously when the battery is fully charged will be considered.

It's hard to get any two mechanics to agree on the cause of this condition. That's because there are actually a number of different things that can make the engine crank slowly when temperatures rise, and they sometimes exist in combination. Included are high cranking circuit resistance, internal engine problems, cooling system problems, and excessive spark advance.

High cranking circuit resistance

When corrosion or loose connections in the starting circuit raise circuit resistance, your battery might have a tough time cranking the engine. And, because resistance increases further when underhood temperature is high, the problem may be noticeable only on hot summer days.

Before even attempting to diagnose the problem, clean the battery posts and terminals, as well as the connection points on the starter motor, starter relay and/or solenoid, if you haven't done so recently. Reinstall the terminals and make sure all connections are tight. Start the engine and warm it to maximum operating temperature by driving it slowly for at least half an hour. Then check starter positive and nega-

tive circuit resistance by measuring voltage drop.

To check positive circuit voltage drop connect the positive cable of a voltmeter that reads in tenths of a volt to the positive battery post and the negative cable to the terminal on the starter. On starters with external solenoids (including most GM cars), connect the negative lead to the large copper connector that joins the solenoid to the starter. Crank the engine with the meter attached. It should read less than 0.5 volt if circuit resistance is within limits.

If you get a reading in excess of 0.5 volt on a car with an external solenoid, attach the negative probe of the voltmeter to the "BAT" terminal on the solenoid where the cable attaches. If there is less than 0.5 volt at this point with the engine cranking but there was more than 0.5 volt at the bridge between

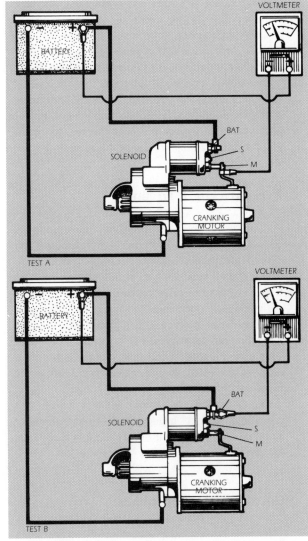

To check for high solenoid resistance on systems with an external solenoid, measure voltage between the battery positive post and the large copper connector that joins the solenoid to the starter (test A). Then check between battery positive and BAT terminal on solenoid (test B). If reading exceeds 0.5 volt at connector (test A) but not at BAT terminal (test B), solenoid resistance is excessive.

the starter and the solenoid, then the resistance problem is within the solenoid.

High solenoid resistance is very common on some GM cars. The problem is due to a buildup of corrosion on the brass disc that transmits voltage to the starter when the solenoid engages. New Delco solenoids have an improved design contact plate, so rather than purchasing a rebuilt solenoid buy a new one from your GM dealer.

If positive circuit resistance was excessive at both points, the problem is in the positive cable or connections. Replace the cable and recheck all terminals for corrosion.

Check negative circuit resistance by connecting the voltmeter negative lead to the negative battery post and the voltmeter positive lead to the starter housing. Make sure you make contact with the bare metal of the housing. With the engine cranking, ground circuit voltage drop should measure less than 0.2 volt. If it is not within specs, check all connections again and replace the ground cable if necessary. If the ground circuit cable attaches to the frame, make sure that the cable joining the frame and engine is in good condition. By connecting your voltmeter positive lead at various points in the ground circuit you can usually pinpoint the problem area.

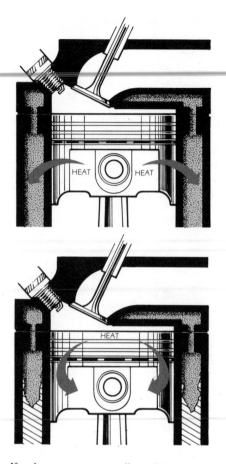

If coolant passages surrounding cylinders are blocked, pistons can expand and stick in the cylinders when the engine is hot.

Excessive spark advance

Slow crank/hot start problems are frequently caused by a combination of high resistance and excessive advance, so it's a good idea to check spark timing even if you think you've solved your problem with a solenoid or cable replacement.

First, attach a tachometer and make sure idle speed is at specification. Then, check timing following the directions on your vehicle information label or in your shop manual. If the manufacturer provides a range of acceptable timing, adjust to a figure at the lower end of the range.

On cars with mechanical advance, check the centrifugal weights inside the distributor to make sure that corrosion doesn't cause them to stick when the engine is hot.

Cooling system problems

Believe it or not, serious cooling system problems can cause hot start/slow crank problems. If coolant passages surrounding engine cylinders are blocked with crud and corrosion, heat from the pistons won't be transferred to the coolant. This causes the pistons to expand to the point where friction between them

and the cylinder walls makes the engine difficult to turn. In many cases, coolant temperature will remain within the acceptable range.

This can sometimes be remedied by a power backflush combined with a cooling system cleaner. In severe cases cylinder block replacement may be your only recourse.

Prevention is the best solution. If you take good care of your car from the time you first purchase it, the yearly cooling system backflush and coolant replacement will prevent severe buildup of crud. Coolant should be a mixture of clean water and an antifreeze recommended by the car manufacturer.

Ordinary overheating problems can also cause an engine to crank slowly when hot.

Internal engine problems

Any internal engine problem that produces friction can cause the engine to crank slowly. And since most clearances tighten up when the engine is hot, it's most likely to happen then.

You can tell if your engine is hard to turn by removing the plugs and attempting to turn the front crankshaft bolt with a torque wrench. It should break away at 90 lbs. or less and should turn with application of 70 lbs. or less. Unfortunately, it's quite difficult to get at the front crank bolt on most cars, thanks to accessories and the radiator. In most cases, you'll have to do a lot of disassembly work first.

Obviously, internal engine damage might occur in combination with and/or as a result of blocked cooling system passages. And the torque wrench test can't tell you for sure that the problem is due to one or the other. So before disassembling your engine or asking your mechanic to do so, make sure you've exhausted more conventional remedies.

Fast crank, no hot start

What about cars that crank fast when the engine is hot but still won't start? This is another very common problem that can leave you stranded when you least expect it. Again, the causes can be multiple, but the problem is usually the result of a choke system failure, a fuel flooding problem, a serious vacuum leak, fuel starvation, or an intermittent electrical failure. Of course, if your car is in need of a tuneup and maintenance items like plugs and air filter are on their last legs, you should correct this situation before looking for more unusual causes.

Choke problems

The scene is repeated over and over again in supermarket parking lots during the heat of summer. After a futile attempt at starting his car, the driver jumps out, throws the hood up, unscrews the air cleaner and jams a screwdriver in between the choke plate and carb body. After starting his car, he reverses the procedure, slips in behind the wheel and drives away.

If you're numbered among the supermarket screwdriver starters, it's time for you to pop the hood and solve the problem that makes this ritual necessary. The culprit could be incorrect choke adjustment, but you must also consider the possibility of a carburetor flooding problem as discussed in the next two sections. Although the screwdriver holds the choke flap open, that may only be necessary due to engine flooding. You can't assume that the choke is the cause of the no-start.

Choke adjustment and cleanup, though, are the first two things you should consider, and in some cases the scrub brush work may be all that's necessary. Make sure the engine is cold. Then, using a small solvent brush and a can of carb cleaner or an aerosol can of carb cleaner, remove all the varnish and accumulated dirt from the linkage arms and choke assembly. Make sure you clean every piece that is connected to the linkage or choke flap.

Because there are a considerable number of different choke mechanisms used on recent carburetors,

Before attempting to adjust a choke, clean all of the choke system parts, using a can of carb cleaner and a solvent brush or, if you prefer, a can of aerosol carb cleaner.

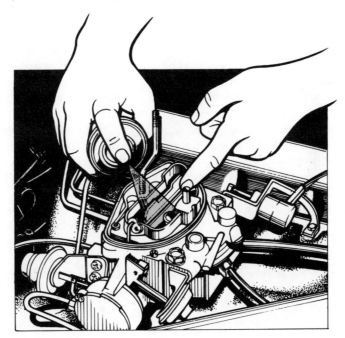

To remove the slotless screws that retain some choke housings, make your own slots with a hacksaw. You'll probably have to remove the carb from the engine.

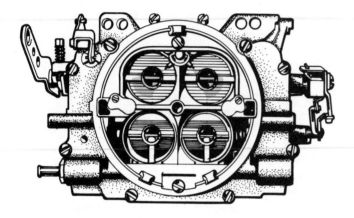

To check for fuel starvation, remove the air cleaner, hold the choke flap open and stare down into the carb barrels. Then open the throttle and watch for fuel spray from the accelerator pump nozzles.

we can't provide exact directions or specs for checking each. In order to do this job properly, you'll need a service manual—either the carmaker's manual or one of the general repair manuals on the market. We can tell you that most choke systems require at least three adjustments: vacuum break, choke flap closing, and fast idle. Some call for as many as five or six different adjustments.

The choke flap closing mechanism is usually the culprit here, since it's the tightly closed flap that make the hot engine hard to start. But the choke flap mechanism is connected to the other choke system components and they can sometimes cause it to bind.

On most systems, a temperature-sensitive bimetal coil, mounted either on the carb body or within a stove on the intake manifold, opens and closes the flap. On some, the coil is heated electrically; on others, exhaust heat is used. Adjustment is frequent-

ly accomplished by turning the housing that surrounds the bimetal coil until a pointer aligns with a specified point on a scale that is attached to the carb body. On others, the housing is mounted in a fixed position and adjustment is made by bending a linkage rod or lever. Sometimes the correct choke flap position must be gauged with a rule, or, as on many GM cars, with a drill bit or rod gauge.

On most cars, the choke housing is mounted with rivets or slotless screws to discourage tampering. To remove rivets, drill them out. To remove slotless screws, cut a slot in each with a hacksaw blade. In either case you'll probably have to take the carburetor off the engine first.

Choke flap sticking can become a problem on very old carburetors or poor rebuilds where the choke flap bushings have worn to the point where the flap won't stay in one position and can't be properly adjusted.

Bowl vent boilover

When you park your car, heat from the engine is transferred to the fuel remaining in the carb float bowl. The temperature increase is accompanied by rising pressure. This pressure has to be relieved or fuel will be forced into the intake manifold. Once the manifold becomes soaked with fuel, the engine floods and can be started only by holding throttle and choke flap wide open. You can usually tell if your engine is flooded with fuel when you open the hood. If you're greeted with a powerful gasoline odor, the engine is most likely bogged down with a manifold full of puddled fuel.

On most cars, the carb float bowl is vented to the evaporative emissions canister. You'll find the large black canister somewhere to the side of the engine. On some older cars the bowl may be vented to the inside of the air cleaner. In either case, the vent must be open when the engine is shut off or high pressure within the bowl will force fuel through the carb metering circuit.

Check the bowl vent and any connecting hoses for possible blockage. If they're okay, take a look at the canister. If the bottom of the canister is open, you can usually replace its filter. If a closed canister drips fuel from the bottom, replace it and troubleshoot the evaporative emissions system according to directions in your service manual.

Internal carb leaks

If you find that your bowl vent system is normal but your engine continues to flood when shut off hot, the carburetor probably has an internal leak. Unfortunately, this type of leak is very difficult to pinpoint and equally hard to fix. The only reasonably sure way to stop the drip is by replacing the carburetor.

Before you invest in new hardware, make sure your engine is running at normal temperature. Even a good carburetor may spit fuel into the engine if it's running 30 or 40 degrees above normal operating temperature.

Vacuum leaks

If your engine is hard to start hot but does not seem to be flooded with excess gasoline, a vacuum leak could be the source of your difficulty. Check all hoses for splits, kinks and other signs of damage. If the hoses are old and brittle, replace them. Make sure all hoses are connected in the manner illustrated on the vehicle information label.

In addition to making hot restarts difficult, a vacuum leak will cause a rough idle. To find a vacuum leak that is not the result of an obviously defective hose, use a needle nose pliers to squeeze off each vacuum hose near its source while the engine is idling. When the roughness clears up, you've found the leak. If the hose itself is okay, the component it's attached to is the culprit.

An EGR valve that sticks open qualifies as a vacuum leak, as it allows the engine to draw air through the exhaust passages when you're trying to start it. On most engines you can check the EGR valve by applying vacuum to it while the engine is idling. When the vacuum signal causes the valve to open, the engine will idle roughly. When you release the vacuum, the valve should close and proper idle should be restored. If the application of vacuum to your EGR valve does not cause it to open, check your service manual for EGR test procedures.

Fuel starvation

While excess fuel is a common cause of hot start problems, fuel starvation can also be the culprit. In these cases, the engine cranks until the pump has filled the float bowl sufficiently. Then it finally starts.

You can tell if your engine is getting a supply of fuel by removing the air cleaner and climbing right up on top of the engine so you can see down the carburetor barrels. (Do this while the engine is off and the starting problem is present. Take care not to burn yourself on hot engine parts.) While holding the choke flap open, crack the throttle. You should see fuel shoot out the accelerator pump nozzles. If you don't, check the fuel filter, fuel pump and carburetor float adjustment. One of these should prove to be the problem.

Intermittent electrical problems

Some electronic parts can fail temporarily when underhood temperatures are excessive. Unlike our previous examples, the engine usually will not start even with a long cranking period if this type of problem is present. Rather, it will start only after having cooled off for an hour or two.

Vacuum leaks can cause hot starting problems. Excessive spark advance can contribute to a hot start/slow crank condition. For info on spark advance adjustment and vacuum hose routing see the vehicle information label, which you'll find in the engine compartment.

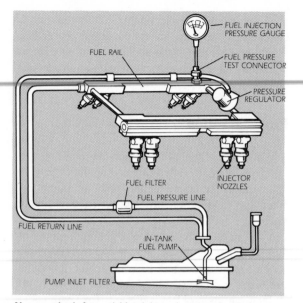

You can check for a sticking injector by measuring fuel system pressure after shutdown. The injection pressure gauge is attached to the Schrader valve found on the fuel rail of most systems.

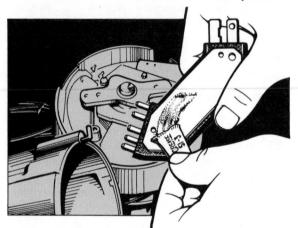

Applying silicone dielectric grease to the back of a GM ignition module reduces the chances of heat damage and hot restart problems.

The most likely offender in these cases is the electronic ignition module. Off-brand discount-priced modules seem to be more likely to fail than name-brand or original equipment types.

If you buy a new module and it is not the source of your problem, you're stuck with it, as electronic parts are not returnable. Some mechanics, who maintain a good inventory of such parts, will "substitute test" and reinstall your old module if it was not the source of the problem.

Fuel-injected and computer-controlled engines

Because most injection systems remain pressurized after the engine is shut off, a fuel injector that sticks open can flood the engine and foul one or more plugs. Given enough time, the fuel evaporates and the engine starts easily, but for the first hour or so after shutoff starting can be extra tough.

On port injected engines (one injector per cylinder), a sticking injector can sometimes be located by checking the plugs half an hour after shutoff. If a plug is fouled or wet, it's likely that the injector for that cylinder is leaking.

A lack of wet plugs doesn't necessarily rule out dripping injectors. A visual check of the injectors is the best way to test. On throttle body injection systems (injectors within a carb-like throttle body), the injectors are easy to observe, and you can simply warm the engine, shut if off, remove the air cleaner and watch the injector(s) to see if there's a drip. On some port injected systems you can lift the injectors and fuel rails out of the ports to watch for drips.

A check of system pressure is also useful in tracking down leaking injectors. If pressure drops continuously after shutoff, a leaking injector could be the cause. But other problems—like a faulty fuel pump check valve, a leaking pump connection or a bad pressure regulator—can cause pressure loss as well.

On most systems you can measure pressure by attaching a fuel injection pressure gauge to the Schrader valve that is mounted on the fuel rail. When attaching the gauge, wrap a rag around the gauge connector to catch any fuel leakage.

On any car with a computer-controlled fuel system, you should perform the basic diagnostic checks when a driveability or starting problem occurs. In most cases, however, a system problem is indicated by a glowing CHECK ENGINE light.

Timing Your Engine for Performance and Economy

MORT SCHULTZ

■ SMOOTH, POWERFUL, EFFICIENT ENGINE performance is impossible if the ignition spark does not occur at exactly the right time. That's why a check of initial spark advance is necessary when your car is tuned up or when poor performance symptoms suggest that a spark advance problem is present.

Such symptoms include hesitation, lack of power, poor fuel economy, overheating, detonation and high idle emissions.

The initial spark advance figure is always given in degrees. This figure describes the relative position of the piston at the moment of spark. An advance specification of 5° BTDC means that spark occurs five crank-shaft degrees before the No. 1 cylinder's piston reaches the top of its bore, or top dead center. This specification is called *initial* because it is measured while the engine is idling and with all spark control devices disabled.

Spark control devices are necessary, because the piston moves faster at high rpm and because the spark advance requirements of an engine change as load changes. These devices vary the amount of advance under different conditions.

On most cars, this variation is accomplished by means of a vacuum diaphragm and centrifugal weights. The vacuum diaphragm moves the points or electronic pickup within the distributor cam or trigger and, thereby, changes the moment of spark. Centrifugal weights on the top of the distributor shaft move the rotor in relation to contacts within the distributor cap, again changing the moment of spark. Late-model cars equipped with computer-controlled systems may vary spark timing electronically. Since electronic, centrifugal and vacuum advance mechanisms are not adjustable, unless internal components are changed inside the distributor, only the initial spark advance adjustment is generally checked. However, when a check of the initial advance finds it okay, but symptoms of incorrect spark advance persist, the operation of the internal secondary advance mechanisms should be checked.

Magnetic timing

For many years, stroboscopic timing lights have served as the principal means of checking ignition timing. Now, however, there's a better—but more expensive—way to check ignition spark timing: the magnetic timing meter.

Magnetic timing is also called monolithic timing and electronic timing. It's done by connecting the test instrument to the car battery and inserting an electronic probe into a socket near the engine's crank hub or flywheel. Then you connect an inductive pickup clamp to the No. 1 sparkplug cable.

The probe electronically senses its position rela-

tive to an index mark on the hub or pulley. The inductive pickup tells the meter when the plug fires. The magnetic probe tells the meter what the crank position is at that moment. The meter translates this information into a spark advance reading.

At the same time, the meter can record engine revolutions per minute (rpm). Therefore, the meter eliminates the need for a separate tachometer. Setting initial timing requires that you make the adjustment with the engine running at a speed specified by the manufacturer. You can find tuneup specs in most owners manuals or in books such as the *Popular Mechanics Motor Car Care Guides* or *Saturday Mechanic Car Care Illustrated*. The tachometer function also permits precise measurement of mechanical and vacuum advance operations at engine speeds above idle.

With a timing light, you have to be able to observe crankshaft position as the plug fires. With a timing meter, you obtain numerical readouts of ignition advance. Readouts are checked against engine manufacturer specifications. By checking advance at speeds above idle, vacuum and centrifugal advance mechanisms can also be checked.

The stroboscopic timing light can also be used to check vacuum and centrifugal advance. However, since the total advance of many cars approaches 45° at high engine speeds, the scale that is attached to the engine for checking idle speed advance won't serve for this purpose. To check high speed and intermediate advance with a conventional timing light, you would have to mark your crankshaft pulley with degree indications up to about 50° or install one of the timing tapes that are generally available for some engines through high-performance parts outlets.

Buying a timing meter

Before deciding that you want to set timing electronically, check to see if your engine has a timing socket. If it doesn't, you can't use a meter.

If you buy a meter from an auto parts dealer, make sure you can return the equipment if the probe doesn't fit the socket on your engine.

Most people aren't ready to shelve their timing lights. Either their engines don't have magnetic timing sockets, or they don't want to pop for a meter (figure on spending at least $200).

Even if your car doesn't have magnetic timing sockets, you can still time most ignition systems using a light. But accuracy depends on how you do it. Let's run down the steps.

1. Note the initial spark advance figure on your underhood vehicle information label. If the label is missing or illegible, get the information from another source.

2. Make the specified timing mark stand out by painting it white or coating it with white chalk. Also paint or coat the pointer or index mark.

3. With the engine off, connect a tachometer, following the instructions that come with the instrument. Some timing lights have a built-in tachometer, as well as a distributor advance scale. They cost more than conventional timing lights, even more than some magnetic timing meters. But you may want to look into them if you're in the market for both a timing light and tachometer.

If you have a GM car equipped with a High Energy Ignition (HEI) system that has the ignition coil inside the distributor cap, but the engine doesn't have a diagnostic connector, you'll need an adapter to connect the tachometer. The adapter hooks to the terminal marked TACH on the distributor, and the tachometer is connected to the adapter.

If your GM engine has a diagnostic connector, attach the tachometer to terminal No. 6 of the connector.

You can probably buy a tachometer adapter from an auto parts store. If not, you can order it from Borroughs Tool and Equipment Corp., 2429 North Burdick St., Kalamazoo, Mich. 49007 or from Kent-Moore Tools, 29784 Little Mack, Roseville, Mich. 48066.

You can also use the same adapter on a Ford or AMC engine that has a cover over the terminals of the SSI (Solid State Ignition) coil.

4. Connect the timing light according to instructions that come with the instrument. Hopefully, your timing light has an inductive pickup, so you can clamp the pickup right on the sparkplug cable going to the No. 1 cylinder. If your timing light is not an inductive type, place an adapter between the No. 1 sparkplug and its cable, and connect the timing light lead to the adapter.

If you don't have an adapter, don't time the engine before you get one. Piercing the sparkplug cable to connect the timing light lead ruins the cable. It can cause a hard-to-trace engine misfire. Voltage jumps to ground through the broken cable insulation before it gets to the sparkplug. The sparkplug, therefore, can't fire.

5. If your distributor has a vacuum advance (many 1981-'82 models don't), you probably have to disconnect the vacuum hose from the vacuum advance chamber and plug the end of the hose with a pencil or golf tee. If this is a requirement, it says so on the vehicle information label in the engine compartment. Other requirements, such as the speed at which timing should be checked, the point to

which the engine should be warmed, and what accessories should be on or off during the test, will also be noted on the decal. On cars equipped with electronic spark control, the label may instruct you to unplug an electrical connector. *Do this with the ignition turned off.*

6. Start the engine and adjust idling speed, if necessary. Then, if nothing blocks your view, aim the timing light at the specified timing mark and sight down the center of the light barrel. Hold the light straight.

If you can't get a clear view of the timing mark by sighting down the barrel of the timing light, sight along the side of the light. Get your eye as close to the instrument as possible, but don't get your hand or hair caught in the fan.

The pointer or index mark should line up with the mark and both should appear stationary. If they're not aligned, adjust timing by loosening or removing the clamp that holds the distributor. Keep the specified timing mark under the pulsating flashes of the timing light as you rotate the distributor until the timing mark and pointer or index mark are aligned. If they don't appear stationary, you may have a bad distributor.

Distributor hold-down bolts of some newer cars are hard to reach without specially made wrenches. If you need a special wrench for your car, check your local auto parts store or the parts department of a dealer selling your make of car.

If the distributor housing is stuck, wrap a strap wrench or oil-filter wrench around it and try turning. If it doesn't turn, let the engine cool and give the base of the distributor a shot from a dry chemical fire extinguisher. Then try it.

7. After you set timing, reposition and tighten the distributor-holding clamp. Then, recheck the adjustment to make sure it hasn't wavered. Finally, disconnect instruments and reattach the vacuum advance hose or electrical connector.

If timing marks for your engine are at the rear of the engine and are seen through a hole in the bellhousing, the hole may be fitted with a pull-out rubber or plastic cover to keep out dirt. Reinstall the cover after making adjustment.

Secondary advance mechanism

When initial timing is adjusted to the correct specifications, but symptoms of incorrect spark advance persist, the vacuum and centrifugal advance mechanisms should be checked for proper operation.

Reconnecting the vacuum advance hose with the engine running at 2,000 rpm, while watching the

Magnetic timing meter lets you set ignition timing without timing marks. Readout is more accurate than visual alignment.

Cars with timing mark scale positioned at the engine's rear may also have a magnetic timing probe socket. Look for it.

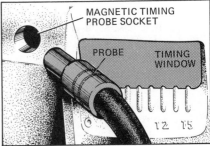

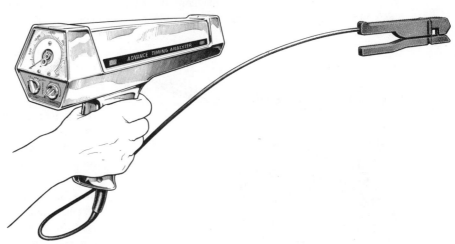

High-priced timing lights have a built-in tach to show rpm and they can give advance-curve information. Lights that have an inductive pickup are easiest to use.

timing indicator with your light, will tell you if the vacuum advance is functional. But a more specific test is necessary to ensure that it's working the way it should. Increasing engine speed while watching the indicator should cause the centrifugal weights to advance the timing. But again, this procedure

doesn't tell you if this mechanism is working *correctly*. It just tells you it's working.

Reasonably accurate tests of centrifugal and vacuum advance functions are fairly easy to perform. But to perform this check with absolute precision, a distributor testing machine is necessary. Either way,

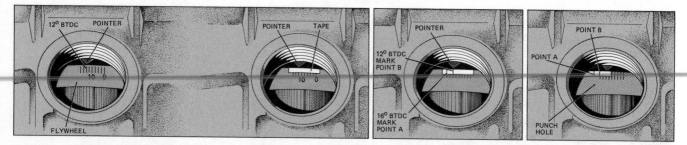

Timing marks can be extended. On some cars, this may be needed just to check timing. On others, you may want to extend the scale to check secondary advance. Here, a 16° scale is being expanded to 20° before top dead center (BTDC). First, lay a piece of tape across the scale. Then, make two marks, A and B, on the tape, representing 4°, the distance between 12° and 16° marks. As shown, move the tape over to add a distance equal to 4° to the scale. Finally, mark 20° point with a punch.

you need vacuum and centrifugal advance specifications for your car. These aren't on the underhood information label, but they're included in most repair manuals, such as the *Motor Auto Repair Manual*. Because specifications may vary within a single model year, the various applications are generally listed by distributor number. As an example, here's the procedure for checking secondary advance mechanisms on a 1978 Ford Fairmont with distributor No. D7EE-CA.

Centrifugal advance is checked with the vacuum line to the distributor disconnected and plugged.

Specifications indicate that centrifugal advance for this distributor should begin with 1° advance at 800 rpm. At 1,500 rpm, total centrifugal advance should be 1° to 3½° at 2,500 rpm. This distributor should provide 7½° centrifugal advance total. To check, accelerate the engine while watching the marks on the timing indicator with your light. Again, this is much easier to check with a magnetic timing meter and tach combo, since some advance specs go

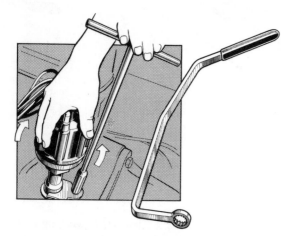

Timing is adjusted by loosening distributor and rotating it one way or the other to get the timing mark lined up with the pointer or index mark. A special wrench may be needed to get at distributor hold-down bolt. Wrench fits between the distributor and brake vacuum booster and beneath air injection reactor control valve of GM J-cars.

beyond the range of the timing marks on the crank pulley or indicator scale.

If the indicator scale on your engine doesn't extend to the range necessary for checking advance mechanisms, you can extend its range by measuring the width of a 5° increment of the scale and then painting additional pulley marks.

A hand vacuum pump is necessary for accurate testing of vacuum advance. Figures for vacuum advance are given as a certain amount of advance at a specific vacuum level.

The specs for our Ford distributor call for 13¾° vacuum advance at 15¾-in. vacuum. The vacuum advance should begin operating at 2.3-in. vacuum. To check, adjust idle to a point below that figure where centrifugal advance begins, in this case, 800 rpm. Then attach a hand vacuum pump to the distributor's vacuum diaphragm with the engine idling.

Point your timing light at the scale and begin pumping up vacuum. Note the point where timing starts to advance. Continue pumping until you reach the vacuum figure where advance should be full. Compare the amount of advance indicated on the crank pulley to the specification. You don't have to split hairs to see if it's within half a degree. Just check if it's working approximately the way it should.

Again, on most cars you'll have to extend the timing scale on the crank pulley if you're using a light, rather than a timing meter. Remember, if the increase in idle speed that results from the vacuum advance raises the idle above the figure where centrifugal advance starts, it will throw off your reading.

Some mechanics disable the centrifugal advance by securing it in position with little strips of duct tape while they're checking vacuum advance. But this is only practical on distributors where the centrifugal advance weights are directly under the rotor.

If the vacuum advance diaphragm is defective, replace it.

If the centrifugal advance is not functioning, it could be the result of sticking due to rust or lack of lubrication. The centrifugal advance can also fail because of weak springs or worn advance weights. Worn advance weights may result in excessive centrifugal advance, while worn springs would result in the advance coming in at a lower rpm than specified.

Troubleshooting Fuel System Problems

PAUL STENQUIST

■ FUEL SYSTEM PROBLEMS ARE among the most difficult to solve, particularly for anyone working without professional tools like emissions analyzers and oscilloscopes. These problems are tough because the fuel system is really seven different systems. Because of this complexity, the mechanic rules out other causes of engine problems before turning to the carburetor. Of course there are obvious exceptions, but for the normal range of no-starts, hesitations, stumbles, misses, backfires and burps a thorough check of maintenance items and internal engine condition should precede any attempt to diagnose a fuel problem.

However, most diagnostic checks can be completed satisfactorily with a minimum of equipment. Even electronic ignition diagnosis can be performed with an inexpensive analyzer.

Carburetor troubleshooting is another story. While some tools are available to help with specific troubles, the most helpful tools for diagnosing fuel problems are priced beyond the range of do-it-yourself mechanics. Instead, the part-time fuel system diagnostician must rely on his eyes and ears plus his knowledge of systems that control engine fueling and symptoms that malfunctions can provoke. Saturday mechanics must weigh the symptoms, such as surging, hesitation or rough idling, and logically determine which of the carburetor or fuel-supply components is the likely cause.

Most cars on the road today use a conventional carburetor to control fuel and air intake. For fuel to burn well, this ingenious device must maintain an air/fuel ratio of about 15 to 1. Connected to the engine cylinders by intake manifold runners, the carburetor provides fuel and air in response to pressure drops created when the pistons move down on intake stroke. It also responds to the driver's control, maintaining that relatively accurate air/fuel ratio as the throttle plates open and close. To do this efficiently under various conditions, a typical carburetor depends on at least six different systems: fuel reservoir, main metering, idle, enrichment, accelerator pump and cold start.

While most carburetors employ variations of the same systems, they come in many sizes and shapes, and fall within three classes: one-, two- and four-barrel. Barrel refers to throttle bores in the carburetor, so these classes are based on the number of throttle bores the carburetor has.

Four-barrel carburetors are designed to open the secondary barrels—the two rear ones—only when the pedal is pushed past the ¾ mark or so. This type of carburetor is called a two-stage design. There are also two-stage, two-barrels in use. All two-stage carbs have a choke flap on the primary side only.

Before the carburetor can do its job, fuel must be delivered by the pump and tank system. If you understand how that system and the six systems within the carburetor function, you will be well on your way to a working knowledge of conventional fuel systems. In the following subsections we'll discuss each system and explain what happens when it fails.

Fuel delivery system

The fuel delivery system of a carbureted engine consists of a mechanical fuel pump, a filter and the tank. Fuel delivery problems are easy to recognize because they produce a very clear symptom: The car behaves as though it has run out of fuel. Usually the engine dies at high speed. Sometimes it will restart when you ease off the throttle. If not, it can often be started with the key, but may die again. This will occur primarily under heavy load conditions, such as hill-climbing.

The first thing to consider when you have a delivery problem is the filter. If it isn't new, replace it. On many cars, it's behind the carburetor inlet nut. Before loosening the nut, be sure the engine is cold and lay a rag under the inlet. Then remove the nut and pull the filter out. Note any difference between the front and rear of the filter. Many have a check valve on one side. Other cars have in-line fuel filters.

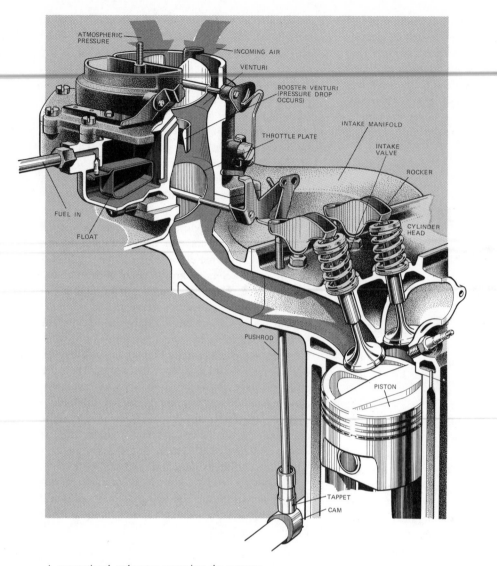

ATMOSPHERIC PRESSURE

INCOMING AIR

VENTURI

BOOSTER VENTURI (PRESSURE DROP OCCURS)

INTAKE MANIFOLD

INTAKE VALVE

THROTTLE PLATE

ROCKER

FUEL IN

FLOAT

CYLINDER HEAD

PUSHROD

PISTON

TAPPET

CAM

A conventional carburetor recognizes the pressure
drops created when pistons move down in their bores
and supplies fuel in proportion to the volume of air
drawn in.

Canister-shaped with a nipple on each end, these are spliced into a fuel line.

If the new filter doesn't solve a fuel delivery problem, the pump pressure should be tested. Disconnect the fuel line at the carburetor and attach a fuel-pressure gauge. Run the engine at idle on the fuel in the carburetor float bowl and read the pressure. Generally, it should be between 4 and 7 pounds per square inch (p.s.i.), but it would be best to check the exact figure. If pressure is too low, replace the pump.

If pressure is okay, check for pumping capacity. Disconnect the fuel line at the carburetor and hold it in a graduated container. Look at the second hand of your watch, while an assistant runs the engine until it pumps one pint into the container. At idle speed, it should produce a pint in about 30 seconds. If there are lots of air bubbles in the fuel and capacity is low, there may be a small hole in the line between tank and pump.

If the pump is producing full pressure but will not deliver enough fuel, suspect a restricted fuel line, clogged tank or clogged purge canister or tank vent. If the tank is full of dirt, you should see some when you disconnect lines. Restrictions are usually caused by kinks in fuel lines. A clogged canister or vent will produce a sound of air being drawn into the tank when the gas cap is removed; the car also should perform satisfactorily without the gas cap. If the system appears okay but the pump will still not meet capacity specs, have it replaced.

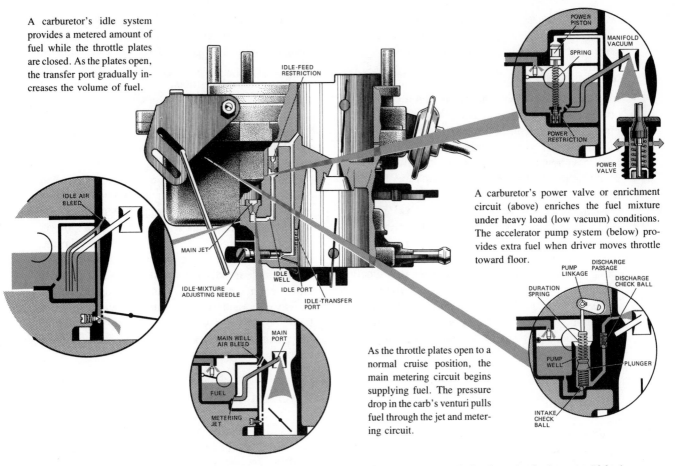

A carburetor's idle system provides a metered amount of fuel while the throttle plates are closed. As the plates open, the transfer port gradually increases the volume of fuel.

A carburetor's power valve or enrichment circuit (above) enriches the fuel mixture under heavy load (low vacuum) conditions. The accelerator pump system (below) provides extra fuel when driver moves throttle toward floor.

As the throttle plates open to a normal cruise position, the main metering circuit begins supplying fuel. The pressure drop in the carb's venturi pulls fuel through the jet and metering circuit.

Fuel reservoir system

When the fuel arrives at the carburetor, the fuel pressure forces the needle valve open. Then the float bowl within the carb begins to fill. As it fills, a plastic or brass float inside rises and pushes the valve closed. When fuel reaches the proper level, the needle closes to prevent the bowl from overfilling.

If the needle doesn't close, the engine will run rich, because the fuel level will continue to rise and fuel will be forced through the metering system and float-bowl vent tube. This condition is typified by roughness, chugging and black smoke. A rich condition will sometimes clear up under load at wide-open throttle, because the engine is using so much fuel the float bowl doesn't overfill.

Several things can cause the needle not to close. One is simply a worn needle or seat. Another is dirt wedged between the needle and seat. This can occur if a car is run without a filter, or if care is not taken to maintain cleanliness when the fuel system is apart. A third cause is an improperly adjusted float system. A very common cause is a plastic float becoming saturated with fuel, and sinking in the bowl. A brass float with a hole in it will also sink.

That brings us right back to the fuel pump. If fuel pressure is excessive, it can hold the needle valve open.

Main metering system

The main metering system provides fuel under all open throttle conditions. Under heavy load and acceleration, it is supplemented by other systems. This system depends on vacuum developed by the pistons moving down in their bores to draw in fuel.

If you look down the throat of a carburetor, you'll see that each barrel has a throttle plate at the bottom and a narrow section or venturi somewhere near the top. There is usually a second barrel, a booster venturi, within the main venturis. When throttle plates are opened, pressure drop created by the pistons causes air to be drawn through the barrels. When air moves through the narrow venturi of the carburetor, the vacuum signal is amplified. The booster venturi amplifies it further.

In the center of the booster venturi, you'll find a tube with a hole in it. This tube leads to a metering passage that is joined to the bottom of the float bowl. Where it meets the float bowl, there is a metering jet.

When air passes through the booster venturi, it literally sucks fuel out of the float bowl in much the same way you can draw liquid through a straw.

If the metering circuit becomes clogged with dirt, the engine will run extremely lean, causing misfire, roughness and stumble at partial throttle/cruising conditions. Idle will probably be okay unless the idle circuit is dirty too. Since it is nearly impossible to tell the difference between an ignition misfire and a lean misfire without an oscilloscope and emission analyzer, it is important that ignition problems are ruled out first.

Many two-stage carburetors meter fuel for the secondary barrel(s) by a valve linked to a secondary air flap. As air rushes through these barrel(s), it pushes the flap open, which opens the metering valve. As air volume increases, so does fuel supply in correct proportion. A two-stage carburetor that performs well on the primary barrels, but causes hesitation, bucking or surging when the throttle is floorboarded, may have a secondary metering system problem.

Idle system

With the throttle at idle the idle adjustment screw or idle solenoid prevents the throttle plates from closing completely. Since air volume passing around the nearly closed throttle plates is not sufficient to draw fuel from the main metering circuit, an idle fuel circuit is provided to connect the fuel reservoir to a small hole in the carb barrel just below the throttle plates. With the engine running, air rushing around the edge of the nearly closed throttle plate causes a pressure drop. This vacuum draws fuel from the idle circuit.

Just above the idle port and bridging the edge of the throttle plate is the idle transfer port. This port, also connected to the idle circuit, provides a transition from idle position to open throttle.

An incorrect idle mixture causes rough running, high emissions and poor fuel economy. A clogged transfer port can cause hesitation, surging or stumble at off-idle throttle positions.

Enrichment system

During open throttle, high load conditions, the carburetor's metering circuit can't provide enough fuel for a suitable air/fuel ratio, so an enrichment or power valve system is provided.

Most enrichment systems consist of a piston and metering rod or a diaphragm-controlled valve. High manifold vacuum keeps the diaphragm closed or the piston down in its bore, preventing fuel from entering the system. As vacuum falls, the spring-loaded piston rises in its bore, pulling the rod out of the metering jet that it restricts, increasing the amount of fuel supplied. With diaphragm-controlled valves, a spring pushes the diaphragm valve open.

If the piston sticks or the diaphragm tears, the enrichment circuit can remain open. This makes the engine rich at light throttle. Fuel economy suffers.

The enrichment valve can also cause a lean condition if it jams in the high vacuum position, or if its fuel inlet port becomes clogged. A nonfunctioning enrichment system will cause loss of power, stumble and surging under heavy load/open throttle conditions. Absolute confirmation of an enrichment valve problem calls for tear-down and inspection. However, a service facility that's equipped with a chassis dyno and emissions analyzer can confirm a faulty power valve without opening up the carburetor. Detonation—spark knock—can also result from an excessively lean condition.

Accelerator pump system

In addition to the main metering and enrichment systems, controlled by engine vacuum, a carburetor needs an accelerator pump system that responds to throttle movement. Without it the carburetor can't supply enough fuel when throttle plates open quickly.

Two types of accelerator pump systems are in use—diaphragm pumps and piston pumps. Diaphragm systems have a spring-loaded neoprene diaphragm that, when compressed by the throttle linkage, delivers fuel to a nozzle or nozzles in the carburetor barrel. Piston-type accelerator pumps use a spring-loaded rawhide piston. A check ball near the discharge nozzle stops the flow when the accelerator pedal is held steady. When the pedal is released, the returning piston or diaphragm draws fuel from the float bowl. A second check valve keeps the charge from leaking back.

If you car hesitates severely when you tromp on the accelerator, your carburetor may have a worn or damaged accelerator pump or a clogged discharge nozzle. By manually operating the throttle while you look into the carburetor, you'll be able to determine whether the pump system is delivering fuel.

Cold-start system

The most important cold-start components—the choke and fast-idle mechanism—are controlled by the carburetor.

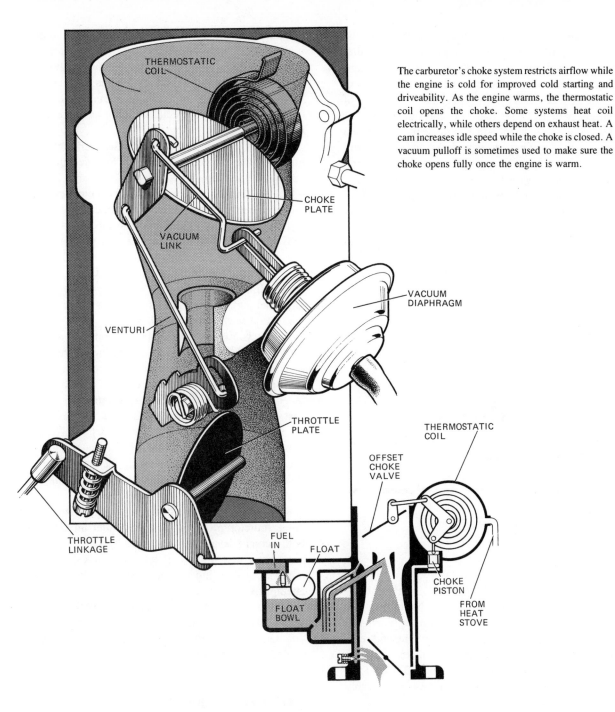

The carburetor's choke system restricts airflow while the engine is cold for improved cold starting and driveability. As the engine warms, the thermostatic coil opens the choke. Some systems heat coil electrically, while others depend on exhaust heat. A cam increases idle speed while the choke is closed. A vacuum pulloff is sometimes used to make sure the choke opens fully once the engine is warm.

The choke is an air flap that partially covers the carburetor barrel(s) when the engine is cold. The restriction created speeds up airflow. Resulting turbulence helps vaporize the fuel injected by the accelerator pump when the throttle is floored for a cold start.

Once the engine is running, the choke continues to limit the air intake, ensuring that the air/fuel mixture will be richer with fuel than under normal conditions and that the increased turbulence will help improve the cold-engine combustion.

The choke flap is usually controlled by a metal coil that expands as it warms. The coil is usually located within a housing on the side of the carburetor. Sometimes it is on the intake manifold.

On the throttle side of the carburetor a bellcrank is connected by linkage to the choke flap. Called the fast-idle cam, it has a series of graduated steps. Resting against the fast-idle cam is a fast-idle adjustment screw attached to the throttle-plate shaft. When the engine is cold and the throttle is floorboarded for a cold start, the choke coil closes the choke flap that pushes the linkage which rotates the fast-idle cam. When the throttle is returned to idle, the fast-idle screw contacts the high spot on the cam.

Choke problems show up most often in the form of difficult cold starting. Generally, this is the result of the choke being set too lean or simply not working. A lean choke adjustment will also make the car hesitate during cold driving. A rich choke adjustment will cause high idle emissions, poor fuel economy and poor driveability. An extremely rich choke adjustment can cause hot-start problems. An improper fast-idle adjustment will also cause cold driveability difficulties.

Whenever such problems occur, all choke-system adjustments should be checked. Most general auto repair manuals provide specifications and adjustment techniques for the more common carburetors. Some can be adjusted using only a steel rule. For others, a choke-valve angle gauge may be necessary.

Rebuilding a Carburetor

PAUL STENQUIST

■ IF YOU ENJOYED BUILDING model airplanes or cars as a youngster, you'll probably have a fine time rebuilding a carburetor. Carburetor repair can be entertaining if you enjoy disassembling and reassembling interesting machines. With the price of some rebuilt carburetors hitting the $200 or $300 mark, the idea of doing it yourself is considerably more appealing.

There is one principal disadvantage to rebuilding your own carb: It may not work when you're finished! As mechanics well know, there's no guarantee of success when you rebuild a carb without testing it on a flow bench as major rebuilders do. The carb could fail to work properly due to a porous casting or extensive internal blockage—even if you perform a flawless rebuild. For this reason, some mechanics won't rebuild carburetors in the shop.

The Saturday mechanic has an advantage here. You know the pitfalls going in, and if you're willing to take a chance, you can save a lot of money by rebuilding your own carb.

Another factor to consider before you decide to do it yourself is the complexity of the carburetor in question. The novice carburetor mechanic should avoid some of the more complex designs, such as the Rochester Quadrajet or the Ford Variable Venturi carbs, which require special tools for accurate set-up.

Some of the most commonly used carburetors, however, are also the most simple. Included among them. are the popular Rochester 2GC and 2GE, which are found on millions of GM cars produced in the last quarter century; the various one-barrel Carter, Rochester and Holley designs; the newer GM 2SE and E2SE Rochester two-barrels; the Autolite four-barrels found on many mid-'70s Ford and Mercury V8s; the Carter Thermoquad and AFB four-barrels found on some Chrysler V8s and virtually any other carb that doesn't have a tremendous number of components or special systems.

Before you even consider taking your carburetor off the intake manifold, you should have carefully diagnosed your engine performance problem. Fuel system troubles are sometimes easily confused with other types of engine performance problems. The best mechanics never try to repair an engine by throwing new parts at it until they get lucky. Instead, they logically and systematically attempt to eliminate possibilities until they locate the true culprit. ''Troubleshooting Fuel System Problems'' outlines a plan for fuel system diagnosis.

Remember, too, that all fuel system problems are not carburetor problems. Incorrect fuel mixture—both rich and lean—can be caused by a malfunction somewhere else in the fuel system, so a test of fuel pump pressure and output should precede any attempt to repair your carburetor.

If your fuel tank is contaminated to the point where you must change fuel filters frequently, have your tank professionally removed and cleaned before beginning other repairs.

Carburetor removal

The first step in the repair procedure is the removal of the carburetor from the car. Begin by removing the air cleaner. Most air cleaners have a vacuum line for control of the hot air system. This line connects to a manifold vacuum source. Disconnect the line from the air cleaner's thermal valve. Mark it with a color-coded or number-coded piece of tape, so you won't confuse it with other vacuum lines that will have to be disconnected. Disconnect the hot air duct that runs from the exhaust manifold to the air cleaner and remove the entire air cleaner assembly from the engine compartment.

With the air cleaner removed, study the carburetor and note any linkage, wire or hose attachments that will have to be disconnected before the carb can be lifted from the engine. Mark the vacuum lines—you'll find at least one more in addition to the one you've already removed—remove them and lay them aside. If there's more than one wiring connection, mark them as well before you disconnect. The throttle linkage and transmission shift valve linkage (on cars with automatic transmission) are usually secured by circlips or ball-and-socket connectors. Remove these, taking care not to lose any clips. If the carburetor has a manifold-mounted choke heater, you must disengage the choke linkage, as well.

The next step is disconnecting the fuel line. Place a rag under the fuel line connection to catch spilled fuel. Then, using a tubing wrench that provides a secure grip, loosen the fuel-line nut. Use an open-end wrench to hold the fuel-inlet retainer nut, which is part of the carburetor. If you don't, you might twist the fuel line. If you don't have a tubing wrench, you can try loosening the fuel-line nut with an open-end wrench, but you might round it off. If you do that, use locking pliers to remove it, and then replace it.

Once the fuel line has been disconnected, loosen the fuel-inlet retainer nut while the carb is still on the engine. This will save you having to wrestle with it on the bench. Then, loosen and remove the four bolts securing the carburetor to the intake manifold. You'll probably have to use a box wrench on most of them. Don't use an open-end wrench unless you have to because of limited access.

With the carburetor off the car, examine it until you find a model number. It might be stamped or printed on the float bowl, or it might be on a small metal tag secured by one of the float bowl screws. Determine the make and model of the carb, such as Rochester 2GC or Carter BBD.

Armed with this information, head for your local parts store. (If you have trouble finding the model and ID number, take the whole carburetor with you.) Ask the counterman for a rebuilding kit. Make sure the kit comes with instructions before you purchase it. The instructions should include an exploded view of the carb, which demonstrates how the parts fit together, plus instructions for making the various adjustments, and a list of specs for the different cars on which the carb is used. It may not include specific step-by-step assembly and disassembly procedures, but it should, at least, include a list of the various components that indicates the order of removal and reassembly.

While you're at the parts store, buy a new fuel filter and—unless you have access to a carb-dip cleaning tank—a can of engine degreaser spray.

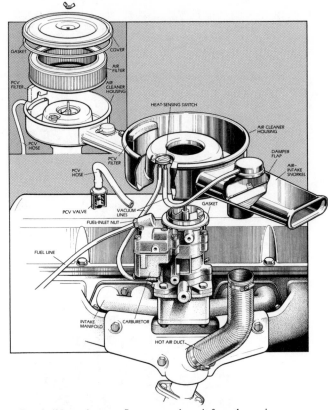

To rebuild a carburetor, first remove the unit from the engine. Label every wire, hose, duct, line and linkage before you remove them from the air cleaner or carb. Unscrew the fuel-inlet nut before removing the carb from the manifold.

Find a large, well-lighted work area before you even open your carb kit. Kitchen tables are great, but the rest of the family will undoubtedly object to the gasoline odors that will permeate the house if you do the job indoors. A basement or garage workbench is best.

Open the carb kit, examine the instruction sheet and familiarize yourself with the parts included in the kit. You'll find a variety of gaskets, some new clips, some little steel balls, a new needle and seat assembly, a new accelerator pump (in most cases) and a gauge for measuring float height adjustments.

Carburetor disassembly

Begin the disassembly procedure in the order prescribed in the instruction sheet. You'll probably begin with the fuel-inlet retainer nut (which you've already loosened) and proceed to disconnect the various linkages (accelerator pump, choke, fast idle) that join the bottom half of the carb to the top half, or air-horn assembly.

Many carburetors are equipped with a choke housing that contains a thermostatic coil. On most late-model carbs, the cover of this housing is secured

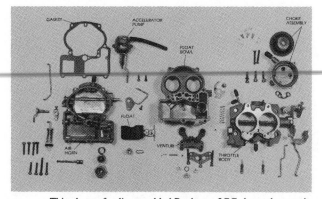

This photo of a disassembled Rochester 2GC shows three main body components (air horn, float bowl and throttle body) surrounded by removable subassemblies, gaskets, jets, check balls, screws and linkages. Replace old parts with new ones in kit.

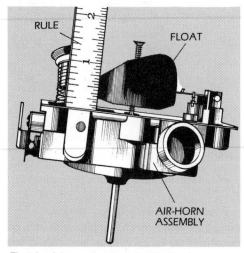

Float level is usually checked with the air horn inverted. Use steel rule or gauge in the kit to measure and adjust the float level.

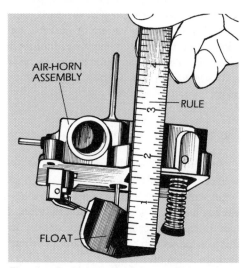

Float drop is checked with air horn upright. On most carbs, drop can exceed specs if needle doesn't wedge against float.

with rivets to prevent tampering with the choke adjustment.

To remove a choke cover that has been riveted to its housing, drill the head of each rivet until it falls off. GM specifies a No. 21 drill bit for removal of the cover on many of its Rochester carbs. Once the head has fallen off the rivet, drive out the shank of the rivet with a small drift.

After you've completed all the preliminary disassemblies, the instructions will probably direct you to remove the air-horn screws and air-horn assembly. Next will be the float assembly and accelerator pump. These parts are frequently attached to the underside of the air horn, although they are located in the bottom, or float bowl, half of the carb in some designs.

The float bowl will contain the metering jets, some check balls and, in many cases, a power valve assembly. All of them will be removed. In many cases, the float bowl can be disassembled from the throttle plate beneath it.

The idle adjustment screws are located in the throttle plate. On many late-model carbs, they're tamper-proof. You may have to remove a plug to gain access to the idle mixture screws.

Once the carb has been completely disassembled, examine the float. If it's made of brass, shake it to see if there's fuel inside. If there is, the float has a leak and must be replaced. If the float is plastic, you should replace it as a precaution. Some plastic floats absorb gas with time and become too heavy. This can affect performance. If you have a float scale and a list of specs, check it. Otherwise, it's best just to replace it. Most parts stores carry a wide range of replacement floats.

Cleanup and reassembly

The cleanup procedure is the worst part of the rebuilding job. Mechanics immerse the metal parts in a chemical cleaner, known as carb dip, for an hour or so. Then they rinse the parts in water and dry them with compressed air. This cleaner can be used for other part-washing jobs, so it might not be a bad idea to purchase a small container.

You can also use a drain pan and a spray can of carb cleaner. Simply lay the parts in the pan, spray them and let them soak for 10 or 20 minutes. Renew the spray if it starts to evaporate. Then rinse the parts in hot running water and blow them dry if possible with an air compressor, not a hair dryer. Blow drying is important because you can direct the air into the various passages, insuring that they're not blocked. If you don't have an air compressor, buy a can of the compressed air sold in camera stores for cleaning photo equipment.

If the parts aren't clean after one treatment, repeat the procedure. Cleaning is probably the most important part of a rebuild. Many carb failures are the result of dirt.

Once cleanup is complete, examine all parts for cracks or porosity. If the carb is equipped with a power valve piston or metering rod piston (see your parts list), examine it for scoring or galling. You can polish it lightly with crocus cloth. Don't attempt to polish the metering rod itself or to straighten a bent metering rod. Damaged metering rods must be replaced. This is usually not a parts store item, but many new car dealers' parts departments do stock individual carb components.

Reassembly usually begins with the installation of the needle valves in the throttle plate assembly. Screw them in only until they are finger-tight, then back them out two to four turns as an initial idle adjustment (or as indicated in your carb kit instructions).

Before you're very far into the reassembly, you'll be installing the float and needle seat assembly in the air horn. At this point, you must make the float adjustments. You'll find specs and instructions for this job in the adjustment section of the instruction sheet.

Generally there are two adjustments: Float level is adjusted with the air horn inverted and the needle seat in a closed position. (This is probably the most critical carb adjustment of all.) The other float adjustment is usually called float drop, and it's made with the air horn in an upright position. In this case, you may not have to be quite as cautious, as an amount in excess of the spec is okay, as long as the float will retain the needle without binding at maximum drop.

When you reinstall the air horn on the float bowl assembly, make sure you don't knock the float out of adjustment. If the carb has a piston-type accelerator pump that hangs from the air horn, make sure it fits properly into the pumping chamber in the float bowl.

Adjustments

Once you have completed the reassembly procedure, you'll have several adjustments to make, most of which can be done with the carb off the car. These will include a choke adjustment, fast idle adjustment, vacuum break adjustment and a choke unloader adjustment. (On carbs that are more than 10 years old, you may have fewer adjustments to complete.)

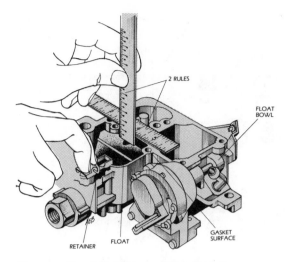

Float assembly of this Rochester 2SE is inside the float bowl, rather than under the air horn. On such carbs, you can use two rules to measure the distance from the gasket surface to the float at the point most distant from retainer/hinge.

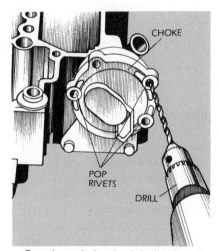

Cover is attached to the choke housing with rivets, rather than screws, on late-model carbs. Drill out rivets to remove the cover.

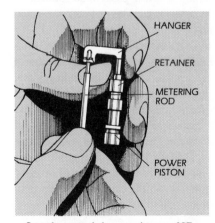

Scored or corroded power piston on 2SE can be polished lightly with crocus cloth. Replace any damaged metering rods.

Fixing Your Mechanic's Most Common Goofs

PETE WARREN

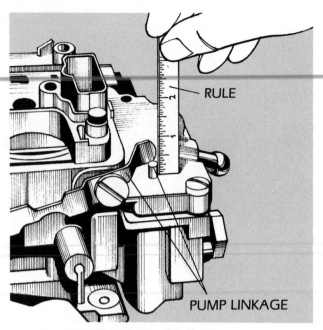

Kit will contain instructions for adjustments that must be made after reassembly. Here, pump linkage of a 2SE is set to specs.

RULE

PUMP LINKAGE

Perform each adjustment in exactly the manner described on the instruction sheet. This will make a tremendous difference in driveability.

On some late-model GM carbs, like the 2SE and E2SE, you will need a choke angle gauge to make certain adjustments. However, you can complete enough of the adjustments without this tool to get the car running. Then, if you'd rather not invest in this specialized but inexpensive tool, you can take the car to a mechanic for the adjustment.

Even if you can complete all the adjustments yourself, you may want to take the car to a competent engine mechanic for final adjustment of the idle mixture—particularly if your state has an annual inspection program. A few degrees of adjustment on an idle-mixture screw can make or break the emission inspection.

When you have reassembled the carburetor, reinstall it on the intake manifold and properly reconnect all the wires, hoses, ducts, lines and linkages that you labelled and disconnected in the beginning. Then reinstall the air cleaner and its vacuum lines.

Unless your car has an electric fuel pump, it will not restart until the engine has turned over enough for the mechanical pump to fill the float bowl. Prime the carburetor by dumping a few spoonsful of gasoline (one at a time) down the carburetor throat until the engine will start and run without stalling.

■ IF YOUR CAR IS running poorly, perhaps an out-of-date mechanic is the reason. Too often we hear the excuse, ''Can't do any better. It's the emission controls.'' That's sometimes valid, but it's also used by mechanics who just got left behind when the auto industry began to clean up tailpipe emissions.

The computer-equipped car is one source of service hassles for mechanics who haven't kept up with the technology. However, many problems are caused by ignorance of engine control systems that have been around since the 1960s, and not all of them are emissions related. Many times, if the ill-trained simply left things alone, the cars would run a lot better. But instead they've disconnected and bypassed critical systems. Unfortunately, the things they left alone were worn-out parts that required extra effort to replace.

Here are many of the obvious underhood errors that should have been fixed, but were not. If you discover one of these problems and choose not to fix it yourself, find a professional who *has* kept up to date.

Disabled EGR

Exhaust gas recirculation valve disconnected, resulting in ping.

The vacuum hose was taken off and plugged, because someone was convinced that recirculating exhaust gas back into the engine had to be bad, even if it does reduce emissions (see lead illustration). Well, because it reduces peak combustion temperatures, it also prevents ping on most cars.

Port vacuum bypass

Vacuum spark advance hoses rerouted, resulting in ping.

One of the most common steps is to bypass anything between the distributor vacuum advance and the vacuum source. In some cases, the bypass just results in excessive spark advance when the engine is hot, but in most of those we've seen the problem was too much advance applied on takeoff.

On a Chrysler, for example, the carburetor and distributor hoses were disconnected from the Orifice Spark Advance Control (OSAC) valve on the air cleaner and one hose was run from the carburetor base to the distributor (Fig. 1). The OSAC valve delays spark advance between idle and part throttle.

On other cars, a distributor vacuum advance hose was connected to the intake manifold or carburetor base. Either one is a source of manifold vacuum, instead of the original equipment source, which was a port above the throttle plate. Manifold vacuum is highest at idle and still relatively high going to part throttle. Port vacuum is zero at idle and builds up gradually as the throttle is opened up to part throttle.

Improper advance

Ignition timing set incorrectly, resulting in ping or poor performance.

Even mechanics who wouldn't touch computers know there is a procedure to be followed before checking ignition timing, generally a wiring connector to be grounded or to be taken apart.

Because an AMC six-cylinder engine didn't have a computer, the timing was set the conventional way. However, it had a Ford-type ignition system with an ignition module containing a timing-retard circuit that must be canceled before any timing check and adjustment is made. The car's underhood decal that gave the procedure was missing, but a mechanic who was up to date would know what to do. The procedure, which also applies to many Fords, is to unplug the two-wire (yellow and black) connector from the module and connect a jumper wire across the male terminals (Fig. 2).

Vacuum-break failure

Choke vacuum break failed, resulting in poor gas mileage and black smoke on startup, plus rough idle and poor driveability when warm.

When the engine starts, the vacuum break diaphragm link should pull in, but if the diaphragm fails, it won't (Fig. 3).

We've seen cars on which the carburetor was replaced to correct poor mileage and black smoke on startup, but the old defective diaphragm unit was

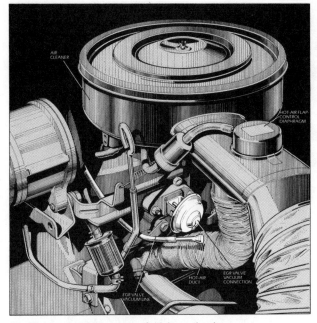

You'll get pinging because of high combustion temperatures if your mechanic disconnected the EGR valve and plugged the vacuum line.

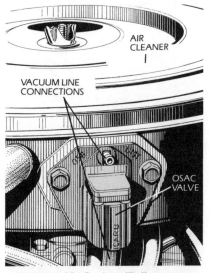

1 Bypassed OSAC valve will allow excess vacuum advance and often cause pinging.

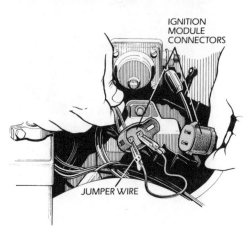

2 Ford-type electronic ignition modules must be jumped to set timing correctly.

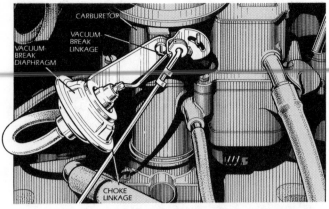

3 When a vacuum-break diaphragm falls, the choke may stay closed, causing poor mileage and black smoke. If old diaphragm is reinstalled, even a new carb won't help out.

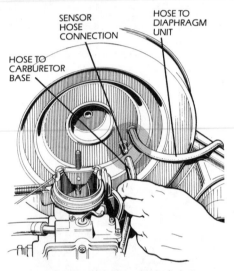

4 Bypassing thermostatic air cleaner sensor locks system in the heat-on position.

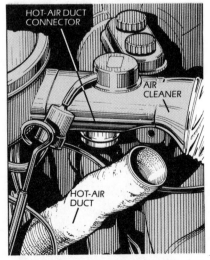

5 A disconnected carburetor hot-air duct will cause cold hesitation and stalling.

transferred to the new carb, so the problem remained. In one case, the car was used in short-trip operation, and warm driveability was passable because the cooling system thermostat was stuck open and the engine warmed up very slowly. In another case, the sparkplugs were removed, found to be fouled, and replaced, but nothing else was done.

Temperature sensor bypass

Thermostatic air cleaner sensor bypassed, leaving system stuck heat-on, resulting in poor performance with the engine warm.

The temperature sensor in the air cleaner controls vacuum to the diaphragm unit that operates the flap in the snorkel. As the engine warms up, the sensor should reduce vacuum, so a spring forces the flap to pivot from heat-on to heat-off.

In this case, the two hoses—one from the carburetor base to sensor, the second from sensor to diaphragm unit—were replaced with one hose from the carburetor base to diaphragm unit (Fig. 4), so the flap was always in the heat-on position. Cold starts were fine, but once the engine was warm, the hot air coming in contributed to overheating (and leaning out) of the fuel mixture, reducing performance.

Unheated intake air

Thermostatic air cleaner disabled, resulting in hesitation and stalling until the engine fully warmed up.

Unless the thermostatic air cleaner flap goes to heat-on position when the engine is started cold, the engine will run poorly for several miles.

There are several ways we've seen the system disabled. Inadvertently, the hot-air duct from the heat stove on the exhaust manifold was left disconnected at one end (Fig. 5) or the vacuum hose at the air cleaner sensor was unplugged. However, we've also seen the vacuum hose at the diaphragm unit pulled off and plugged, and the hot-air duct left out completely, and both were deliberate acts.

Disabled idle stabilizer

Digital idle stabilizer on a VW Rabbit bypassed, resulting in rough idle.

The stabilizer, on engines with fuel injection, makes continuous small adjustments in ignition timing to keep idle within a specified range. It takes at least a moderately knowledgeable mechanic to know about this part, and to remove the connectors and plug them into each other to correctly perform an ignition timing check (Fig. 6). However, the mechanic forgot to plug the connectors back into the stabilizer when the tuneup was done.

Disabled idle solenoid

Idle solenoid failed and idle speed set on low-speed screw instead of at the solenoid, so the engine diesels when shut off.

The electric idle solenoid was introduced in the late 1960s. Its job is to permit the throttle to remain open far enough to hold a suitable idle speed, yet allow the throttle to close almost completely when the engine is turned off to prevent dieseling. But some mechanic apparently still didn't know about it. When it failed, the engine began to stall. Instead of replacing the solenoid, he turned up the idle using the low-speed idle screw (Fig. 7). So the throttle didn't close when the engine was shut off.

Stuck EGR valve

Idle speed turned up to reduce rough running caused by exhaust gas recirculation valve stuck in the open position, resulting in dieseling.

In this case, the idle speed was controlled only by an idle-speed screw—no idle solenoid was originally fitted. At the throttle opening required for factory-recommended idle speed, the engine normally wouldn't diesel. However, with the wider throttle opening from the too-high idle speed, it did diesel. Further, the engine ran almost as rough even at the high idle speed.

On some cars, you can see or feel the EGR valve stem and operate it with a screwdriver to make sure the valve will move (Fig. 8). If you can't, unbolt the valve and operate it from the inside end to be sure it's free.

Kickup solenoid failure

Idle kickup solenoid failed and the engine stalled when the air conditioning was turned on.

In an attempt to correct this, the idle-speed screw was turned, raising the idle speed so the engine dieseled when shut off. On many cars the correct idle-speed throttle position does not cause a dieseling problem (often because the idle speed is kept low), but there is a solenoid, used to provide an idle-speed

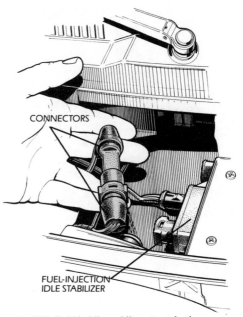

6 VW Rabbit idle stablizer must be by-passed for timing checks, then reconnected for smooth idling.

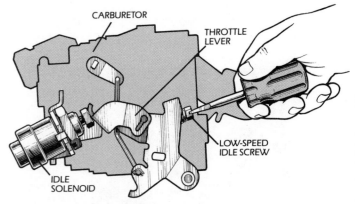

7 If idle speed is set using screw when an idle solenoid fails, dieseling will result.

kickup only when the air conditioning is turned on. In this case, the high idle speed did not always stop the stalling when the a/c kicked in, and it added the dieseling.

PCV system disconnection

Positive Crankcase Ventilation valve pulled out and not pushed back into its grommet, resulting in oil flow into the air cleaner (Fig. 9).

The oil splashed around and helped plug the filter (reducing performance and mileage) and also was pulled into the combustion chambers (resulting in oil loss).

Cause: When the PCV valve was out, a flow reversal occurred in the crankcase ventilation system. Air rushed into the engine through the PCV

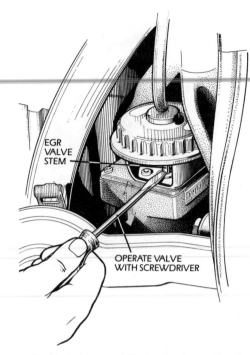

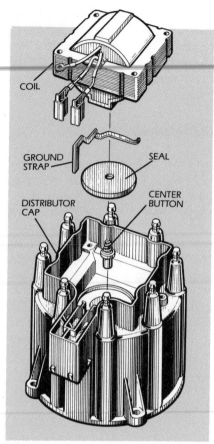

8 Check for a stuck EGR valve by working the EGR valve stem with a screwdriver.

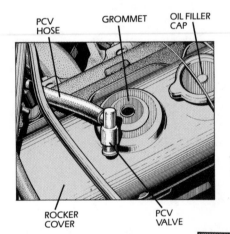

10 Omission of the center button in GM HEI systems will cause short plug life.

9 An inoperative PCV valve can cause oil to flow up into the air-cleaner housing.

11 Swivel-joint sockets and ratchet extensions may be needed to change plugs, but regular replacement is vital.

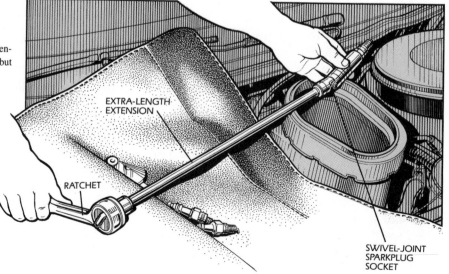

valve opening and oil vapors and droplets flowed up the fresh-air intake, into the air-cleaner housing.

HEI shortchange

High Energy Ignition distributor cap "button" left out when cap was replaced, resulting in short plug life and erratic performance.

The center button in General Motors HEI distributor caps is a separate part, normally included with a new cap (Fig. 10). The old cap's button and the rotor were burned out (a problem that has occurred on HEI systems) and when the new cap and rotor were installed, the old coil and rubber gasket were transferred, but no one looked inside the box to get the new center button. Perhaps the center button was left out of the box, or was not included with that brand, but the installer should have had a cap that included one.

Inaccessible sparkplugs

Difficult-to-reach sparkplugs never changed, so the engine idles roughly and runs poorly.

The problems of reaching some of the sparkplugs on the Chevy Monza V8 are well known, but a couple of other cars also have inaccessible sparkplugs that were never changed.

The plugs in the rear bank of the 2.8-liter V6 in the transverse-engine, front-drive GM X-cars were very difficult to reach on 1980 models, but the access was improved when an air pump was installed instead of the Pulsair valve assemblies. In either case, the job looks worse than it is.

The rear plug on many installations of an inline American Motors six-cylinder also is a tough one, but if you have a very long extension, it can be removed, albeit with some difficulty (Fig. 11). But a lot of AMC engines are running on only five cylinders.

Part **III:**

INSIDE
YOUR ENGINE

Troubleshooting Oil Consumption Problems

PAUL STENQUIST

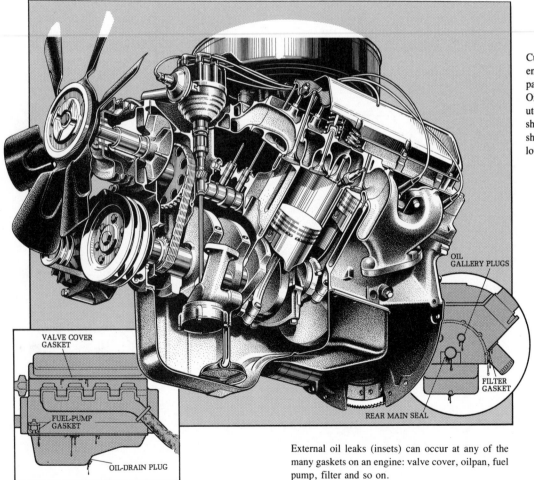

Cutaway of typical V8 engine shows major parts of its oil system. Oil pump (and distributor) are driven by a shaft and gear on camshaft. Oil pickup is at lowest point of oilpan.

OIL GALLERY PLUGS

FILTER GASKET

VALVE COVER GASKET

FUEL-PUMP GASKET

OIL-DRAIN PLUG

REAR MAIN SEAL

External oil leaks (insets) can occur at any of the many gaskets on an engine: valve cover, oilpan, fuel pump, filter and so on.

■ HAS YOUR VEHICLE'S THIRST for motor oil forced you to join the ranks of those poor unfortunates who carry a substantial part of the nation's petroleum reserve in cans in their trunks? Are you serenaded by the rolling and clunking of errant oil cans every time you accelerate or come to a stop? Do you occasionally find yourself at the side of a dark highway, flashlight gripped between your teeth, trying to direct a wind-whipped stream of oil into that little opening in your car's engine?

Maybe it's time to solve your engine's oil-consumption problem. A lot of vehicle owners assume that the solution to an oil-use problem will be expensive. And while it's true that repairing some of these can be costly, a great number of oil-consumption problems can be fixed quite inexpensively.

The first step toward the solution is to determine whether the loss results from internal or external leakage or both. Your parking space should provide a good clue. If a puddle of lubricant always is left behind, your vehicle is obviously leaking something. But remember, it could be transmission or differential oil.

An engine that leaks oil internally, into the combustion chamber, will produce blue exhaust smoke under one or more conditions. The list includes idling, accelerating, decelerating, after prolonged idling, or after fire-up. The conditions that provoke exhaust smoke can help you determine the source of the oil.

External leakage

External leaks are difficult to pinpoint because there are many locations from which lubricant can leak, and because the vehicle uses more than one type of lubricant.

You can identify the area of leakage and the type of lubricant by leaving white paper under your parked car. Engine oil leaks will leave dirty spots, while transmission fluid leaks will leave pink spots. By tracing the point of leakage on the vehicle, the source can sometimes be determined.

However, if the entire underside of the engine is covered with wind-swept oil, the drip method of locating a leak may only reveal the spot where the lubricant is collecting before dripping to the ground. Sometimes, the tracks of oil can be traced to the source. Remember that since the oil is blown to the rear as the car moves, the source will be a point farther forward.

In some cases, it may be necessary to clean the engine before attempting to find the leak. Use one of the commonly available engine cleaning solutions. Cleaning agents come in aerosol cans. You simply spray the cleaner on the dirty engine, allow it to soak in for a while and then hose it off. Several applications may be necessry to clean a filthy engine. You should do a particularly good job on the underside.

Once the engine is clean, repeat the drip test without driving. Let the engine idle for 20 minutes over the paper. Race the engine occasionally while it's idling to prevent overheating. Shut the engine off. If there are no spots on the paper, leave the car in place for a few hours.

The point of leakage should now be fairly easy to trace. If the leak is near the top of the engine, it may not drip down to the paper. But you should be able to spot the dripping lube on the clean engine.

In either case, if you still can't find the leak, you can try one of the black light kits available for tracing oil leaks. These kits include a fluorescent substance that's added to the oil. When the black light is aimed at the leaking lube, the leaking oil glows brightly.

Most engines have rocker cover, timing cover, oilpan and fuel pump gaskets. Some engines have valley or pushrod cover gaskets. On some V-type engines, the intake manifold seals the valley, and intake manifold end-seals are used. These are all common sources of leakage, and the leak can

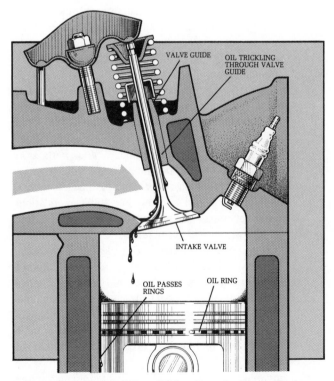

Internal leaks occur when oil is sucked into the combustion chamber by one of two routes: either up past the piston rings or down past the valve guides and the valve.

sometimes be difficult to spot. If the rear end-seal leaks, oil may collect on the block behind the manifold or it may leak down between the bellhousing and the engine block. In the latter case, it may lead you to believe that the source of the leak is in the oilpan gasket or rear main seal.

In some cases, a considerable amount of disassembly work may precede the installation of a gasket. This is particularly true of oilpan and timing cover gaskets. You'll want to consult a repair manual before attempting either of these repairs.

Tighten bolts carefully

Occasionally, a gasket leak can be repaired by tightening a few bolts. However, don't tighten bolts excessively in an effort to stem the flow. Use a torque wrench and tighten only to the manufacturer's specification.

Modern gaskets are generally installed without adhesives. But in many cases, a fast-drying adhesive must be used to hold the gasket in place for installation. We have found that, when installing oilpan, rocker cover, fuel pump or timing cover gaskets, it's advisable to secure the gasket to the respective component first with a fast-drying adhesive and then allow it to dry before installation is attempted. Check the instructions that come with the new gaskets for any additional information concerning adhesives. When reinstalling components, torque all fasteners to the correct specification in gradual steps.

Some of the new powerplants are assembled with RTV (room temperature vulcanizing). RTV adhesive is used *in place of* conventional gaskets. On other engines, an anaerobic form-in-place chemical sealant is used in a similar manner. Your parts store counterman should be able to tell you if either compound is necessary for repair. All he has to do is look in the gasket catalog. For some applications where chemical sealant was used at the factory, gaskets are provided for repair.

Most powerplants have a flexible seal surrounding each end of the crankshaft. These are usually known as the timing cover seal (front) and the rear main seal (rear). Timing cover seal leaks come from behind the front pulley of the engine and are easily misdiagnosed as timing cover gasket leaks. Repair of a timing cover seal involves disassembling the front of the engine. In most cases, the radiator must be removed. Consult a repair manual before attempting such a task. If the old seal wore a groove in the collar

of the crank damper, the damper assembly will have to be replaced along with the seal.

Rear main seal leaks come trickling down from between the oilpan and the flywheel. To repair a rear main seal leak you must remove the oilpan. The rear main seal is located in the last of the main bearing caps or in a seal holder behind the last main bearing cap. On some engines, the oil pump must be removed so that you can gain access to the rear main bearing cap.

The main seal has both upper and lower halves. Once the cap or seal retainer has been removed, the ends of the upper half will be visible. On some engines, the upper half can be "walked out" by holding it against the crankshaft with a punch while an assistant slowly rotates the crank. Once the seal has been dragged around to the lower position, it can be pulled out. Again, consult a repair manual before attempting a rear main seal job.

Most engines have a camshaft expansion plug in the back of the block above the crankshaft. If this plug leaks, it can mimic a leaking rear main seal. On some engines, you can see above the crank by using a flexible light probe. On other engines, you may not discover a leaking cam plug until the rear main seal job fails to stop the dripping lube. In any case, the repair of the cam plug calls for removal of the engine or transmission.

Internal leakage

If lubricating oil leaks into an engine's combustion chamber in significant amounts, it can produce several undesirable results, not the least of which is that large cloud of blue smoke that forms at the rear of the tailpipe. But smoke isn't the only negative effect of oil consumption. The presence of oil in the combustion chamber sometimes causes detonation. Furthermore, the fact that the engine operates without sufficient lubricant much of the time can also lead to friction damage.

There are two principal ways that oil can enter the combustion chamber—through the valve guides or past the piston rings. But oil can also reach the chambers through the PCV system fresh air hose or, on some engines, past the intake manifold gaskets. There are several clues that can help you distinguish among the causes of internal oil consumption.

If blue smoke is present only when the vehicle is first started after several hours at rest, the problem is probably bad valve guides. The same is probably true if the smoke appears only when the engine is first

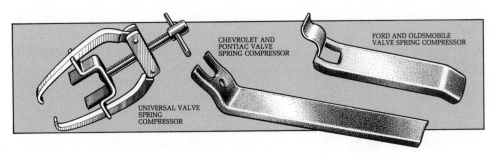

Repairing oil leaks at worn valve guides is a do-it-yourself job. One of the few special tools needed is a valve spring compressor. It is available for different cars, and also comes in a universal model. Spring compressors can often be rented by the day.

accelerated after extended idling. On the other hand, if smoke appears only when the engine is under load and continues throughout the rpm range, the oil rings probably are worn out or stuck in their grooves. However, as valve guides continue to wear, they can produce oil smoke under most operating conditions.

Before attempting a diagnosis, remove all the sparkplugs. If only some of the plugs exhibit the caked-on, oily black deposits that indicate oil consumption, you will be able to limit your troubleshooting to those cylinders.

Valve guide wear is a very common problem on today's high-temperature engines, and is certainly the principal cause of oil consumption. The valve guides are the bushings that hold the intake and

exhaust valves. They are fitted to within a couple thousandths of an inch of the valve stem diameter and are sometimes capped at the top with a seal. You can check the valve guides for wear by pressurizing each cylinder with an air leak tester or a plug-hole air-hose adapter. An air-leak tester consists of an air compressor, a regulator, a hose and an adapter that screws into the sparkplug hole.

To check valve guides, remove the valve cover, attach the air fitting to the first sparkplug hole or the sparkplug hole of the first cylinder that shows evidence of oil fouling. Then turn the engine until that cylinder is at top dead center, and pressurize the cylinder.

Remove the jam nut, ball and rocker assembly for

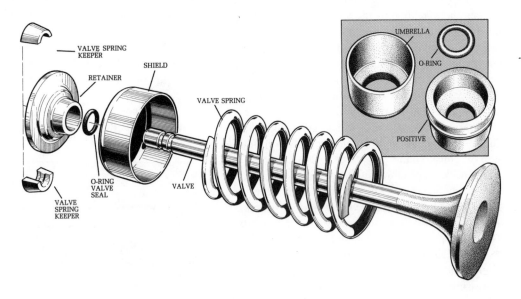

Parts of a typical valve assembly (above) include the valve itself, spring, retainer, and split keeper, or lock. Some cars also have a metal shield and/or an O-ring seal near the top of the valve stem. Replacement seals (inset) are available in various styles: the O-ring; the umbrella type, which slips over the valve guide; and the positive type, which locks onto the guide.

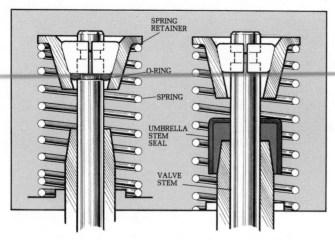

Two typical valve seal arrangements are shown above. Both have a funnel-shaped spring retainer and a split keeper, or lock, that fits into a groove on the valve stem. The setup on the left has an O-ring in another groove; the one on the right has an umbrella seal.

the intake valve. If all of the rockers are mounted on a shaft, remove the shaft assembly. (You'll need a manual that shows torque specifications to reinstall the rocker assemblies.)

Obtain an on-the-engine valve spring compressor. There are several types available, and they can be rented from most tool rental outlets. Tap the retainer of the intake valve for that cylinder with a worn socket and hammer. Then compress the valve spring and remove the spring, retainer and keepers.

Note the condition of the valve stem seal. If it's not on top of the guide, you'll find it in the form of a rubber O-ring in the valve stem's lower groove. If you have a mid-'70s car that was equipped with neoprene seals rather than the newer, more durable Viton seals, they may be cracked or broken. If they are, the replacement of the seals may be all that is necessary. However, you should also check the guides. New seals on worn guides will do little to stop oil consumption.

To check the condition of the guide, release the air from the cylinder while holding the top of the valve stem. *Don't let go or you may end up disassembling the engine!* Move the valve down ¼ inch in its guide. Then attempt to wiggle the stem back and forth. If it moves a visible amount, the guides are worn excessively, and the head will have to be removed for professional guide and valve seat service. Once the guides are renewed, the valve seats must be reground.

If the intake guide for the particular cylinder is okay, check the exhaust guide, as well. Exhaust guides generally have more clearance than intakes, but you should be able to produce only a barely perceptible lateral movement.

Reassemble the valve, retainer, spring and split valve keeper units carefully. If O-ring–type seals are used, they should be pushed into the proper groove before the split valve keepers are installed.

If you find that only the valve seals are damaged, continue compressing springs and replacing seals, one valve at a time. We once solved a serious oil-consumption problem on a mid-'70s AMC V8 by replacing all of the seals, which had disintegrated.

Engines that use the intake manifold as a pushrod cover, like the small Chevy V8s, can sometimes draw oil through a leaking intake manifold gasket. This will mimic bad guides to some extent. However, the idle will be very rough and if the sparkplugs are removed, you'll find that only one or two are oil-fouled. A vacuum gauge can help confirm a leaking manifold gasket since idle vacuum will be low and unsteady.

Some engines can draw oil through the PCV system's fresh air tube if the filter is missing. You should always make sure that the PCV system is functional before attempting to diagnose an oiling problem.

If the oil-return holes that allow oil to drain back to the pan become clogged, an engine may begin to consume oil through the valve guides even if they're not excessively worn.

If you find that oil is unable to drain to the bottom of the engine, try to clear the drain holes before any additional diagnosis is attempted. Clogged drain holes can also aggravate a PCV oiling condition.

Some technicians have told us that using certain types of aftermarket rocker covers can lead to oil consumption through the PCV system if the internal baffling of these covers differs from the original equipment.

If all other potential causes of oil consumption have been ruled out, consider the oil rings. Bad oil

Oil rings should be forced out against the cylinder walls to make a tight seal. Leaking rings may be worn or just stuck.

rings are usually accompanied by bad compression rings, but not always. Generally, if the oil rings are worn, you'll find that the cranking compression of the cylinders is below the minimum. However, the presence of the oil can sometimes mask the compression problem.

If the engine pushes a substantial amount of smoke and hot air through the oil filler cap when it is removed with the engine running, the compression rings are probably worn. If air comes rushing out through the fresh air tube or oil filler cap when you pressurize a cylinder to check the valve guides, the compression ring seal is bad, and the oil rings are probably worn as well.

However, remember that oil rings can leak without the compression rings leaking. If the oil rings stick in their grooves, the engine will burn oil. Sometimes they can be loosened by driving the car for a short period of time with a crankcase full of light viscosity oil, such as SAE 10W, and a thin oil additive designed to free sticking lifters and oil rings. *Don't* use one of the heavy, sticky oil additives for this purpose. Run the engine until it is extremely warm. Place a piece of paper over the radiator if necessary, but don't overheat the engine. Then change the oil, using your normal fill.

Of course, the ultimate solution for oil rings that cannot seal the combustion area is a complete teardown and rebuild. Before you agree to this expensive job, make sure you have eliminated all other possible sources of oil leakage.

Diagnosing Engine Compression Leaks

PAUL STENQUIST

■ HAVE YOU EVER BEEN forced to live with a powerplant that just wouldn't idle smoothly, even after a tuneup and carburetor adjustment? Or how about that older, high-mileage engine that still runs

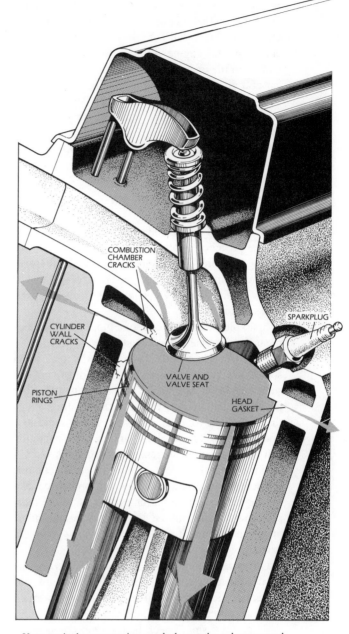

Your engine's compression can leak past the valves, around sparkplug threads, past the piston rings, through cylinder wall or combustion-chamber cracks, or around the head gasket.

reasonably well, but lacks the punch it once had and drinks fuel as though it had a hole in the gas tank?

In both cases the culprit very well may be poor sealing of cylinder pressure within the powerplant. A pressure leak is most likely to occur at the rings, the valves or the head gasket. But pressure can leak through cracks in cylinders or cylinder heads, as well. And, of course, severely damaged pistons or worn piston ring grooves (lands) will serve as escape routes for precious cylinder pressure.

Correct cylinder pressure is essential to satisfactory vehicle operation. If an engine is unable to compress the air/fuel mixture as much as it should, the affected cylinder will not operate at maximum efficiency and the engine will lose power. And since a wider throttle opening will be required to propel the car at a given rate, more fuel will be consumed.

If only one or two cylinders have a defective compression seal, the engine will lope or miss while idling. If cylinder pressure is leaking through an intake valve, backfire may result at some speeds.

Check the ignition system

A check of ignition system components should always precede any attempts to diagnose an internal engine problem. This should include at least sparkplug cleaning, inspection and regapping, and a check of all secondary components, including cap, wires and rotor.

Sparkplug condition can sometimes provide clues regarding internal engine condition.

Oily wet plugs with large deposits of carbon sometimes indicate defective piston rings, but the same condition can result from a number of other problems that are not related to ring sealing. Plugs that are slightly darker than others may indicate a poor compression seal, but again the same condition can be the result of various other problems.

If the internal problem is simply one of oil control, replacing or cleaning the plugs will probably make the engine perform better for a while, but if the same plug fouls again within a couple of thousand miles, you can assume that a serious oiling problem exists.

Oil consumption problems are by no means always related to compression sealing problems, but a check of the compression seal should be performed when an oil consumption problem is noted.

Some mechanics check fuel system components before checking compression seal when a misfire or power loss problem arises. However, carburetor diagnosis is usually more difficult than internal engine diagnosis—unless you're equipped with an emissions analyzer—so the typical Saturday mechanic will usually try to rule out compression seal problems as a cause of misfire or poor power before turning to the carburetor. (See ''Troubleshooting Fuel System Problems.'')

Checking cylinder pressure

The most basic method of checking for a compression leak is by measuring cranking cylinder pressure with a compression gauge.

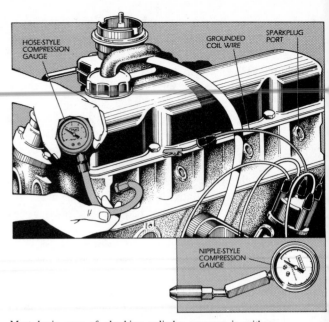

Most basic way of checking cylinder pressure is with a compression gauge, available in two basic types. Gauge attached to the plug port has a hose that screws into plug threads. Gauge at right has rubber nipple that's held against plug hole to get a reading.

Compression gauges are generally available in two basic types: One is fitted with a rubber nipple that is held against the plug hole to obtain a reading, while the other has a hose attachment that is screwed into the plug hole. The second type is easier to use, but with some care either can be used satisfactorily on most engines. On engines where access to the plug holes is limited, the hose type must be used.

Before beginning a compression test, remove all of the sparkplugs. If you don't have a remote starter switch that you can wire between the battery and starter relay or solenoid, you'll have to have a helper crank the engine from inside the car.

You have to make sure that your battery remains fully charged for the complete test, because compression readings will drop if the engine cranks noticeably slower. The best solution in this case is to perform the test while the battery is connected to a charger.

Open the throttle valves and choke valve completely. You should provide some means of holding them open. The throttle can sometimes be held open by placing an appropriately sized object between the idle screw and fast idle cam. With the throttle all the way open, the choke unloader should push the choke partway open. You may need a piece of wire to hold it all the way open.

Disconnect the negative wire from the coil and cover the terminal end of it with insulating electrical tape. On GM HEI ignitions disconnect the bat terminal from the distributor. Turn the key to the on position, even if you're using a remote starter switch.

With the compression gauge in place on the first cylinder to be tested, crank the engine five times or until you get a maximum reading. Write down the gauge reading. Move on to the next cylinder and take a reading, cranking the engine the same number of times you did for the previous reading. Continue until all cylinders have been tested.

Interpreting gauge readings

All of your readings should be within 75 percent of your strongest cylinder. Furthermore, the pressure reading of each cylinder should equal the minimum suggested by the vehicle manufacturer. Minimum pressures are found in the spec tables of most general auto repair manuals.

With a small four-cylinder engine, however, you may want all of your cylinders to fall within 85 or 90 percent of each other. On a large V8, strong cylinders can compensate easily for their weaker brothers, but a small engine may suffer a considerable loss of performance and smoothness with a compression loss of 25 percent in one cylinder. It's all a matter of how fussy *you* are about the way your car runs, weighed against the cost of repairing the compression leak.

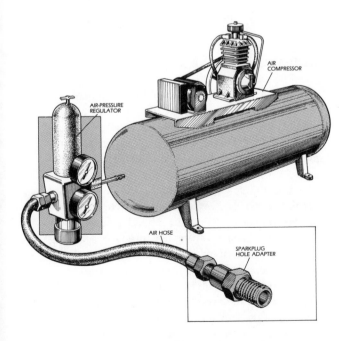

Homemade air tester can help locate the source of compression leaks. It can be made from an air hose, a regulator and a sparkplug hole/air hose adapter. Once a cylinder has been pressurized, your ears can pinpoint the leak.

Locating leaks

The compression test won't tell you where the engine is leaking compression, just that a leak exists.

Mechanics used to squirt oil in the cylinders in an attempt to distinguish valve leaks from piston ring leaks, but this method will only reveal grossly leaking valves, because the oil volume raises the cylinder pressure and may therefore mask a slight valve leak. On the other hand, the oil may fail to seal seriously worn or damaged rings, causing you to conclude erroneously that the valves are the source of the problem. It can also mask a leaking head gasket.

The best method of pinpointing compression leaks is an air test, which can be performed with either a cylinder leakage tester or homemade air test device. The idea here is to pressurize each cylinder with compressed air and then look for the spot where it leaks out.

Performing an air test

A homemade air tester can be fashioned from an air hose, a regulator and a sparkplug hole/air hose adapter. This last item is threaded to fit the plug hole on one end and has an air hose connector on the other end. You should be able to purchase one at your local auto parts store. If your air compressor develops less than 90 p.s.i., you won't need the regulator.

A commercial cylinder leakage tester will provide more than just an indication of where the leak is located. It will also tell you what percent of the compressed air charge is leaking out of the cylinder. This can help you determine how serious the leak is.

The cylinder leakage tester offers another advantage. If your engine has a bad compression ring seal *and* an internal oiling problem (the two don't necessarily go together), a cranking compression test may fail to reveal a poor compression seal due to the presence of oil in the cylinder.

In this case, the cylinder leakage tester can help you diagnose a compression leak, because it is not as easily fooled by the presence of oil in the cylinder as the compression gauge. However, the homemade air tester cannot measure the seriousness of a compression leak. All it can do is locate it.

Determining TDC

The air leak or cylinder leakage test must be performed while the cylinder being tested is at top dead

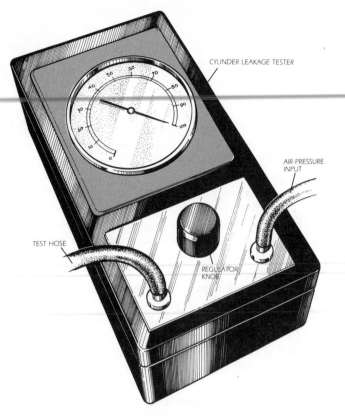

CYLINDER LEAKAGE TESTER

AIR-PRESSURE INPUT

TEST HOSE

REGULATOR KNOB

A commercial-type cylinder leakage tester can help locate a leak. It will also show what percentage of the compressed air is leaking past the rings.

center on its compression stroke. There are several ways to determine TDC.

The crankshaft pulley or flywheel of your engine is marked for No. 1-cylinder TDC. If the No. 1 cylinder is on compression stroke, the distributor's rotor should be pointing to the No. 1 plug wire. (Check a manual if you don't know how the cylinders of your V8 engine are numbered. Nearly all four and six cylinders are numbered front to rear.)

If you have good access to the crank pulley, you can mark it for top dead center of the other cylinders. TDC of an eight cylinder occurs every 90°. TDC of a four cylinder occurs every 180°.

If you have a six-cylinder engine, TDC occurs every 120°. A flexible tape measure can be used to measure the circumference of the pulley. The circumference is then divided by half the number of cylinders, and the pulley is marked in increments of a length equal to the quotient.

For example, on a six-cylinder's pulley, measuring 18 inches in circumference, the TDC marks would occur every six inches. One mark is already there. You would make two additional marks.

Assuming that the firing order is 153624, the mark that you make 120° counterclockwise will be TDC, cylinder 5. The second mark that occurs as

you continue to rotate the engine clockwise will be TDC, cylinder 3. On the engine's next clockwise rotation, the original TDC mark will be for cylinder 6. The second mark will be TDC/2, the last mark TDC/4.

Another method is to use some type of device to signal you as each cylinder rises to the top.

Some mechanics use a whistle which has been inserted into the end of a hose that is attached to one of those previously mentioned plug-hole/air hose adapters. When the contraption is screwed into the plug hole and the engine is turned, the whistle will shriek loudly on the compression stroke, but will stop abruptly as TDC is reached.

On some engines, you can easily see the top of the piston come up in the bore on compression and exhaust. You can tell which stroke (compression or exhaust) the engine is on by removing the distributor cap. If it's on compression stroke, the rotor should be pointing to the sparkplug wire for the cylinder in question.

Once you're sure that the engine is on TDC for the cylinder to be tested, screw the adapter into the plug hole, adjust the air pressure regulator to 70 or 80 pounds and attach your air hose to the adapter. If you're using a cylinder leakage tester, set the leakage meter at zero before connecting the test hose to the sparkplug adapter. If the engine is not exactly at TDC, the air pressure may force the piston down in the bore. If that happens, you may have to use a wrench to hold the engine in place while you perform the test.

Listening for leakage

With the air supply connected to the cylinder, listen for compression leakage through the exhaust pipe, crankcase oil filler hole, carburetor opening (with the PCV hose disconnected), adjacent sparkplug holes and the edges of the cylinder head sealing areas.

A leak through either of those last two locations suggests a bad head gasket. If air seems to be rushing out the carburetor, you have a bad intake valve.

Leaking exhaust valves will produce a hissing noise in the exhaust pipe. If you detect air hissing out through the oil filler hole, the rings are worn.

After listening for air leakage at all locations mentioned above, remove the radiator cap and look for bubbles in the coolant. Their presence would indicate a leaking head gasket or cracked cylinder head.

Remember that you're looking for the point of *excessive* leakage. There will always be some leakage past the rings. If jiggling the engine with a wrench on the front pulley increases the size of the leak significantly, the ring lands may be worn.

Exhaust valve leakage can be caused by dirt on the seat.

Some mechanics like to tap firmly on the top of the exhaust valve stem with a brass hammer while checking cylinder leakage. This will release a burst of air past the valve which can help dislodge any particles that may be creating a leak. It can also temporarily seat a valve that may not seat well under operating conditions, due to a worn valve guide. So this practice can be somewhat deceiving. If you do stop an exhaust valve leak in this manner, crank the engine two complete revolutions and see if the leak recurs. If it does, the problem is probably the result of a worn guide.

Using a commercial tester

If you're using the commercial cylinder leakage tester for the air leak test, you'll get a percentage reading of cylinder leakage.

The leading manufacturer of this type of equipment specifies 20 percent or more as a failure level. Race car engine builders usually look for less than 5 percent cylinder leakage. Again, it's all a matter of how fussy you are. Most high-quality production engines that we have tested leak less than 10 percent.

When testing a cylinder that showed evidence of oil fouling on the sparkplug, allow the air hose to remain connected to the cylinder for at least five minutes. This will blow excess oil past the rings, if the ring seal is poor, allowing a more accurate reading.

After the No. 1 cylinder has been leak tested, continue checking other cylinders that failed the cranking compression test.

You may want to test all cylinders if you have a commercial leakage tester. You should obviously leak test any cylinders that showed evidence of oil fouling. If you marked your crankshaft pulley for TDC locations, the second cylinder in the engine's firing order should be tested after No. 1. Simply rotate the engine to the next mark.

As explained previously, it will take two full revolutions to bring all cylinders to TDC. If you're using the whistle or eyeball method to determine TDC, you can simply move on to the next cylinder on the bank.

Plugging the hole

Once you have determined the source and the seriousness of a compression leak, a repair decision must be made. Some leaks may not be worth repairing.

For example, a leaking compression ring that falls right at the 25 percent failure figure on the cranking test and produces perhaps 30 percent leakage with the commercial cylinder leakage tester may not be worth repairing, particularly on an older vehicle. On the other hand, a leaking exhaust valve that produces the same loss of pressure may be worth repairing due to the fact that the job is much less costly and time-consuming, particularly if you can replace your own cylinder head.

If you find that your engine needs new piston rings, a complete engine rebuild is called for. The powerplants of 15 or 20 years ago were frequently re-ringed right in the car. The mechanic simply pulled the heads, dropped the pan and knocked the pistons out. He would then hone the cylinder walls while standing on a fender, install new rings on the pistons and new bearing inserts on the rods and drop them in.

If your mechanic tries to tell you that he can repair your late-model, small-displacement engine in such a manner, find a new mechanic. Today's engines are built to much closer tolerances, and, consequently, repairs involve considerably more precise measurements and expert machine work.

Don't take a chance on haphazard repairs. If your engine failed in original equipment form, you certainly don't want it rebuilt to specs that are even looser than the original equipment specs.

Troubleshooting Valve Train Problems

PAUL STENQUIST

■ IS YOUR ENGINE PLAGUED by the annoying tick of a noisy valve lifter? Does it lack the power it

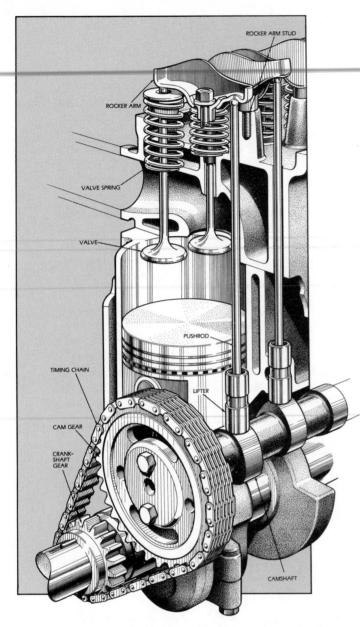

Typical valve train in a pushrod engine consists of the crankshaft and camshaft timing gears and the timing chain that connects them, the camshaft, lifter, pushrod, rocker arm, valve and valve spring. Hydraulic lifter takes up play.

once had, or does it idle unevenly? It may be suffering from a valve train malfunction.

Perhaps the most annoying of all common powerplant problems is the noise that is produced by excessive clearance in the valve train of a pushrod engine.

This noise is distinguished from other taps and ticks that can trouble an engine by its regular, measured beat, which increases in frequency as engine rpm increase. If the condition is allowed to continue, expensive valve train parts will eventually be damaged.

In most modern pushrod engines, hydraulic lifters are responsible for taking up the slack in the valve train. When the cam rotates to the zero lash position and the valve closes, pressurized engine oil is supposed to fill a cavity in the lifter, taking up any extra clearance and providing a cushion within the lifter that will dampen the mechanical forces acting on the rest of the valve train. If the lifter is not able to retain this oil, or if there is more clearance in the valve train than there is supposed to be, noise will result.

If the ticking noise occurs only when the engine is first started and disappears after several minutes of running, it should be considered normal. This happens because valve spring pressure forces the oil out of lifters that were on the top of the cam lobes when the engine was shut off. When the oil is cold, the lifters may take a few minutes to refill.

If the lifters are intermittently noisy at idle or low speeds, there may be dirt in the lifter valving system, or some of the lifter's internal parts may be worn. The only certain cure is to replace the lifters. You can sometimes locate the lifter that is making noise by applying considerable pressure to the pushrod end of the rocker arms, one at a time, while the engine is idling with the valve cover(s) off. Use a piece of wood or a hammer handle to push on the pushrod ends of the rockers. Each lifter should collapse and begin to make noise. If one of them doesn't, it is probably already collapsed and making noise.

If your engine is equipped with stamped rockers that are retained on a stud by a ball and nut, they'll probably squirt oil all over the engine compartment if you start the engine with the valve covers off. Oil shields that prevent this are sold at parts stores.

Of course, an intermittent lifter noise cannot be detected unless it is present while you're looking for it. Most professional mechanics advise their customers to replace all the lifters if the noise is frequent enough and loud enough for a repair to be necessary. If one lifter is worn or dirty enough to make noise, the others are probably in a similar condition.

If your lifters are continually noisy while the engine is at low speed or idling, but become quiet at high speeds, they probably are worn and should be replaced. The wear causes excessive clearance in the working parts of the lifter. However, the same condition can result from low oil pressure or an engine oil that is too light in viscosity. Measure engine oil pressure at idle before you spring for a new set of lifters.

If your engine is not equipped with an oil pressure gauge, you can connect one to the engine oil gallery to get a reading. In most cases, you can remove the sending unit for the oil pressure light and insert the gauge's hose fitting in its place. Specifications for oil pressure can usually be found in a shop manual. The manual should also be able to pinpoint the location of your engine's oil pressure sending unit.

If your engine is quiet at idle and low speeds, but develops a ticking noise at higher speeds, the lifters may be drawing air along with their oil supply. A low engine oil level can cause air bubbles in the oil, as can a leak in the suction side of the oil pump or oil foaming due to overfilling the crankcase.

If your lifters are noisy both at idle and at high speed, they are probably badly worn or clogged with sludge and varnish. On the other hand, this kind of lifter noise can result from wear or damage in other parts of the valve train. If the cam lobe or lifter face is worn, if a rocker arm or valve stem is badly worn, or if a pushrod is bent, constant valve train noise will result. Engine oil pressure that is excessively low, both at idle and higher speed, can also produce a constant valve train noise.

Valve train inspection

First, check engine oil pressure. There's no point in doing extensive valve train repair if the parts aren't being lubricated.

If the noise is rather loud, you probably can determine which cylinder and valve it's coming from while the engine is shut off. Just remove the valve covers and rotate the engine, stopping approximately 30° after each valve returns to its seat. With the engine in that position, check for clearance by wiggling the rocker back and forth. There should be virtually no clearance. If you are able to move the rocker back and forth from pushrod to valve stem, something is wrong.

Once you've located the offending members, begin disassembling valve train pieces and look for excessive wear. To remove stud-type rockers, turn the engine until the rocker has released the valve and spring, then remove the nut from the stud and lift the rocker off. On most modern engines, the nut locks against the stud, and only has to be torqued down to specs for reassembly.

Some engines mount all of the rockers on a single shaft that is secured to the cylinder head by support stands and bolts. On most engines, the entire rocker stand can be unbolted without causing any difficulties. However, on some engines the rocker stand bolts also serve as head bolts. In those cases, check the shop manual for specific disassembly recommendations. (You can tell if the rocker stand bolts are

doubling as head bolts by their size. If they're as big as the head bolts, they probably serve a dual purpose.)

Inspect the rocker arm. Is it smooth and free from galling at the points where it contacts the pushrod, valve and ball? Or, if it is a shaft-mounted rocker, does it rotate freely and with little noticeable clearance on its shaft?

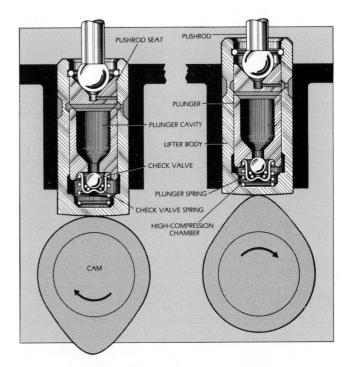

When a hydraulic lifter is down (left), pressurized engine oil enters the plunger cavity via tiny holes. This pushes the two parts of the lifter body apart, increasing the effective height of the lifter and eliminating any play that may be present in the valve train. As the cam raises the lifter (right), the check valve closes, trapping the oil as a result. When the lifter fails, oil is allowed to escape so that the valve can close completely.

If a rocker arm is damaged in any way, replace it. To replace a shaft-mounted rocker, the cotter pin on the end of the shaft must be removed, and the rockers and the springs that separate them are then removed from the shaft. If the shaft is worn, it, too, should be replaced. When reassembling the rockers and shaft, lubricate the parts with engine oil, and make sure you install all springs and washers in the correct sequence.

If you find a bad rocker, don't stop there. Remove the pushrod of each suspect valve mechanism. Examine the ball or cup at each end for chipping or galling. Roll the pushrod on a flat surface. It should roll smoothly. If it goes, "kathump, kathump," it's bent and must be replaced.

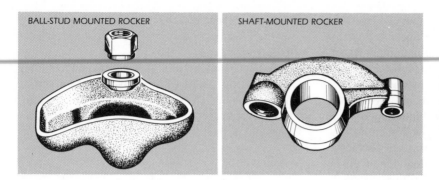

BALL-STUD MOUNTED ROCKER

SHAFT-MOUNTED ROCKER

Stamped rocker arms (left) pivot on ball studs and are held to studs by a locknut and washer. Studs can be staggered. Cast rocker arms (right) are mounted on shafts, so all rockers must be in a straight line. Rockers with adjusting nuts have solid lifters.

Digging deeper

If you found only a damaged rocker, you may want to button up the motor and hope there's no further damage within, because on most V8 and V6 engines, the intake manifold or the valley cover under the intake manifold must be removed to inspect the camshaft or to replace the lifters. If you found a bent pushrod, chances are that something else—perhaps a worn camshaft—caused the push-rod to bend.

If you have a dial indicator, you might be able to tell if the cam lobes are worn without removing the manifold. Warm up the engine and remove the valve cover. Then rotate the engine until the valve in question closes, and mount a magnetic-base dial indicator on the cylinder head so that its shaft rests against the top of the valve retainer and is parallel to the valve stem. Find the valve lift spec for your engine in a shop manual, and rotate the engine until the valve opens.

If the valve doesn't open as much as the manual says it should, the cam may be worn. Check a few other lobes for comparison. If they're all within 0.010-inch of the spec and each other, the wear is probably normal and should not be a problem. However, if there is considerable variation from lobe to

lobe, the cam might be excessively worn and some further inspection is in order.

Don't condemn the cam just on the basis of the indicator test. The readings can be distorted by lifter leakdown. On the other hand, don't be surprised to find, upon inspection, that you need a new cam. They don't seem to last very long on many recently built powerplants.

The cam and lifters may be accessible for inspection through a side cover or lifter cover on some six- and four-cylinder in-line engines. However, after removing the cover, you may also find that only the lifters can be examined, and that the camshaft must be removed for inspection.

The same is true of some V8 and V6 engines. Sometimes, even after removing the valley cover and intake manifold, the camshaft cannot be easily examined.

If inspection is necessary, the only alternative may be to remove the cam. This involves removing the fan and water pump assembly, the front timing cover, the timing gears and chain, the radiator and grill. Once these parts are out of the way, and the lifters have been pulled out of their bores, the cam can be removed. A shop manual will include specific instructions for camshaft removal.

Sometimes, simply removing and examining the lifters can give you a good indication of camshaft condition. If you're willing to climb right in on top

To remove a shaft-mounted rock-er arm, first remove the bolts and the support stands. Remove the cotter pin at the end of the rocker shaft and slide off the rockers, springs, washers and spacers (if any). Make notes or a sketch so that you can reinstall everything in the right order.

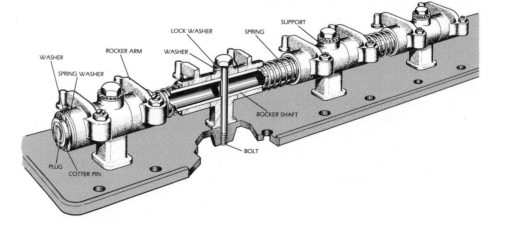

LOCK WASHER   SPRING   SUPPORT

WASHER   ROCKER ARM   WASHER

SPRING WASHER

ROCKER SHAFT

BOLT

PLUG   COTTER PIN

of the engine with a small illuminated probe, you may be able to do a fair job of examining the cam through the lifter holes.

Once you've removed the lifter galley cover, valley cover and/or intake manifold, you may find that you can't extract the lifters from their bores, even with the special extractor tools sold for this purpose. This is the result of a slight ridge that sometimes forms on the bottom of the lifters. On some high-mileage engines, you may have to pull them out with locking pliers; on other engines, you may have to disassemble the engine.

If you have to resort to locking pliers, you might as well replace all of the lifters, because you'll certainly damage them. If you intend to just inspect and reinstall lifters, keep them in order by placing them in a numbered egg carton. Each one must be reinstalled on the same cam lobe. If all valve train components on the offending valve mechanism appear to be in good condition, the lifter is the source of the noise.

With the lifter out of the bore, inspect the cam lobe if possible. Is it pitted or flaking? Is the top of the lobe ridged or does it appear to be flattened out in comparison to the other lobes? If so, or if the bottom of a lifter is cup-shaped or galled, the cam is damaged and must be replaced.

Some mechanics won't replace lifters without replacing the cam. Sometimes, a new set of lifters will wipe out an old cam almost immediately. You're always taking a calculated risk when you replace one or more lifters without renewing the cam. If you replace the cam, replace all lifters, too.

Slop stop

Timing chain wear is probably the second most frequent valve train problem. On most engines, particularly V8s and V6s, a chain connecting the crankshaft and camshaft is responsible for driving the cam and maintaining it in proper relation to the crankshaft. As the chain ages and begins to stretch, the camshaft retards, causing a loss of low-speed response and torque. If your engine has relatively good compression, but lacks the punch it had when it was new, it may be that the timing chain has stretched. Once the chain stretches to the point where it can hop all the way off the teeth of the gears, the engine may "jump time." This condition is evidenced by an engine that dies and won't restart. It usually backfires and burps as you try to start it.

If you suspect that your engine has jumped time, rotate it to the ignition timing mark on the

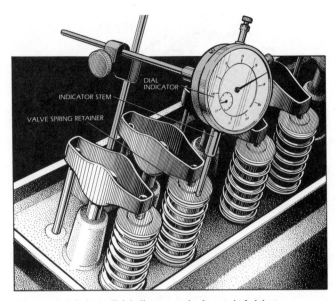

Use a magnetic-base dial indicator to check camshaft lobes without diassembling the engine. The indicator should be mounted to the cylinder head with its shaft parallel to the valve stem and touching the retainer. If valve does not open to specs, suspect a worn cam.

crank pulley. Make sure both valves for the No. 1 cylinder are closed. You can do this by placing your finger over the sparkplug hole while a helper rotates the engine toward the timing mark. You should feel and hear air compressing in the cylinder if the valves are closed. Stop at the timing mark and remove the distributor cap. Check to see that the rotor is pointing to the No. 1 cylinder sparkplug wire.

If you find that the rotor is pointing to No. 1, try to determine if the trigger wheel is aligned approximately with the distributor's magnetic pickup (or, on engines with contact points, that the points are just beginning to open). If so, the ignition is in time, so the camshaft must also be approximately in time, and is probably not the source of the no-start problem.

If you suspect that your timing chain has stretched to the point where it is affecting engine performance, there are a couple of ways you can check it. The most reliable way is to remove the timing cover and check for chain deflection. Once the cover has been removed, turn the engine until the timing chain starts to turn the cam. The chain will then be tight on one side of the gears and slack on the other side. On the loose side, measure how much you can move the chain back and forth. If you can move it more than a half inch, timing chain wear is excessive; replace the chain and drive gears.

When a new cam is installed, the cam must be properly phased in respect to the crankshaft. On most cars, there are marks on both the crank gear and

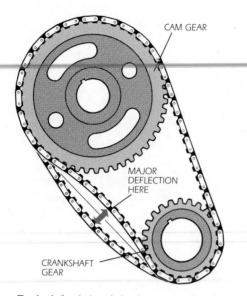

CAM GEAR

MAJOR
DEFLECTION
HERE

CRANKSHAFT
GEAR

To check for timing chain play, remove the timing cover and turn the engine until chain is tight on one side and loose on the other. Check play on the loose side.

cam gear that must be aligned on the centerline of the cam and crank bores. Again, consult a shop manual for specific instructions for your vehicle.

Some camshafts are gear-driven, including many GM in-line four- and six-cylinder engines. To check for excessive wear on a gear-driven cam, the timing cover must be removed, and clearance between gear teeth checked with a feeler gauge. It should be at least 0.002-inch, and should not exceed 0.006-inch.

Excessive clearance on cam gears won't affect timing dramatically, but will produce noise and eventually result in total gear failure.

Solving Oil Pressure Problems

PAUL STENQUIST

■ THE FIRST THING YOU notice might be the soft glow of an idiot light when your engine is idling. Or perhaps the needle of your oil pressure gauge has begun to drop out of the safe range. Or maybe you've just noticed that your engine ticks and clatters much more than it used to. They're all clues that could point to an oil pressure problem. If you don't act right away, extensive engine damage can result.

A magnified view of an engine's crankshaft journal and bearing surfaces makes it very easy to understand why a loss of lubricant can be so critical. Although these surfaces appear completely smooth to the naked eye, they're actually covered with little peaks and valleys. If the journal and bearing come into direct contact at high speed, the resulting friction quickly generates heat that can cause the metal parts to seize.

On the other hand, if these moving parts are separated by a film of lubricant, the sliding friction is replaced by fluid friction. Because the molecules of the lubricant move freely when they encounter high or low spots on the machined parts, they offer little resistance to movement. Consequently, heat generation is minimized, protecting the surfaces.

Delivering the lube

Modern automobile engines are equipped with a full-force lubrication system that pumps oil to most moving parts (see lead illustration). Oil is drawn into a pump through a mesh screen submerged in the oil pan.

In most systems, the pressurized oil is first pumped through the filter. The filter or filter mount is equipped with a bypass valve so flow will not be interrupted if the filter clogs.

The filtered oil is then pumped into the main oil gallery. Oil is usually supplied to hydraulic lifters and main bearings by means of passages connected to this gallery. Oil routed to the lifters is then directed up to the rest of the valvetrain, via a separate passage or through the pushrods. Main bearing lube travels through drilled passages in the crankshaft journals to the connecting rod bearings. Oil spray from between the connecting rod pairs, or in some cases, from a small passage in one side of each rod cap, lubricates the cylinder walls and piston pins.

Low oil pressure is the result of problems in the pump or delivery circuit. If the pump can't supply enough oil to fill the galleries, pressure will be low. If there is an overly large opening in the circuit that allows oil to escape too easily, low oil pressure will result. Improper oil viscosity or oil dilution can also make pressure readings drop below spec, as pump efficiency is dramatically affected by the thickness of the lube.

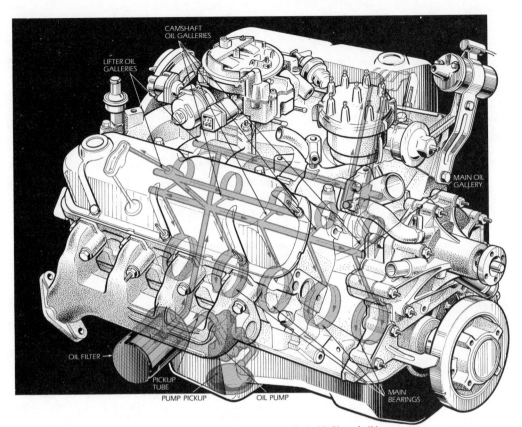

Modern engines have pressure-fed lubrication systems that are supplied with filtered oil by a mechanical pump.

Checking oil pressure

If you feel that your engine's oil pressure is lower than it should be, you can confirm your suspicions with a remote gauge.

Purchase a mechanical-type oil pressure gauge and installation kit from an auto parts store (Fig. 1). The installation kit will include a number of pipe fitting adapters, one of which can be installed in your engine in place of the idiot light switch. If your car already has an oil pressure gauge, install the adapter in place of the stock gauge sending unit. The pressure test will confirm the low reading of your stock gauge.

Manufacturers' specifications for oil pressure vary. To be absolutely sure that your engine's lube system is operating reasonably close to full capacity, you should check oil pressure test specs for your car in a general service manual or in the vehicle manufacturer's manual.

Generally, two figures are given, one for idle oil pressure and one for 2,000-rpm pressure. In most cases, your pump should be able to provide about 10 psi at idle with a fully warmed engine and 25 psi or more at 2,000 rpm. Some makers, however, call for considerably more pressure.

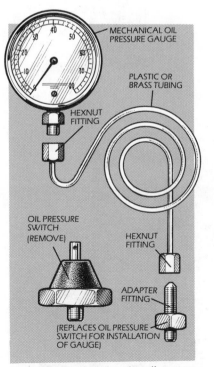

1 To read the actual engine oil pressure, install a mechanical gauge in place of the stock idiot light or indicator.

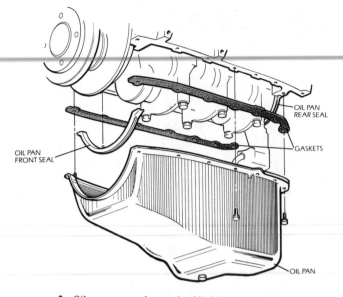

2 Oil pan removal may be blocked by steering linkage, requiring the engine to be jacked up. Attach gaskets and seals securely before reinstalling.

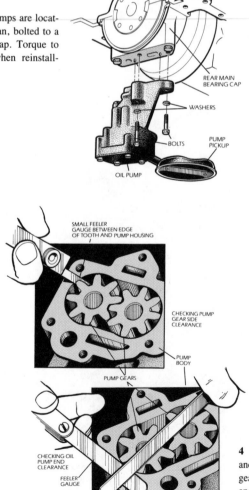

3 Most oil pumps are located inside the pan, bolted to a main bearing cap. Torque to correct spec when reinstalling.

4 On spur-gear type pumps, critical clearances to be checked are those between the gear edge and housing, and between gear ends and the bottom plate of the pump.

If your test finds that oil pressure is okay but the idiot light continues to glow, replace the oil warning light switch. If a new switch doesn't turn the light off, check the oil light switch circuit for problems.

Solving low-pressure problems

If you found that oil pressure was below the recommended figure at idle but within the acceptable range at higher speeds, check the engine idle speed. It may be below specs.

Oil pressure that is somewhat low at one or both test points can be caused by motor oil that is of incorrect viscosity or has been diluted with gasoline. Try an oil change, using the manufacturer's recommended oil viscosity for the weather conditions.

If the oil change solves your pressure problems and you find that the drained oil is heavily diluted with gasoline, find the cause of the dilution before putting the car back in service. It may have been caused by an engine misfire that allowed unburned fuel to run down past the rings, or, on carbureted cars, it may be the result of a ruptured fuel pump diaphragm.

A clogged oil filter can also cause a loss of pressure. If your filter has been on the car for more than a few thousand miles, change it and retest.

Pulling the oil pan

Having eliminated simple causes, further diagnosis requires removal of the oil pan on most powerplants (Fig. 2). On some engines, however, the oil pump is externally mounted and can be checked without removing the pan. If this is the case on your engine, proceed to the section headlined "Checking the oil pump."

On some cars, oil pan removal is a simple task, but on most it is quite difficult and may involve loosening the engine mounts and jacking or lifting the engine. The starter motor or other components may have to be removed to get to the pan bolts.

Specific instructions for oil pan removal are found in both general service manuals and vehicle manufacturer manuals. On some "short skirt" type engines, the pan will have to be dropped more than a few inches before it will clear the main caps, crank counterweights and oil pump.

Checking the oil pump

If your engine suffered a total loss of oil pressure, the cause is most likely a broken oil pump drive.

Most oil pumps are driven by a shaft that joins the pump to the distributor drive gear or by an intermediate shaft that is fitted with a gear and driven by the cam. If the drive mechanism breaks, a total loss of oil pressure will be the result. Another possible cause of total oil pressure loss is a missing oil gallery plug.

In addition to the simple causes mentioned previously, partial loss of pressure can be the result of a worn pump, a clogged pump pickup, a hole in the pickup tube or broken tube or excessive bearing clearance. Less likely causes for partial loss of pressure include leaking gallery plugs and porous block castings.

Since you have to remove the oil pan on most engines to check any of the more likely causes, you ought to check all of them before buttoning up. On high-mileage engines, low pressure is frequently caused by a combination of pump and bearing wear.

Once the pan is off, remove the pump from the engine. It's held in place on the block or on a main bearing cap by one or more bolts (Fig. 3). In most cases, the pickup tube is attached only to the pump, although on some engines it may be retained by a bolt. On engines with external pumps, the pickup is usually bolted to a machined surface inside the crankcase.

If the pickup tube is pressed into the pump, leave it in place. If it's pinned or bolted to the pump, remove it for inspection. Examine the pickup and pickup tube for possible air leaks. Check also if there is clogging of the pickup screen.

Disassemble the oil pump by removing its bottom cover. Hold the pump in a vise between two pieces of wood or brass jaws. On some engines that have externally mounted pumps, the cover (as well as the gears and relief valve) can be removed without unbolting the pump from the engine.

On the pump cover or body, you'll probably find a hexhead or expansion cup plug. The pump relief valve and spring are installed behind this plug. Remove the plug, valve and spring, and check to see how the valve moves in its bore. If you find that it is stuck in its bore or fits so loosely that you can move it sideways any discernible amount, it could be the problem. Replace the valve and the pump or cover as necessary.

If your oil-pressure test found that pressure was okay at idle but lower than specified at a higher speed, a weak relief valve spring might be the source of your trouble. Some manufacturers provide a specification for relief valve spring length. (A weak spring will be shorter than a good one.) Measure your spring and compare it to spec.

Under the pump cover, you'll find the pumping mechanism. Two types are commonly used. One

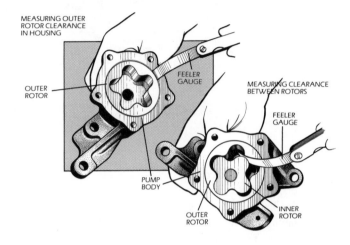

5 Lobed rotor-and-ring-type oil pumps must have clearances checked between the outer rotor and pump body, and between the inner and outer rotor lobes.

utilizes a driven, lobed inner rotor that turns a surrounding lobed ring or outer rotor. The other variety uses two spur-type gears, one of which is attached to the drive shaft.

Inspect the gears, pump cover and pump body for signs of wear and scoring. Obvious damage is grounds for replacement. If you're in doubt about pump condition, check clearances with a feeler gauge.

To check spur-gear–type pump, measure clearance between the top of the gears and the pump body's gasket surface using a straightedge (small steel ruler) and a feeler gauge (Fig. 4). Lay the edge of the rule across the gasket surface and insert the feeler gauge between it and the gears. You'll find specifications in a service manual. Using a narrow feeler gauge, check clearance between the edge of the pump gear and the pump body.

If your car is equipped with a lobed rotor-and-ring–type pump, you should at least check clearance between the center rotor and the pump body gasket surface, between the outer rotor and case, and between the inner rotor lobes and outer rotor lobes (Fig. 5). Chrysler provides specs for checks of cover flatness, rotor thickness and outer rotor diameter.

Measure clearance between the center rotor and gasket surface with a straightedge and rule. Check clearance between the high points of the two rotors and between the outer rotor and the pump body with a feeler gauge. For the 2.2-liter Chrysler, the specs

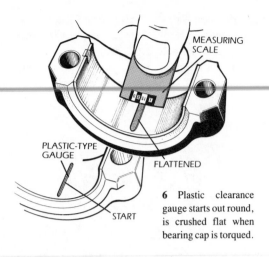

MEASURING SCALE

PLASTIC-TYPE GAUGE

FLATTENED

START

6 Plastic clearance gauge starts out round, is crushed flat when bearing cap is torqued.

are .01 in. (maximum) and .014 in. (maximum), respectively.

Check cover flatness with a rule and feeler gauge, laying the side of the rule across the center of the cover and inserting the feeler gauge into any low spots below it. If the pump is not up to spec, it must be replaced.

Before reinstalling a spur-gear–type pump, pack the gear cavity tightly with petroleum jelly. Fill lobe-and-ring–type pumps with motor oil.

Checking bearing clearance

As bearing clearance gradually increases due to normal wear, the lube oil escapes more easily from the force-fed circuit and pressure drops. Because some of the lube escapes prematurely, certain parts don't get enough. If main bearing clearance, for example, is excessive, the rod bearing oil supply will be inadequate.

The bearing clearances of an assembled engine can be checked using a plastic gauging material (Fig. 6). This product, which is best known by Perfect Circle's trade name Plastigage, will provide accurate measurement of bearing oil clearance when it's crushed between the bearing and the crankshaft (Perfect Circle, Dana Corp., P.O. Box 455, Toledo, Ohio 43692). Purchase two different sizes of the material at an auto parts store so you can measure clearances from .002 in. to .006 in.

To check main bearing clearance, remove main caps two and four (on five-main-bearing engines) or two, four and six (on seven-main-bearing engines). Insert paper shims that are at least .010 in. thickness between these bearings and the crank and reinstall the caps. This will lift the crank off of the other bearings to check clearance.

Remove each of the other bearing caps one at a time and wipe all oil from journal and bearing. Then, place a piece of the gauging material on the center of the bearing in such a way that it spans the width of the bearing. Install the cap, torque it to spec and remove it without turning the crank. Now, compare the crushed strip of gauging material to the scale on the package. This will give you the clearance figure.

If the strip is so wide that it's off the scale, or if it hasn't been flattened at all, use a different size gauging strip to get an accurate reading.

Check clearance of the other main bearings in the same way. Then, move your paper shims to journals one and five or one and seven and check the clearance of the bearings that previously supported the shims. Record all the numbers on a piece of paper, along with the part numbers and any size indication on the bearings (Fig. 7).

Check rod bearing clearance in a similar manner. Remove rod caps one at a time. Place the gauging strip on the rod cap bearing and reinstall, torquing to spec.

If you have a micrometer, check the rod throws for taper and out-of-round by measuring each throw at both ends and at points on the circumference that are 90° apart.

Compare your figures to manufacturer's specs. If rod journal taper or out-of-round are in excess of what the manufacturer allows, the engine will have to be rebuilt.

However, if the crankshaft is otherwise okay, but clearance is in excess of manufacturer's allowance, you can probably tighten it up by replacing the bearings with "undersize" bearings. (Undersize bearings are actually larger than standard; they're

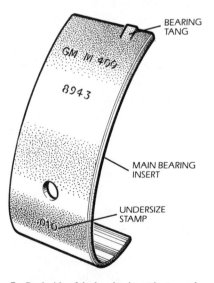

BEARING TANG

GM M 400

8943

MAIN BEARING INSERT

.010

UNDERSIZE STAMP

7 Back side of the bearing insert is stamped to indicate undersize dimension.

called undersize because they're for use with under-size cranks.)

For most applications, bearings are sold in standard as well as .010- and .020-in. undersize. In each of these sizes, bearings can be purchased with an additional .001-in. or .002-in. undersize. The extra bearing material makes up for too much clearance.

Determine which bearings you need by calculating how much the present clearance exceeds ideal specified tolerances. Go to the parts store armed with bearing part numbers and any undersize indication that may have been found on the back of the bearings. A knowledgeable counterman will have no trouble helping you choose the proper replacements for your crankshaft's bearings.

After installing the new bearings, check all clearances again. Check all rod and main bolt torque readings twice, and reinstall the oil pan.

Troubleshooting Your Cooling System, Part I

MORT SCHULTZ

■ PERHAPS 3 MILLION MOTORISTS are marooned each year by disabled cooling systems. You don't have to be among them.

Cleaning and refilling cooling systems is important, of course, but it's no guarantee that cooling-system parts won't fail. So, if you don't want to wind up waiting for a tow truck, make sure you include the inspection of parts in your regular maintenance schedule.

Those parts you can get at easily should be checked frequently. The others you can test less often.

However, every cooling-system part should be examined at least once a year. This means hoses, radiator pressure caps, thermostat, fan and drive belts, radiator, water pump and engine drain plugs.

Start with hoses

Hoses will fail faster than any other cooling-system component. Fortunately, they are visually in full view and easy to inspect.

Although hose life expectancy is approximately 25,000 miles, don't take chances. Inspect your hoses every couple of months.

Just squeeze 'em, but do so with the engine turned off and cold. If a hose isn't firm and doesn't regain its shape as soon as you release pressure, replace it. Scrap a hard or mushy hose, one that shows cracks under pressure or one that's swollen.

Don't forget to include inlet and outlet heater hoses in your inspection. They're as much a part of the cooling system as the upper and lower radiator hoses. Some cooling systems also have a thermostat bypass hose jutting off the water pump. Check this, too. Remember—if any hose suddenly splits, the cooling system will lose most or all of its coolant and shut the vehicle down.

Tips to ease replacing hoses

Replacing a bad hose requires that you drain the radiator below hose level, loosen clamps and twist the hose off its connectors (radiator necks). You may encounter resistance, but don't use excessive force or a prying tool. You might damage a connector, and that could result in a major repair.

So, slit the hose lengthwise at three or four points. Use a sharp knife, such as a drywall knife. Be careful not to slice into the connector. Then, peel the hose off. As for old clamps, throw them away. New clamps are inexpensive.

Worm-drive clamps are easiest to work with, but they do have a tendency to vibrate loose; so be sure to tighten the clamp screws every so often.

Replacement radiator hoses are molded or flexible (accordion-type). Although they're a bit more difficult to install, use molded hoses; we think they hold up better.

Generally, replacement hoses come in one size—long. You usually have to cut them to fit between connectors. If the hose is too long, it will peak and may restrict the flow of coolant.

To cut a new hose, measure the old hose before you throw it away. Mark off the length on the new hose and use a sharp knife to make the cut.

This isn't as simple as it sounds, because you want a square end. If the cut end is slanted, the hose may not fit securely on the connector.

To get a square cut, slide the clamp on the new

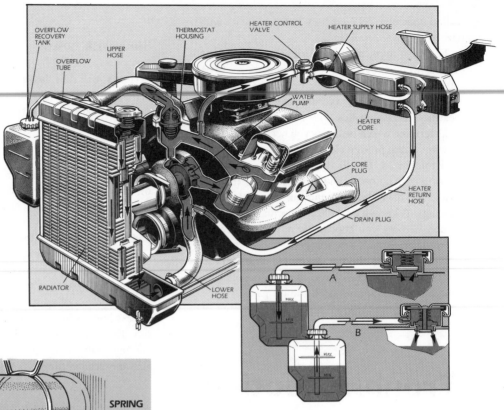

OVERFLOW RECOVERY TANK

OVERFLOW TUBE

UPPER HOSE

THERMOSTAT HOUSING

HEATER CONTROL VALVE

HEATER SUPPLY HOSE

WATER PUMP

HEATER CORE

CORE PLUG

HEATER RETURN HOSE

DRAIN PLUG

RADIATOR

LOWER HOSE

A

B

In a closed-loop overflow system, excess pressure is blown off into the reservoir bottle (A). Vacuum created when engine cools draws the fluid back into the radiator (B).

To remove a stubborn hose, slit it with a blade. Take care not to gouge connector.

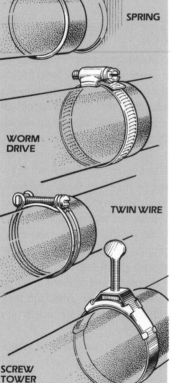

SPRING

WORM DRIVE

TWIN WIRE

SCREW TOWER

A collapsed lower radiator hose is the result of a failed stiffening spring. When you replace this hose, make sure that the spring is of the right type and length for the application.

Of the various types of hose clamps, the easiest one to use is the worm-gear type.

hose. Place it so that one side is on the measurement mark. Tighten the clamp. Now, use the side of the clamp for a guide as you cut the hose.

There is a way to make the installation of a molded hose less of a battle. First, use a wire brush to clean off the connectors. Then, coat the connectors with a waterproof sealer. Do not put any sealer inside the hose. It may flake and fall into the radiator.

Now, slip the clamps onto the hose and dip the ends of the hose in coolant (ethylene glycol). The coolant acts as a lubricant and makes it easier for you to push the hose fully onto the connectors.

Finally, slide the clamps into place. Generally, inlet and outlet connectors of the radiator have a round protuberance. Make sure that the clamp is behind this bead. In any case, place the clamps about ¼ inch from the ends of the hose.

Tighten the clamps snugly, but don't use excessive force. If you do, you could deform the connector. Refill the radiator, start the engine and make sure that no coolant is leaking from around the ends of the new hose.

That lowdown lower hose

That lower radiator hose is a sneaky devil. It has a coil spring inside that can lose tension. This causes the hose to collapse at higher engine speeds, cutting off the flow of coolant. The result is overheating on the highway.

To make sure this won't happen, have someone start and accelerate the engine as you watch the hose. (Keep away from the fan, belts and pulley.) The hose should stay in shape. If it flattens, replace it.

The lower radiator hose can cause another problem if you have to replace it. Make sure the one you get has a coil spring in it. Lower radiator hoses are entering the market without springs. This isn't a problem if you're replacing the old hose because it's cracked or leaking. Just transfer the spring from the old one to the new hose.

However, you can't do this if you're replacing the hose because of a weak spring, so keep looking until you find a new hose with a spring. If you can't find one, go to an auto salvage yard and get one off a junker. Just make sure it's the correct length.

Keeping the pressure on

The radiator pressure cap is reliable, but it doesn't last forever. It has two important jobs. If it fails to do them, the cooling system will overheat.

One job is to seal the cooling system. The cap gasket pushes against the radiator filler neck to do this. Sealed, the cooling system builds up pressure that raises the boiling point of coolant. For example, the boiling point of a 44 to 56 coolant-water mixture is raised approximately 50° at sea level, and a higher engine operating temperature is more efficient.

The second job the radiator cap has is to release pressure when it reaches a critical level. Depending on the cap design, a pressure vent, cap gasket or a rubber washer around the rim of the cap will move when the pressure gets too high, and pressure is released.

In older cars, this pressure is released through an overflow hose that extends down the side of the radiator. As it's released, some coolant flows from the radiator through the overflow hose and is lost.

Newer cars are equipped with sealed overflow systems. As the pressure is released, the coolant flows from the radiator through the overflow hose into a plastic tank. When the engine cools, vacuum created in the radiator draws the coolant back into the radiator.

Capping it off

Here's what you should know about servicing pressure caps:

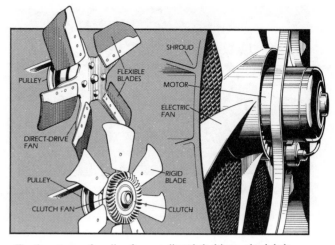

The three types of cooling fans are direct-belt-driven, clutch-belt-driven and electric-motor-driven. All three can be tested, using different procedures for each one.

■ Never remove one from a hot radiator. As careful as you are, there's always a chance that hot coolant will gush and scald you. Burns are the main injury suffered by those who work on cars.

■ Wash the cap in water and examine the gasket or gaskets. Whenever a crack is found, replace the cap.

■ If the cap has locking tabs, be positive that neither one is bent. If a tab is bent, replace the cap.

■ Press down on the spring. It should offer strong resistance. If there is but slight resistance, replace the cap.

■ Attach the cap to a cooling-system analyzer and pump up the pressure so that the dial records the pressure stamped on the cap body. If the pressure falls off rapidly, the cap is not functioning properly. Replace it.

Analyzers (pressure testers) are sensitive to small air leaks which can cause the pressure to drop off slowly. Don't be fooled and replace a good cap. If you're not losing coolant, keep the cap in service.

■ If a replacement is called for, buy a new cap that's designed for your cooling system. Doing otherwise will result in a loss of coolant and overheating. Furthermore, aluminum radiators require the use of aluminum radiator caps to prevent galvanic action that results in corrosion.

■ Inspect the radiator filler neck to check for bent tabs and rim. Also, make sure that the neck is firmly soldered to the radiator tank. A damaged filler neck will have to be replaced.

■ Replace the overflow tube and/or plastic tank if either one is not in good shape.

■ Finally, in many cars with plastic coolant recovery tanks, radiator caps have to be secured so that an arrow or mark on the cap will line up with the overflow tube. This is your assurance that the valves

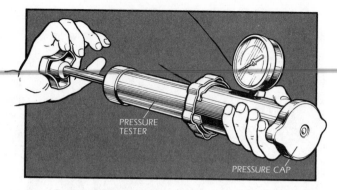

Cooling-system pressure analyzer is a must for checking the integrity of the system and radiator cap. To test the cap, attach tester and pump the handle until pressure on the gauge matches that stamped on cap.

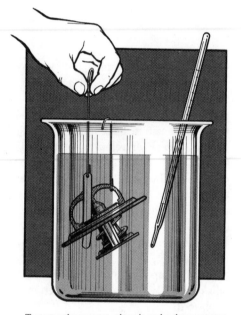

To test a thermostat, place it and a thermometer in water under heat. Check temperature when thermostat opens.

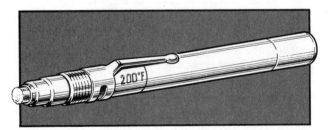

Crayons sensitive to temperature can check a thermostat without the need to remove it from the engine. Such crayons can be had from many laboratory supply houses. See text for instruction in how to use them.

are in place to permit the release of pressure and syphoning.

Pressure-testing the system

With the engine cold and turned off, remove the radiator pressure cap. Make sure the radiator is filled; then wipe the filler neck clean.

Attach the tester securely to the filler neck and pump up pressure until the tester gauge reads the level at which the cooling system is rated. This rating is stamped into the top of the radiator cap.

Watch the gauge needle. If it falls, keep the system under pressure and examine for coolant leaks.

Suppose the needle drops, but you don't find a leak. What do you do then?

Loosen the tester and start the engine. Let it run until it reaches normal operating temperature. Now, tighten the tester.

Caution: Be careful when doing this test. With the cooling system tester connected and the engine running, pressure builds up quickly. Don't let pressure exceed 20 p.s.i. When it starts coming close, loosen the tester carefully. Hot coolant may spew out, so be ready to jump back.

If the needle fluctuates, there's probably a combustion leak because of a bad head gasket.

If the needle doesn't fluctuate, race the engine and watch the tailpipe. If a heavy amount of white smoke (steam) is expelled, it may indicate an internal coolant leak because of a cracked engine block or a cracked cylinder head.

One way of verifying an internal leak is to examine the oil dipstick. If water globules are mixed in with the oil, there's an internal leak.

Tips on thermostats

Most thermostats contain a wax pellet that expands when heated and contracts when cooled. The pellet is connected to a piston that operates a valve.

When the pellet heats and expands, it forces the valve open. As the pellet cools down and contracts, pressure is released, and a spring allows the valve to close. In other words, with a cold engine the thermostat valve remains closed. This keeps coolant out of the radiator and forces it to circulate through the engine, so that it warms up quickly.

As the engine gets hot, the pellet expands, the thermostat valve opens and coolant is allowed to flow into the radiator, so cooling can take place before coolant starts to boil.

COOLING SYSTEM, PART I   77

There are, therefore, two ways of recognizing that a thermostat has become defective:

1. The engine overheats. The thermostat valve may become stuck in the closed position, thus preventing the coolant from working its way into the radiator.

2. The engine warms up slowly, with the result that little or no heat comes from the heater. The thermostat valve is stuck in the open position.

Gauges better than lights

Owners of cars equipped with temperature gauges can determine if one of these problems is developing much better than can car owners having only temperature warning lights. With a gauge, you can see if temperature is staying below normal. Not so with a light, which will turn off the instant you start the engine and goes on again only if the engine overheats—if it's working as it should.

Furthermore, a thermostat that's causing overheating often begins to stick gradually—that is, over a period of time. As the situation gets worse, the engine will run hotter and hotter. This you can readily determine with a temperature gauge, but a warning light goes on only when the problem reaches a critical point—too late to be of help.

Replacing a thermostat

Admittedly, removing the thermostat every year for testing is a real pain. You have to drain the coolant then unbolt and remove the thermostat housing—which will destroy the gasket—in order to get at the thermostat.

You have to hang the thermostat in a pan filled with water, so that it's fully immersed; then heat the water as you keep one eye on the thermostat valve and the other eye on a thermometer. When the thermometer records the temperature stamped on the thermostat body, the valve should be wide open. If not, you have to replace the part.

Then, to reinstall the old thermostat or install a new one (make sure it's rated at the temperature specified by the car manufacturer), you have to clean the housing surfaces and install a new gasket.

An easier test

Here's an easier way to test the thermostat. General Motors advocates the use of temperature sticks. These are pencil-like devices that contain wax

materials that will melt at specific temperatures. The temperature rating is specified on each stick.

You'll need two temperature sticks, or crayons, to test the thermostat—one that's rated at approximately 25° below the rating of the thermostat in your car and the other rated at about 10° above your thermostat.

If the thermostat in your car is rated at 195°F., you should use crayons rated at 169°F. and 206°F. These crayons are available from Omega Engineering, 1 Omega Drive, Stamford, Conn. 06907. They cost $5 each.

When the engine is cold, remove the radiator-pressure cap. Clean the thermostat housing and rub wax from each stick onto the housing.

Start the engine and run it at a fast idle. As the "low-temperature" mark (169° F., for example) starts melting, look in the radiator (not the overflow tank). You should *not* see coolant moving (flowing). If coolant is flowing, it's a sign that the thermostat valve is probably stuck open.

Now, before the "high-temperature" mark (206° F.) starts melting, you should see coolant flowing. If you don't, the thermostat valve is probably stuck closed.

Fanfare

Your car has a direct-drive, clutch-type or electric fan. Direct-drive and clutch-type fans are driven by belts, and bad belts are the most common cause of fans not working. If the fan isn't working, air can't circulate through the radiator to carry heat away, and overheating results.

So, to avert trouble because of a direct-drive or clutch-type fan that suddenly poops out because of a bad belt, inspect the belt for cracks, grease, frayed edges, or any other damage. Also, make certain that the belt is tight.

With the engine off and cold, look for bent and cracked fan blades. Replace the fan if blades are damaged.

If you have a clutch-type fan, turn the fan. It should rotate freely, but you should feel slight resistance. Also, check the area for a fluid (silicone) leak from the clutch. If the fan is hard to turn or there is a leak, replace the fan.

As for an electric fan, there is no test to determine if the switch and motor are about to fail. However, it is possible to test the heat-sensitive actuating switch which turns the fan motor on and off. These automatic switches are usually bolted into the engine block or cylinder head and their sensing ends are in direct contact with coolant. When the engine coolant reaches a specified temperature, the switch opens or closes a circuit and switches on the fan. A workshop manual will tell you at what temperature this should happen.

You test this switch in the same way you would check a conventional wax-pellet thermostat, but you must also make a circuit using a 12-volt power source and a test light in addition to a thermometer.

Immerse the sensor and the attached wires into a pan of heating water and keep an eye on the thermometer and test light. When the switch reaches its design temperature, the light should go on.

Troubleshooting Your Cooling System, Part II

MORT SCHULTZ

■ COOLING SYSTEMS ARE PRONE to two common types of maladies: leaks and clogging. Both problems can result in an overheated engine and possible terminal engine damage. But both can be prevented, in most cases, if you take the time to understand how your cooling system works, then take proper preventive steps. Repairs are another matter we'll discuss later.

But first, remember this caution: *Never attempt to work on a hot cooling system. And never open a radiator cap on a hot system.* The coolant is under pressure and is hotter than boiling water. Make sure the system is well cooled down.

Now, let's take a look at the problems.

Leaks

A cooling system is a sealed system. Coolant is lost only if it boils and evaporates, or if a leak develops. If there's a leak, you may spot a puddle under the car. If there's no puddle, the leak may be internal. So how do you know if your cooling system is sound? You can make an accurate evaluation by using a cooling system pressure tester, as described in Part 1.

Leaks often occur around the top hose connector. This is a weak-link point. Cooling system pressure is greatest here, and the connectors put a tug on the hose. Another place where leaks occur is the seam between the top tank and top header plate. The header plates (there's also a bottom header plate) are those parts of the radiator core to which the top and bottom tanks are soldered. Leaks happen when solder falls apart due to excessive pressure, heat and/or corrosion.

Leaks are also common at the corners where top and bottom tanks join the header plates. Corners flex as they alternately heat and cool off. This expansion and contraction may cause corner seams to open.

Less common are leaks from a split tank and from radiator tubes. There are a bunch of these tubes running from the top to the bottom header plates.

Clogs

Tubes clog more often than they spring leaks. To prevent clogging, which keeps hot coolant trapped in the radiator, the cooling system has to be kept clean. This means draining and flushing the entire system, and then refilling it with new ethylene glycol anti-freeze.

An annual treatment is recommended for newer radiators with $3/8 \times 3/32$-in. tubes. With older radiators, which have tubes that are $1/2 \times 3/32$ in., you can get by with a 24-month cleaning.

Identify your radiator

There are two types of radiators: downflow and crossflow. Downflow radiators have tanks on the top and bottom of the core. Crossflow radiators have tanks on the sides of the core. The core is that portion of the radiator consisting of tubes and airway fins.

Coolant from the engine enters the top tank and circulates through the tubes. The liquid is cooled by air flowing through airway fins, which are connected to the tubes. Coolant then enters the bottom tank and is recirculated to the engine.

Radiators may also be classified according to the materials from which they're made—all metal or a combination of plastic and metal. The majority of cars have all-metal radiators. For the most part, tanks, header plates and tubes are brass, and airway fins are made of copper.

In recent years, car manufacturers—Ford, GM, VW and most Europeans—have used radiators with plastic tanks and aluminum or copper cores.

If a plastic tank should spring a leak, a special

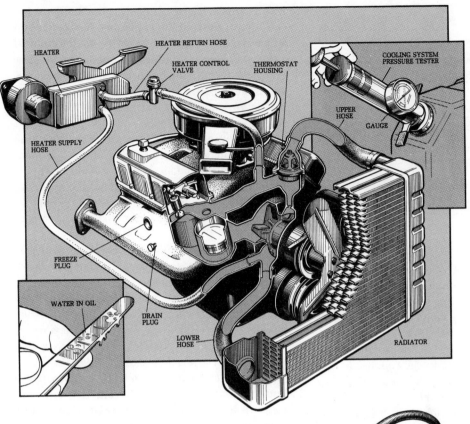

Check indicated areas of the cooling system for leaks while pressurizing the system (inset, above). In addition, check dipstick for coolant in oil (inset, left).

welding unit is needed to seal it. This unit consists of an electric blow-type gun, similar to a hair dryer, for applying a glass-impregnated sealing material. Plastic radiator tanks are made of glass-impregnated nylon that resists high temperature and pressure.

If the radiator in your car springs a leak, you're going to face these choices:

■ Should you try to repair it yourself?
■ Should you take it to a radiator repair shop?
■ Should you buy a new radiator from a dealer parts department?

A good radiator shop will blast out blockages (left) and flow-test a radiator (right) before attempting any repairs. If it fails the flow test, it's dismantled and fixed.

Chemical sealing agents

The first inclination probably is to try to repair it yourself, using one of the many chemical sealing agents on the market. Can a chemical sealer stop a radiator leak?

"Only if the leak is not a structural leak," Frank Finger of Finger's Radiator Hospital in North Brunswick, N.J., points out. "Chemical sealers are only effective for stopping champagne leaks." A champagne leak is a small leak from a porous area, usually a tube. But a chemical sealer may *clog* narrow tube passages, especially if they're already partially restricted.

Use a professional

Should you try to repair a leaking radiator yourself? No. It's a waste of time and effort. Chances are slim that your repair will be effective. Even if you have experience in soldering and have the necessary equipment, you can't just lay a bead of solder on top of a leaking area. It won't work. Here's why.

Suppose there's a leak from a top tankheader plate seam. This area accumulates a thick coating of

Part of the repair procedure for your car's cooling system is to remove all rust, scale and deposits from the core and the tube with a torch. The header tanks are removed for this operation and cleaned.

3). Turn the engine to TDC compression stroke for corrosion between the underside of the tank and along the inside of the header plate. To close this leak, solder has to flow—by capillary action—under the seam to seal the opening from the backside. Solder won't flow and take hold in areas where corrosion exists. In other words, the tank has to be removed and cleaned thoroughly. So does the header plate. Are you equipped to do this?

If the leak is from a connector, the connector has to be cut away and the area cleaned. A new connector then has to be soldered to the tank. Again, simply laying solder along the joint usually doesn't work.

How about a pro?

Yes, there are fly-by-night radiator shops. So how can you be sure the one you go to is reputable? Other than the obvious—talking to friends and relatives who have been in your boat—one way is to find out if the shop is a member of the National Radiator Service Association. About 30 percent of the radiator shops in the country belong to this group. Generally, members are competent and familiar with modern repair techniques. However, if a shop isn't a member, it may not be inferior.

So another way of trying to determine if a shop is competent is to find out its procedure for repairing radiators. A shop manager should be willing to give you, as a potential customer, a tour to see firsthand how the facility refurbishes radiators.

Here's the procedure used by a good radiator shop to get a radiator back into shape.

1. The radiator is put into a tank of caustic solution for cleaning. Then, it's sprayed outside and inside with water under high pressure. It's important that radiators be cleaned before they are leak-tested, since foreign matter inside the radiator may block the

leak and make it appear as if there's nothing wrong.

2. Next, the radiator is put on a flow tester and water is fed through it, by gravity, to determine if tubes are clogged. The mechanic compares the flow rate to the manufacturer's specification. If the radiator doesn't meet the flow-rate specification, the next step is to remove the tanks and clean the tubes by pushing a rod through them.

3. Assuming the radiator meets the flow-rate specifications and doesn't need rodding, all openings are sealed, and an air hose is connected to the filler neck. Then, the radiator is dunked into a vat of water, and air at 15 to 18 p.s.i. is shot through it. Bubbling water reveals leaks and indicates their seriousness.

Suppose a tube leaks? If a chemical stop leak won't seal it, there is a way of salvaging the radiator by cutting out the tube and soldering the openings that are left in the header plates. This shouldn't cause any cooling problems unless a car is used for towing a trailer or city driving. Even so, it's worth a try. A new radiator for a subcompact costs about $90; for a full-sized car, as much as $200.

4. If the leak or leaks can be repaired, top and bottom tanks are removed from the core and cleaned in a machine that blasts them with abrasive glass beads. Header plates are wire-brushed. If a core is leaking and it can't be salvaged, top and bottom tanks usually can be removed from the old radiator, cleaned and soldered onto a new core. This saves the cost of new tanks.

5. Before tanks are soldered back onto an old core that can be salvaged, airway fins are examined and bent fins are straightened.

Remove the radiator yourself

How much do radiator shops charge? Finger's, which has been in business since 1929, charges $40 if a customer brings in the radiator and adds another $27 if they must remove and reinstall the radiator.

It isn't particularly difficult to remove and reinstall a radiator. First, drain the cooling system, remove hoses and disconnect any automatic transmission oil cooler lines. Be careful with those oil-cooler fittings. They're brass and delicate. Many do-it-yourselfers damage them when they take off or reinstall cooler lines. If fittings are damaged, coolant will leak and new fittings will have to be installed, adding to the cost.

Remove parts blocking the radiator, such as the fan shroud and fan. The radiator is held by bolts that attach the radiator mounting brackets to the vehicle. Remove them and draw the radiator out of the car.

Buying a new radiator

If your radiator is shot and you have to buy a new one, get the exact one for your car. By exact we mean one with the correct dimensions.

The best way to order a radiator is to use the original equipment manufacturer number, which is found on the radiator. The number may be on the top tank, on the mounting brackets or on the filler neck. If you can't find the number or if it's been obliterated, determine the radiator you need by measuring the height, width and thickness of the old radiator. Only the core is used for measuring, not the tanks.

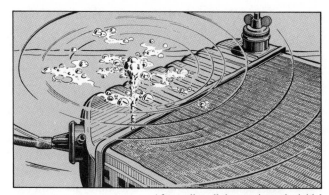

After sealing all the openings, the initial leak test is performed by pressurizing the radiator with compressed air and immersing the unit in water. Bubbles rising to the surface will pinpoint leaks immediately and will provide an indication of their seriousness.

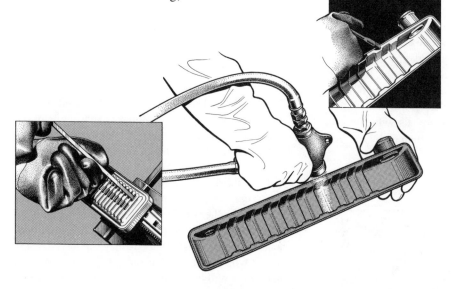

Core tubes are reamed clean with a wire rod (far left). A badly corroded header tank is sandblasted to expose bare metal (left). The solder brazing won't hold if there is any dirt or impurity on the metal. Once the tank is clean, flux is brushed on the surfaces to be brazed (above, right). The flux will allow the solder to flow.

Make sure the radiator is in an upright position; that is, with the filler neck opening facing up. Measure thickness by inserting a length of wire or a thin rod through an airway fin until its end is flush with the other side. Mark the wire or rod and then measure the amount that penetrated the fin.

Don't be fooled into thinking that height is an up-and-down measurement and width is a side-to-side measurement with a crossflow radiator. Height is between the tanks; width is between the mounting brackets.

The ethylene glycol story

One thing's for sure. If you practice sound maintenance, the chances of getting a radiator leak during the life of your car is minimized. Good maintenance involves flushing the cooling system once a year and refilling it with a fresh mixture of ethylene glycol antifreeze, which leads us to another subject—ethylene glycol.

You shouldn't use just any antifreeze. There are superior and inferior products. The inferior ones don't contain ample additives to protect the cooling system against corrosion. How can you tell which

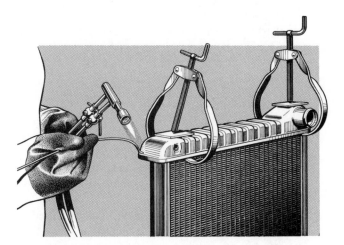

To repair a leaky header tank, you should have a professional clean the unit thoroughly, then braze it. Remove dirt and corrosion before brazing so solder can take hold.

antifreeze is better? Sticking to a brand-name product is your best assurance.

Aluminum parts

If you don't have aluminum components in the cooling system—radiator core, water pump and/or cylinder head—you can use any ethylene glycol antifreeze. However, if your engine contains aluminum parts, a special formulation is needed to resist corrosion better. Aluminum is more susceptible to corrosion than other metals used in automobile cooling systems.

How do you know whether the ethylene glycol you buy is suitable for aluminum? It will say so on the label. If it doesn't say so, don't buy it.

Once you've got your antifreeze, don't try improving it with additives. You may upset the chemical balance. Remember: Your name's not, for example, BASF Wyandotte, which makes Alugard; Dow, which makes Dowgard; DuPont, which manufactures Zerex; Northern Petrochemicals, which makes Peak; or Union Carbide, which manufactures Prestone.

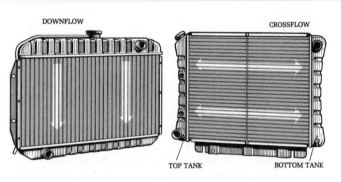

DOWNFLOW   CROSSFLOW

TOP TANK   BOTTOM TANK

Whether your automobile has a crossflow radiator or a down-flow radiator, the basic operating principles are the same. Water flows from the top header tank to the bottom header tank through the cooling fins. Heat is carried off by the rushing air.

Caustic solutions

Aluminum radiators and engine components can also be destroyed by caustic solutions found in some cleaners. To avoid damage, make sure the cleaner you buy says it's recommended specifically for aluminum components.

In fact, to avoid complications, GM recommends that you never use any chemicals to clean an aluminized cooling system. Instead, reverse flush with plain water. Remember, too, that an aluminum pressure cap and an aluminum petcock or drain plug

has to be used with an aluminum radiator. Using parts made of another metal causes galvanic action that leads to corrosion. Stay cool.

Solving Five Tough Cooling System Problems

PAUL STENQUIST

■ EVERY SATURDAY MECHANIC KNOWS it's the heat of combustion that makes a car go. But did you know that your engine generates enough heat to warm a five-room house in the dead of winter?

Only one-third of that heat is converted to power. Another third is carried away with the exhaust gases. The remainder is absorbed by the pistons, cylinder walls, and other engine parts. It's up to the cooling system to control the temperature of these components (see lead illustration). If they run too cold, the engine won't operate efficiently, fuel will be wasted and power will be limited. If they run too hot, spark knock will occur and the engine will be severely damaged. If an engine operates for more than a few minutes without coolant, the pistons can literally weld themselves to the cylinder walls. Cooling system problems require your immediate attention.

Fortunately, most cooling system headaches are easily cured by the experienced Saturday mechanic. In the sections that follow, you'll find outlined five cooling system problems and how to solve them.

Excessive coolant overflow from reservoir

If coolant pours from the reservoir overflow line every time you shut off the engine, or even while the engine is running, something is forcing the coolant out of the system. Of course if the problem happens once and doesn't repeat, it could just be a matter of the reservoir being overfilled. But if it happens repeatedly and you're sure you haven't overfilled each time, it may be due to combustion gases leaking

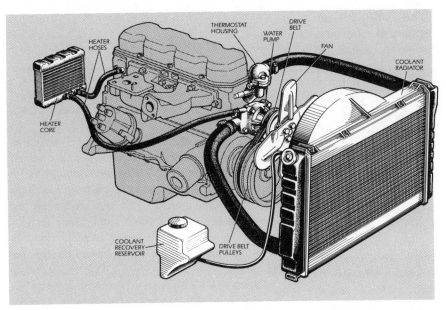

The cooling system's job is to carry combustion heat from engine's coolant passages out to the radiator, where the flow of fresh air can transfer the energy to the atmosphere. If any one component fails, serious engine damage will very likely result.

into the engine coolant jackets or an air leak on the suction side of the water pump.

To determine if an air leak is the source of the problem, remove the lower radiator hose and inspect it for damage on both ends. If any part of the hose is suffering from deterioration or shows other signs of physical damage, replace it. If the lower or upper hose is more than three years old, replace it.

Before reinstalling the lower hose, clean both hose connection areas thoroughly and inspect for any damage that might allow air to be drawn into the cooling system.

If aeration is not the cause of the overflow condition, it could be due to a blown head gasket or cracked cylinder head, which allows combustion gases to enter the cooling system. The easiest way to detect such a leak is with an emissions analyzer (Fig. 1). Ask your mechanic to hold the probe of the analyzer over the filler neck area of the open radiator. The engine must be fully warmed and running. If CO emissions are rising from the radiator, either a head gasket is blown or the block and/or cylinder head is cracked.

If you don't want to pay a mechanic to check for emissions, you can detect most combustion leaks using a cylinder leakage tester or cylinder pressurizing tool. The part of the tool that you need for this test is the air chuck/sparkplug hole adapter—nothing more than an air chuck that screws into your plug hole (Fig. 2). You can buy the air chuck connector from an auto parts store.

To test, remove the upper radiator hose, thermostat housing and thermostat. Reinstall the housing without the thermostat and fill the system with coolant. Remove the plugs and install your air chuck/plug adapter into the No. 1 plug hole. If you

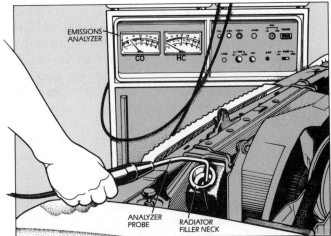

1   Combustion gases leaking into the cooling system, such as through a failed head gasket, can be detected with an emissions analyzer held at the radiator filler neck opening.

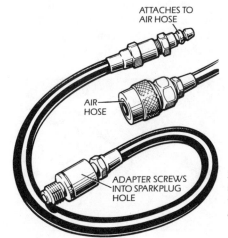

2 Use an air chuck/ sparkplug hole adapter to pressurize individual cylinders.

have a simple child's whistle, attach it to the air chuck end of the adapter with a piece of hose (Fig.

the No. 1 cylinder. You can tell when it's on compression because air rushing from the plug hole will blow the whistle as the piston rises. Attach the air supply.

Watch for bubbles of air in the thermostat housing outlet neck (Fig. 4). A cylinder that produces bubbles has a leaking head gasket or cracked combustion chamber.

Premature V-belt failure

V-belts don't last forever. Three years is about the limit for some highly stressed belts, and replacement every three years makes a lot of sense. You should not, however, have to replace belts more frequently than every three years under normal conditions. If you're constantly changing a belt, try to determine why it fails prematurely.

The way the belt rides in its pulley grooves is one important factor. A conventional V-belt should ride flush with, or slightly below, the top of the pulley groove. If the belt rides too high, it will not fully grip the pulley and the edges of the pulley will wear into the belt sides. If it rides too low, it will bottom out in the pulley groove and slip. Slippage will destroy the belt and the pulley itself.

If the belt appears to ride correctly on its pulleys but still wears out faster than normal, the failure may be caused by misalignment of the pulleys. If space permits, you can detect misalignment by holding a straightedge between the pulleys. Or you can watch the belt while it's running. If it has a noticeable kink or appears to twist as it rides in the pulley grooves, the pulleys are misaligned. To correct alignment, file the mounting areas of the brackets or shim them away from the engine.

Too much maintenance can also lead to belt failure. In most cases, the use of belt dressing should not be necessary and can sometimes weaken the rubber compounds that make up the belt.

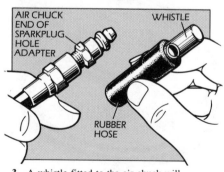

3 A whistle fitted to the air chuck will quickly indicate compression stroke TDC.

Poor heater performance

Most car owners give little thought to their car's heater during the summer. Then, when the weather turns cold, they find out that it doesn't work. A quick check in the summer can pay big dividends.

When the heater is operating, hot coolant is delivered to a radiator-like heater core located behind the dashboard or in the firewall. Outside air or recirculated inside air is forced past the core by a blower fan. The amount of air passing through the core is determined by control doors. Some vehicles are also equipped with a heater control valve that limits the amount of coolant circulated through the core.

The air that blows from your heater outlets when the engine is fully warmed and the heater is set for high heat should be 60 to 70°F. above the ambient temperature. You can check the temperature of the heater's output by holding a thermometer directly in front of the heater outlet. If the temperature is not up to spec and the control doors seem to be functioning properly, either something is restricting the flow of coolant to the core or the engine temperature is too low.

Begin by checking the heater hoses for signs of physical damage. A hose that looks okay on the outside could be restricted on the inside. If the hoses are three years old or older, replace them. If one of the hoses is fitted with a heater control valve, make sure the valve is opening when the temperature control is set to the full WARM position.

Under normal conditions your heater core shouldn't clog. But if you own an older car that has not had its cooling system backflushed on an annual basis or if you've been dumping can after can of cooling system sealant into your radiator, the core could be clogged. If you suspect that it is, disconnect the heater hoses from the engine. Turn all heater controls to the full WARM position. Then attach a garden hose to the heater inlet hose and see if water passes through the core and runs out of the other hose. If it doesn't, the core will probably have to be replaced.

If you find that coolant is reaching your heater core but output is still below spec, your engine is probably running too cool. In most cases, reduced engine temperature is the result of an incorrect or defective thermostat. In some cases, where the thermostat is stuck open or missing, heater temperature may eventually reach an appropriate level but it will take much longer than it should.

To check the thermostat, remove the thermostat

housing after the engine has cooled completely. You should find the thermostat closed. If it's open, replace it with the recommended part. (Don't think you're doing your engine a favor by using a thermostat that causes it to run cooler. Reduced engine temperature causes condensation, which leads to sludge formation.)

If you find that your thermostat is closed, remove it and look for a temperature indication stamped somewhere on the thermostat housing or mechanism. If the temperature indication is lower than that recommended by the vehicle manufacturer, replace the thermostat with the correct unit.

To test a thermostat, suspend it and a thermometer in a pan of water. Heat the water and note the temperature at which the thermostat opens. If it opens too soon, it could be the cause of reduced or delayed heater output.

When installing a new thermostat, follow instructions regarding which end of the unit goes toward the engine. After cleaning all old gasket material from the thermostat housing and water neck, the thermostat fits in the recess provided for it (Fig. 5). Use a new gasket and coat both sides with gasket compound or wheel-bearing grease. Reinstall the water neck and torque the bolts to the recommended figure, usually about 15 ft.-lb.

Engine runs hot

Most cases of overheating are due to obvious reasons: the loss of coolant through a large external leak or the loss of fan or water pump operation due to belt failure. But there are also times when an engine may overheat for no immediately apparent reason.

In order to prevent the boiling of coolant and subsequent overheating of the engine, your cooling system must remain pressurized. Pressure raises the boiling point of the coolant. Even a pin-size hole in a core plug or a leaking radiator cap seal will quickly relieve pressure.

A cooling system pressure test can tell you if you've got a leaker on your hands. This tool is commonly available through auto parts stores. Begin the pressure test by checking the radiator cap, using the adapter that comes with the pressure tester (Fig. 6). The cap should hold an amount of pressure equal to the system pressure specified for your vehicle in your service manual. If it doesn't, it must be replaced.

Once you're sure the cap is okay, attach the tester to the radiator neck and pump the system up to the pressure rating of the cap. If pressure remains steady, the system is leak-free. If leakdown occurs, check all

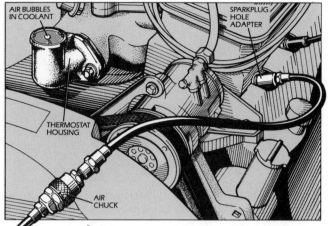

4 Internal leaks of combustion gas into the cooling system can be confirmed by the presence of bubbles in the thermostat housing after pressurizing a cylinder with air.

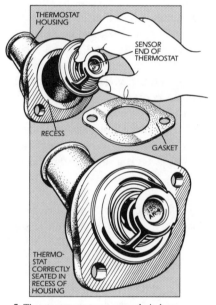

5 Thermostat must seat squarely in housing recess, sensor end facing engine.

hoses, clamps and gasket joints. Inspect the radiator, heater core and water pump vent for any signs of escaping coolant (Fig. 7). Jack up the car, support it on stands and check the core plugs. A deposit of dried coolant could be a clue to a slow leak.

An incorrect water/antifreeze solution can also contribute to a boilover problem. If your coolant contains less than 50 percent antifreeze, you're not getting adequate boilover protection. As you increase the percentage of antifreeze, boiling point rises. However, as percentage rises above 68 percent, freeze protection is lost.

Radiator blockage is a principal cause of overheating problems that do not involve obvious equipment failures. One way to check for severe blockage is to

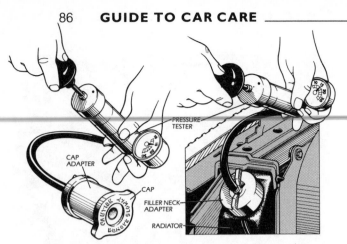

6 A full cooling system checkup must include a pressure test of both the radiator cap (left) and the coolant radiator, hoses and engine coolant passages (right).

remove the radiator cap (while the engine is cool), warm the engine fully and quickly open the throttle. If the radiator core is severely blocked, it won't be able to handle the increased flow that the water pump delivers when you rev the engine, and coolant will spurt from the filler neck. Be extra careful when performing this test. If you stare down into the radiator and crack the throttle, you could end up with severe burns from the coolant.

If the radiator appears to be severely blocked, have your mechanic backflush the cooling system using a machine that can reverse the flow through the radiator. If this doesn't clear the blockage, the radiator will have to be removed for rodding or recoring.

If you've been following our Saturday mechanic maintenance schedule, you flush your cooling system and refill it every year. If this is the case,

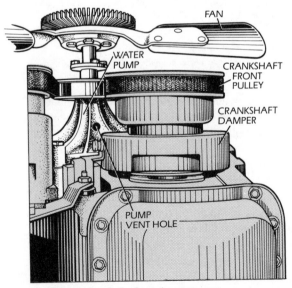

7 When coolant leaks from the pump vent hole (seen here from under the car) it indicates failure of the pump shaft seal.

corrosion should not be a significant problem. If you've neglected your cooling system, some of the passages in your engine could be blocked by corrosion. A professional power backflush and chemical treatment might help. If not, teardown and parts replacement may be necessary.

If none of the above proves to be the cause of your problem, it could be the result of a slipping fan clutch. The fan clutch should permit the fan to freewheel when the engine is cold but should engage as the engine warms. Start the engine cold and listen to the fan as the engine warms. When the clutch begins to engage, the sound of the engine should change noticeably. You can speed the warmup by restricting airflow around the radiator.

Another way to detect a slipping fan clutch is to have a helper shut off the warm engine while you watch the fan. The fan should stop spinning almost immediately. If not, the clutch is malfunctioning.

If you've made all the standard diagnostic checks and still can't find the cause of an overheating problem, you should check for a worn or slipping water pump impeller. You can sometimes get a clue to this problem by watching coolant flow in the top of the radiator with the engine warm. The only way to rule out water pump damage conclusively is to remove the pump and inspect it.

There are a few other unusual causes of overheating that you should consider. One is a restriction in the exhaust system, such as a jammed exhaust heat riser valve. In most cases, exhaust restriction will also cause performance problems, accompanied by a reduction in manifold vacuum. Overheating can also be caused by brake drag. Other potential causes include the same things that can cause spark knock: the wrong type of gasoline, EFE or hot-air system failure, EGR system failure, severe carbon buildup, incorrect ignition timing or the wrong sparkplugs. In most cases, these conditions will only cause mild overheating.

Unexplained loss of coolant

The coolant level in your reservoir will change somewhat as temperature and operating conditions vary, but it should stay within the recommended limits. If you find that the level drops continuously and there's no evidence of an external leak, the problem is probably due to an internal cooling system leak. Unfortunately, these leaks are hard to find and expensive to fix.

If you find that your oil level is constantly increasing while your coolant level is decreasing, you know where the coolant is going. A foam-like coating on the dipstick is another indication of internal leakage. In some cases, one of the heavy-duty block sealer compounds that you add to the coolant may seal it. Don't use more than recommended as it could clog your radiator and heater core.

If you're forced to disassemble the engine in your search for an internal leak, look for signs of a leaking gasket that could allow coolant to escape into the crankcase. On many engines, the timing cover gasket is a likely candidate. A leak on the periphery of a head gasket that doesn't involve the combustion seal might just dump coolant into the oil.

If you can't find a leaking gasket, the internal coolant leak is probably the result of a cracked cylinder head or engine block. An automotive machine shop can usually find the leak by pressure-testing the cylinder heads and the engine block. Once the leak is found, castings must either be replaced or welded by a shop experienced in cast-iron or cast-aluminum repairs.

Part **IV**:

AUTOMOBILE ELECTRICITY AND ELECTRONICS

Getting the Most From Your Battery

BRAD SEARS

■ OPINIONS DIFFER ON THE most neglected part of a car. Some experts claim that the air cleaner is the most overlooked item, others say it's the sparkplugs. But AAA counts dead batteries as the culprit to win the no-start Oscar.

Keeping the battery of today's car in shape isn't difficult, providing the battery itself is capable of starting the car, and holding a charge.

It may seem foolish to check the battery to make sure it is the right one for the car. Just because the battery fits the carrier tray does not mean it is the right one. A battery must have the capacity, or amperes, needed to start an engine under all conditions in which the car might operate. The capacity of the battery is often tied to the guarantee that comes with it. Many makers offer a particular size battery with a three-, four- or five-year warranty.

The difference between them could be nothing more than the size or number of plates in the battery case. It is the plate surface area, working with the electrolyte, or acid, that determines the capacity of the battery.

How it works

Consider the battery for what it is—a lead-acid chemical reactor. It does not store electricity, nor does it manufacture electricity.

When we turn the ignition switch, a chemical reaction takes place in the battery. This chemical reaction will continue until most of the active material in the battery has been changed into lead sulfate. At this point, the positive and negative plates become chemically similar, and the chemical reaction grinds to a halt. In other words, the battery is dead.

This discharge reaction can be reversed by delivering a current to the battery, thus restoring the chemicals to their original form. The car's charging system, which includes the alternator, is responsible for providing the recharge current while the engine is running.

The capacity of the battery, or the amount of current (amperes) that it can produce without recharging, is determined by the amount of plate surface exposed to chemical action. The battery will lose plate area if the plates are not completely immersed in the acid solution. The plates of a battery will eventually become sulfated and inoperative even with normal care, but overcharging or allowing the battery to become fully discharged will speed up the sulfation of the plates.

Check battery mounts

Two of the major enemies of a battery are vibration and physical shock. When a battery is bolted in place it rides with the car and is somewhat protected by the car's suspension. But when the battery hold-down bracket is left off or has corroded away, the battery will bounce all over and is likely to sustain internal damage.

If the hold-down bracket is missing, you can probably get the necessary bolts and bracket at an auto parts store. If the parts store doesn't have a bracket that fits your car, you can buy the original equipment piece from the franchised dealer.

Some cars use a bracket that hooks into a ridge low on the side of the battery case. It is a small metal plate that's attached to the car by a bolt that threads

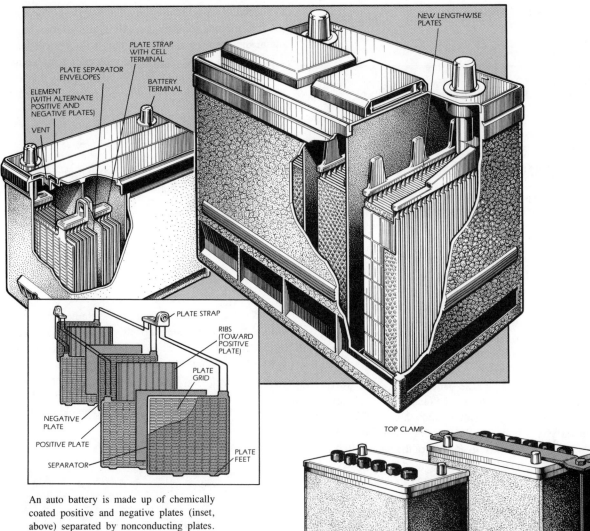

An auto battery is made up of chemically coated positive and negative plates (inset, above) separated by nonconducting plates. Each battery cell contains positive plates, negative plates and separators that are assembled into a unit called an element (small cutaway). Plate straps connect all the negative plates to the negative terminal, or post, while all the positive plates are connected to the positive post. In one new design (large cutaway), the short plates are mounted lengthwise in each individual battery cell.

Hold-down clamps prevent the battery from bouncing around, which can cause internal damage. Bottom clamps require a special ridge around the bottom of the battery case.

into a cage nut on the inner fender well or battery carrier. Some replacement batteries on the market do not have the necessary ridge around the bottom of the case. On some cars equipped with this type of hold-down, the bolt may become corroded. When you attempt to remove it, it will often break. You cannot reuse this type of hold-down without removing the battery carrier, extracting the broken bolt or cage nut, and installing a new cage nut.

If you want to repair broken hold-down bolts, remove the battery and drill a couple of ³⁄₈-in. holes at either end of the battery carrier. Don't attempt to drill the holes with the battery in place. It's easier to

get at the carrier when the battery is removed and, more importantly, it's dangerous to operate electrical equipment near the battery. There is hydrogen gas present around the top of all batteries. Any spark could cause the battery to explode, splashing battery acid all over you, your clothes, and your eyes. For this reason, you should always wear safety goggles when working around the battery.

Removing cables

There is a right and a wrong way to remove battery cables from the battery before servicing. The grounded battery cable, almost always the negative

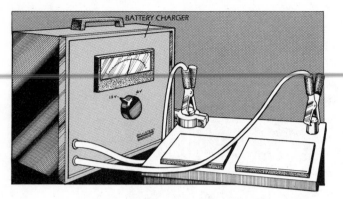

A 6- to 10-amp. trickle charger can recharge most batteries overnight. Fully discharged maintenance-free batteries require fast charging.

to check the fender panel and all of the parts to which the tray mounts for damage. All of the surrounding metal should be cleaned thoroughly with a brush and a baking soda solution, rinsed with plenty of clear water, dried, and painted. The epoxy paint that is used on white spoked wheels gives excellent results.

The battery needs a supply of current to reverse the chemical action that causes discharge. At the same time, the car needs current for the ignition and accessories while it's running. The charging system provides enough for both. If the charging system is not working properly, the battery will discharge excessively, the plates will become sulfated, and the battery will wear out long before its time.

cable, should be removed from the battery first. If you slip and touch a part of the car's body with your wrench, there will not be any spark. However, touching a wrench from the live terminal, usually the positive post, to the car's body will create a dead short plus lots of sparks and heat. At the very least, this will cause the wrench to get hot and burn your hand.

Loosen the bolts on the battery clamps and use a battery clamp puller to ease the clamps off the posts. Now, with the holes drilled, snake a couple of universal-type J-bolts of the correct length into the holes. Stand the bolts up and return the battery to the carrier, then install a universal hold-down bracket across the top of the battery, between the J bolts.

If the battery tray itself is loose, it must be secured. Sometimes a bit of metal fabrication is needed, sometimes just a simple replacement.

Charging system check

The place to start in charging system service is with a check of the alternator drive belt. It should be tight and have about ½ in. of play when you push on it with your thumb at a point halfway along its longest span. Twist the belt over and check it for cracking, glazing or fraying. Any damaged belt should be replaced. A glazed belt may appear to be okay, but it will slip, even when tight.

Watch for corrosion

A battery that has been allowed to float loose in the battery tray will often leak acid that can eat away the inner fender panel, as well as the tray. It's wise

To clean a corroded battery tray (below), use a scraper and a wire brush to remove all corrosion, then spray with epoxy paint. Professional hydrometer gives most accurate indication of battery condition (right). Each cell should read 1.250. Some maintenance-free batteries contain a built-in "eye" to indicate battery condition accurately.

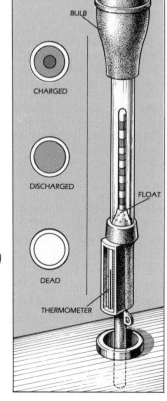

The charging system can be easily tested for general operation with a $20 voltmeter. Set the meter on the 20-v. scale and attach the red lead to the positive battery terminal and the black lead to the negative battery terminal. With all accessories off, the engine warmed up and running at about 1,500 rpm, the voltmeter should read somewhere between 13.8 v.d.c. and 15.3 v.d.c. Any less voltage than 13.8 and the charging system needs work.

This test, of course, tells you only that the charging system is functioning. Considerably more elaborate testing is required to pinpoint charging problems (which will be discussed in the next chapter).

Checking battery charge

You can test the battery for state of charge and capacity with a couple of simple tools. The first one—used on batteries that have removable caps—is a hydrometer. There are many types.

The float type uses a weighted float with numbers inscribed on the barrel. Draw just enough electrolyte up into the tube to raise the float, and read the specific gravity where the fluid level crosses the barrel. A battery fully charged and in good condition will read between 1.250 and 1.300. Each cell should be within .050 points of every other cell. A difference of over .050 indicates that the cell could be sulfated and the battery should be replaced, not recharged. If all cells are even, but well below the 1.250 mark, the battery should be recharged and retested until the hydrometer test gives a 1.250 reading.

The least expensive hydrometer uses five different balls in a glass tube. Each ball is of a different color and weight. As the concentration of acid increases, more balls will float until all of them are floating. This indicates a fully charged battery.

To test the battery, draw fluid from each cell in turn and record the number of balls floating. Return the fluid to its cell and test the next one. Each cell should float the same number of balls. If they don't, you can suspect that the cell with the lower number is defective or sulfated.

If all the cells read low (float only a few balls), then the battery should be recharged. A slow charger can be used and the charging should continue until all of the balls in the hydrometer float (or, until the reading is at least 1.250).

Some maintenance-free batteries have a built-in hydrometer. On many of these, you'll find a little window on top of the battery. Usually, a dark or black "eye" means that the battery is in need of recharge. A green eye means that the battery is at least 75 percent charged. A clear or yellow indicator

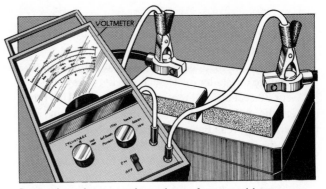

Inexpensive voltmeter can be used to perform several battery tests. Attach the red voltmeter lead to the positive battery terminal and black lead to the negative.

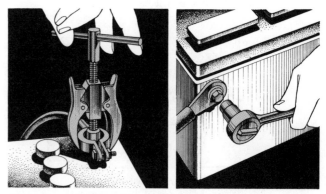

The easiest way to remove battery cables from a top-post battery is with an inexpensive cable clamp puller (left). Loosen the clamp bolt, then use the puller to lift clamp. On side-terminal batteries (right) you merely have to remove the terminal bolt.

means that the battery is defective and must be discarded.

There are many battery chargers on the market, ranging in price from about $50 to $1,000. For the average home shop a simple trickle charger with a 6- to 10-amp. charging rate will suffice. This charger will bring conventional batteries to full charge, but it may take several hours or overnight to do so.

A slightly discharged maintenance-free battery can often be brought to full charge on a small charger, but a fully discharged battery of this type must be charged at very high current levels on professional equipment.

Checking battery condition

Your voltmeter can also be used to check the battery capacity and condition. With the voltmeter still connected to the battery's posts, ground the ignition by removing the coil cable from the distributor cap. Ground the cable to the block with a jumper wire to prevent arcing of the high-voltage spark that could cause a fire, shock you, or damage the ignition system. (On GM cars with HEI ignition, simply disconnect the small lead connected to the BAT terminal on the distributor.)

With the ignition disabled as described above, engage the starter for 15 seconds. Let the system rest for 30 seconds and repeat the test for 15. This time, at the end of the 15 seconds, with the engine still cranking, read the voltmeter and record the reading. If the reading is above 10 volts for a maintenance-free battery—or above 9.6 volts for a conventional battery—the battery and starter are both good.

A low reading will not distinguish between a bad battery or a bad starter. If other conditions lead you to suspect that the battery has lost capacity, you can generally assume that it has.

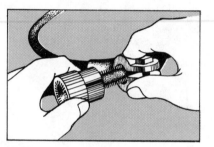

Clean the battery posts and cable clamps (above) with a special wire brush until they are shiny. You should use a battery carrier (below) or strap to lift heavy battery, lessening chance of damage or injury.

Cleaning and reinstalling

To clean and maintain your battery, you will need a wire brush, a clamp and post cleaner, a box of baking soda, a paintbrush, some water and a jar of petroleum jelly. Remove the cables. Mix some baking soda in a container with water to the consistency of wallpaper paste. Use the paintbrush to apply the paste to the top, sides and around the carrier of the battery. When it stops bubbling, flush with clear water. Coat the cable clamps, or terminals, with the mixture, as well. Then flush them with water—plenty of water.

Next, use the post and clamp cleaner to make the posts and inner clamp surfaces bright and shining clean. If the bolts on the clamps are eaten up by acid, replace them. If the clamps fit the posts too loosely, you can use a hacksaw to cut the slot in the clamps wider. This will allow the bolt to pull the clamp shut around the post. If the cable ends are too far gone to give a good connection, replace the complete cable.

Install the cable clamps (positive first, then negative) and tighten each nut and bolt. Care must be taken here. Installing the battery in the reverse polarity will damage the diodes in the alternator, the wiring harness and any electronic or computer equipment on the car. Once the cable clamps are on tight, a light coating of petroleum jelly will prevent corrosion.

Battery maintenance might seem like a lot of work, but getting reliable starts will make the effort worthwhile.

Testing the Charging System

MORT SCHULTZ

■ MAINTAINING, Troubleshooting and repairing the units responsible for producing and controlling electricity in your car isn't such a big deal. Those units are the alternator, voltage regulator and the wiring that connects them to each other and to the units they serve.

As a team, they are called the charging system. The alternator is referred to by some as the a.c. (alternating current) generator and by GM as the Delcotron generator.

Maintenance is a breeze; there's practically none. General troubleshooting is easy, too, because a glance at the warning light or gauge on the dashboard will usually tell you when the system isn't putting out enough juice. Even if the light or gauge isn't working, the battery will serve as a warning. It will soon discharge (go dead) if the charging system fails.

However, one condition you have to be cautious about is failure of the voltage regulator to limit alternator output. Without regulation, an alternator will overcharge the battery, which can ruin components that use electricity.

For instance, bulbs and fuses that can't handle excessive current will burn out. Battery electrolyte (sulfuric acid) will vaporize quickly if too much charging current is supplied. Unless you spot the depleting electrolyte supply soon enough, dry plates will deteriorate, and the battery will die. An overcharged battery can even explode.

In this respect, you're better off with a conventional battery, especially if you're in the habit of removing vent caps and checking electrolyte level once every week or two. If the electrolyte is frequently found to be low, the system is probably overcharging. Even if you don't check electrolyte level you may get whiffs of the gas. It smells like rotten eggs.

A sealed maintenance-free battery offers no latitude. The first sign that overcharging is destroying the battery is when the battery indicator turns pale yellow or clear, but by then it's too late. However, if your car is equipped with a voltmeter or ammeter, you can easily spot an overcharging condition. If battery voltage frequently exceeds 14.5 volts, or if an ammeter shows continuous high charge rates, overcharging is likely and a basic charging system diagnostic test should be performed.

No task too tough

Specific troubleshooting procedures that determine if a fault lies with the alternator, regulator or wiring is a bit more difficult than maintenance and general troubleshooting, but it's not as tough as some people would have you believe.

Only when you uncover a fault inside the alternator does the situation become hairy, but even then you have a choice. You can replace the alternator, which is easy but expensive. Or you can tear it down, test internal components and try making repairs to save yourself some money. Advanced Saturday mechanics certainly have the capability to do these things on some cars. Even Saturday mechanics with limited experience may want to try it. There's nothing to lose.

The only maintenance needed is to check the drive belt, which is something you probably do anyway when servicing the cooling system.

Look for cracks on the underside of the belt, since a cracked belt can break without warning. Also look for oil, grease and hard glaze on the underside of the belt, which will cause a belt to slip on its pulleys. A belt that fails to grip pulleys can't turn the alternator rotor fast enough. The result is a reduction in electrical output.

A belt that has stretched and lost tension may also be the reason why your warning light or gauge is showing reduced current output. Make a quick test by pressing down on the belt with your thumb midway between two pulleys. If the belt deflects more than ½ inch or so, that belt is too loose.

Adjusting belt tension

To remove or adjust an alternator drive belt in most vehicles, loosen the pivot and adjusting arm bolts. If you want to slacken the belt so you can remove it, push the alternator toward the engine. When the belt goes limp, pry it off its pulleys. Then, roll a new belt back on the pulleys. *Caution:* Be sure to get a belt of the correct size for your vehicle.

To adjust belt tension, hold a pry bar against the solid part of the alternator housing and pull the alternator away from the engine until the belt tightens. Pick a solid point. Do not pry against the cooling fins or fan, or you'll damage the alternator.

What's proper tension? That depends on whether you're using the finger method or a belt tension gauge to make the judgment. For accuracy, use a gauge. The most common type has a tang that slides under the belt and two arms that fit on top.

Vehicle manufacturers provide "new" and "old" belt tension specifications in service manuals. Instructions that accompany gauges also give some. Remember: A belt is no longer "new" after it's been used for 10 minutes.

If you don't have a gauge, press down on the belt and continue pulling back on the alternator until the belt deflects about ¼ to ½ inch in the center of the belt's longest span. Then, tighten the adjusting arm bolt and the pivot bolt in that order. Do not tighten a belt so much that it gives less than ¼ inch. A too-tight belt can damage alternator bearings.

Some alternators are equipped with a jackscrew belt tensioner. This is simply a screw that is threaded through part of the alternator bracket. When the screw is turned clockwise, the alternator is forced away from the engine and belt tension is increased.

Some Ford V8s from '79 onward and the '84 Cor-

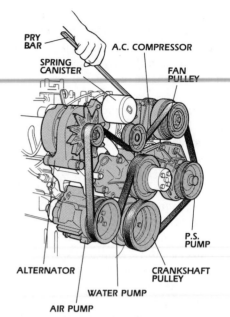

To remove a serpentine belt, place pry bar into tab on spring canister and pull down to raise tensioning pulley. The belt can then be removed easily from the other pulleys so that you can install a new one.

Charging system includes the voltage regulator, the alternator (shown in insets), the battery and the wiring harness that connects them.

A homemade test light can be used to troubleshoot circuits, if you can locate a wiring diagram. Note that a screwdriver is used to disconnect the wiring harness from this Ford voltage regulator.

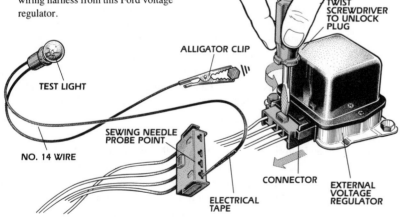

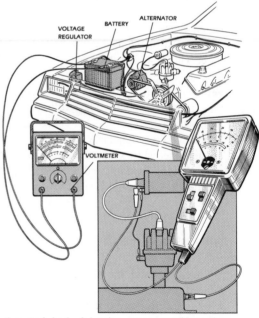

A general check of charging system operation can be made with a voltmeter and a tachometer. The voltmeter should read in tenths of a volt to at least 16 volts. Check the instructions that come with your tach for correct hookup.

vette use a single serpentine belt to drive all engine accessories. It has a spring-loaded tensioner, so it never needs tightening. But it should be checked and replaced if it is cracked, glazed, oil-soaked or frayed on either side (both sides of the belt drive various pulleys).

Squeal is a common sound produced by a slick drive belt or one that possesses minor surface irregularities. An alternator that is developing a bearing problem can also squeal. How can you tell if the squeal is coming from the belt, alternator or somewhere else in the engine compartment? Apply aerosol belt dressing to the belt. If the squeal is no longer present or changes pitch, you have a noisy belt. If the noise stays the same, the trouble may be inside the alternator. Remove the belt and run the engine. If the problem is in the alternator, the noise will disappear.

Test the battery first

When something happens that suggests a charging system problem, you can't overlook the battery.

The battery, alternator and voltage regulator are closely intertwined. When a problem arises that affects one, it affects all. Watch for the following trouble signs:

■ If the vehicle has a warning light and it stays lighted with the engine idling or until engine speed is increased to about 2,000 rpm, the system should be tested. If the warning light doesn't come on when the ignition switch is turned on (engine not running), forget the charging system and test the light circuit (see section below).

■ If the car has a gauge and it shows discharge with the engine running at a speed just above idle, the system should be tested. If the gauge shows neither charge nor discharge with the engine running, test the gauge circuit before turning your attention to the battery and charging system (see section below).

■ If the battery has to be charged or refilled with water often, the system should be tested.

■ If headlights dim excessively with the engine running at idle (but brighten when accelerating), the charging system should be tested.

■ If the engine cranks sluggishly, the system should be tested.

■ If you suspect overcharging, the system should be tested.

■ If the battery discharges completely and the vehicle fails to start, the system should be tested.

The first part of any charging system test is battery inspection and diagnosis (see "Getting the Most From Your Battery," for specific battery service pointers). Once you've determined that the battery is okay, you can proceed to other tests. But first, let's backtrack and discuss what you should do if your warning light fails to glow when you first turn the key or if your gauge needle stays dead center, showing neither charge nor discharge with the engine running.

Checking the warning light

If a warning light fails, the bulb may be shot or there may be an open circuit. You can find out by fabricating a warning lamp test light, using a socket that accepts a No. 97 bulb, two lengths of No. 14 wire, an alligator clip and a probe such as a sewing needle. The drawing on the previous page, lower left, shows how to assemble these parts.

With the ignition switch off, connect the test light alligator clip to a clean metal part, such as a bolt. Then, place the test light probe in contact with the wire terminal on the warning light.

Turn the ignition switch on (do not crank the engine).

If the test light glows, but the warning light doesn't, the warning light bulb is burned out or the bulb socket is defective.

If neither the test light nor warning light glows, there is a problem in the warning light circuit.

Testing the warning light in a GM vehicle with an internally mounted voltage regulator (VR) is done differently. Let's use the Delcotron as an example, since the vast majority of internal VRs are found on GM cars. You don't need to use a test light—only your eyes and hands.

If the warning light glows with the ignition switch off, disconnect the two leads from terminals 1 and 2 on the back end of the Delcotron. If the warning light stays on, there's a short in the circuit between the two leads. If the warning light goes out, the rectifier bridge inside the alternator is defective, so replace it as explained in the next chapter. If your battery has been losing charge, the rectifier bridge could be the source of the problem.

If the warning light does *not* go on when you turn the ignition switch on without cranking the engine, the warning light fuse has blown, the warning light bulb or socket is defective, or there's an open circuit in the No. 1 wire between the regulator and light. This condition can also be caused by a faulty rectifier bridge.

Finally, if the warning light stays on with the engine running, there's most likely trouble with the alternator or regulator.

If a gauge needle doesn't move off dead center, you don't have to go through this fuss. With the ignition switch off, turn on the headlights. If the needle deflects toward *discharge,* the gauge is working. If the needle doesn't move, there's a loose connection at the gauge, an open circuit in the gauge wiring, or the gauge itself is on the fritz.

Troubleshooting alternators

When it comes to testing an alternator and regulator, someone may ask, "Don't we have to use an adjustable carbon pile (rheostat) and ammeter?"

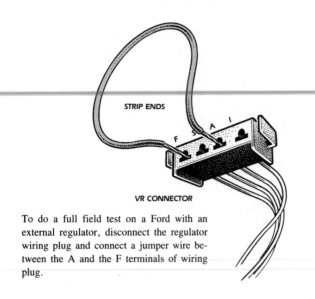

STRIP ENDS

VR CONNECTOR

To do a full field test on a Ford with an external regulator, disconnect the regulator wiring plug and connect a jumper wire between the A and the F terminals of wiring plug.

No, you don't have to. However, you can't be absolutely certain that a charging system is capable of delivering full current without doing a carbon pile load test.

But a basic test of charging system effectiveness can be performed with a voltmeter. The voltmeter should read in tenths of a volt and be capable of measuring at least 16 volts.

While this test can't actually measure alternator effectiveness under all conditions, it can determine if the battery is being charged by the system. It can also tell you what part of the charging system is at fault if the battery is not being charged.

To test a charging system that has an *externally* mounted regulator, warm up the engine to avoid the possibility of a cold regulator giving false test results. Then, turn off the engine and all electrical accessories and lights. Connect an engine tachometer, following the instructions that come with the tach. Then, attach the voltmeter's positive lead to the battery's positive post and the voltmeter's negative lead to the battery's negative post.

Make a note of the voltmeter (battery voltage) reading. It should be no less than 12 volts. If it is less, the battery is undercharged, so charge the battery. Take another reading and record this battery *base voltage*.

Now, start the engine and slowly increase speed until the tachometer records 1,500 rpm. This is called the *no-load test*. When the voltmeter needle stabilizes, read the meter. You'll get one of two indications:

1. If the voltage reading exceeds the base voltage by 2.0 volts or less, skip down this page to the load test.

2. If the voltage reading exceeds the base voltage by *more* than 2.0 volts, you're faced with a faulty regulator, a bad regulator ground or a short circuit in

the wiring harness between the regulator and alternator.

Remove, clean, reinstall and tighten the regulator attaching bolts. Also, clean off the surface on which the regulator sits to assure a good ground.

Do the no-load test again. If you now get a reading that exceeds the base voltage reading by *more* than 2.0 volts, either the regulator is defective or there is a short in the wiring harness. Check the harness for abuse. If you don't detect any, try replacing the regulator.

Note: When mounting a new regulator, see that the mounting surface is clean, bolts are as tight as possible and the ground wire from the alternator, if there is one, is secured under one of the mounting bolts.

If you find a short in the wiring harness, you may still have to replace both the regulator and the wiring, since the short may have damaged the regulator.

Doing a load test

Do the load test next to find a problem in a charging system having an externally mounted regulator. With the tachometer and voltmeter connected as for the no-load test, start the engine. Turn the heater or air conditioner on and set the blower at high speed.

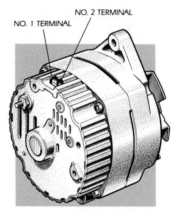

NO. 2 TERMINAL
NO. 1 TERMINAL

To check warning light of a GM charging system with an internal regulator alternator, remove wires from terminals 1 and 2.

Turn headlights and all electrical accessories on. Increase engine speed to 3,000 rpm and note the voltmeter reading. One of the following will result:

1. If the voltage exceeds base voltage by 0.5 volts or more, the charging system is at least capable of keeping your battery charged under normal conditions.

2. If the voltage increase is less than 0.5 volt, the regulator, the wiring or the alternator is defective. "Full fielding" the charging system can help you pinpoint the problem.

How to full field a vehicle

To full field a late-model Ford with an externally mounted regulator, turn off the engine, disconnect the regulator connector and connect a jumper wire between the "A" and "F" terminals of the regulator plug.

To full field a late-model Chrysler with an externally mounted regulator, turn off the engine and disconnect the green field wire that connects the regulator to the alternator field terminal at the alternator. Then connect a jumper wire from the alternator field terminal to ground.

With either system full-fielded, repeat the load test. If voltage exceeds base voltage by 0.5 or more volts, the regulator is defective and must be replaced. If the increase is less than 0.5 volts, the problem is in the wiring or alternator. There are tests that can help determine which, but they vary a great deal from vehicle to vehicle. However, the alternator is usually the source of the problem. If a visual check of the wiring harness for the alternator/regulator doesn't show signs of abuse or heat, you can be reasonably certain that the alternator is the source of your difficulty.

If the alternator is defective, it will have to be removed from the vehicle for further testing and repair.

Caution: In doing the tests we've just discussed on a vehicle that has a catalytic converter, try to wrap things up within a total engine running time of five minutes. If you exceed this, there's a possibility you'll damage the converter. If you must go beyond five minutes, turn off the engine for 30 minutes so the catalyst can cool down before you continue testing.

Testing and Repairing Alternators

MORT SCHULTZ

■ AS EXPLAINED in the preceding chapter, you can test a charging system that has its voltage regulator (VR) inside the alternator without having to use an ammeter and adjustable carbon pile—instruments that many swear by.

When we speak of inside-the-alternator, or integral, voltage regulators, the GM Delcotron is the usual example. Ford produced some cars having integral VRs, but not enough to talk about. Chrysler never has, except for its Japanese-made, 2.6-liter engine.

Suppose that the charging system warning light of a car with a Delcotron glows when the engine is running, or its battery discharges continually, its ammeter gauge shows constant discharge, or its voltmeter gauge shows a constant loss of voltage. Once you rule out the battery itself, the alternator drive belt and warning light malfunctions as possible causes, then the trouble is probably a faulty regulator or alternator. There's an easy test you can make to find out which one it is.

Begin by connecting a voltmeter that reads in tenths of a volt to the car's battery. Connect the negative lead to the negative post, positive lead to positive post. Attach a tachometer according to the instructions that came with the unit. If you have a GM car with HEI ignition and the instructions for your tach tell you to connect one lead to the negative terminal of the coil, attach it to the TACH terminal of the HEI distributor instead.

Check battery voltage before starting the engine. If it is less than 12, charge the battery.

Start the engine and rev it to 3,000 rpm. Turn on all accessories and lights and note the battery voltage. It should exceed your first reading by at least 0.5 volt.

If it does, the charging system is at least functional and the battery discharge condition may have been the result of a current draw, such as a short or a glovebox light that doesn't shut off. Check all accessories that are supposed to shut off by themselves, or that you might have failed to shut off.

If voltage did not exceed your base reading by at least 0.5 volt, either the alternator or the regulator is not functioning properly. To determine which, you'll have to "full-field" the system. To full-field the Delcotron, insert the tip of a screwdriver into the D-shaped hole in the alternator end frame until it touches the metal tab on the rotor brush (see Fig. 1). Rest the screwdriver on the side of the hole.

With the screwdriver in place, repeat the 3,000-rpm voltage test. If voltage still doesn't exceed base by 0.5 volt, there is probably some type of serious alternator malfunction.

If full-fielding causes voltage to exceed the base reading by at least 0.5 volt, the unit's integral regulator is probably defective and should be tested further or replaced. The fact that the alternator charges when full-fielded doesn't guarantee that the regulator is defective. A bad field winding or open stator winding in the alternator will produce the same result.

What if the Delcotron warning light glows when the ignition switch is turned off? Pull the connector off the Delcotron terminals 1 and 2. If the warning light goes off, replace the rectifier bridge in the alternator (see section below). If the warning light continues to glow, there's a short between the wires that feed terminals 1 and 2.

Replacing a faulty integral VR

After removing a Delcotron alternator from the vehicle (disconnect the battery cables before you start), use an awl to scribe a mark across the two halves of the case, which are called "end frames." Use these to realign the end frames when you reassemble the unit.

Then take out the four throughbolts, insert a screwdriver in the slot between the two end frames and pry them apart. Lay the drive pulley end frame and rotor (front half) on a clean surface. Place a piece of tape over the slip ring's bearing to keep dirt out.

The regulator is attached to the rectifier end frame (rear half—see Fig. 2). Mark the stator coil and the housing for reassembly reference, as you did the end frames. Then remove the nuts that secure the stator coil wiring to the terminals inside the housing. Separate the coil from the housing. Remove the diode-trio screw and lift out the wire resistor and diode assembly. The brush holder and voltage regulator may be removed by unfastening the two remaining screws. If any of the screws have special insulating washers or sleeves, make sure they are reinstalled in the same location when the new regulator-brush unit is installed.

When you install the regulator-brush unit, reattach the diode assembly ground strap securely to the diode-trio screw and make sure other screws are properly secured.

Delcotron tests

While the unit is disassembled, you can make additional tests. The stator of all model Delcotrons is tested for grounding by holding one probe of an ohmmeter on the metal core ring and touching the other probe to each lead terminal, in turn (Fig. 3). If the three readings don't indicate high resistance, replace the stator.

Also test the stator for an open circuit: Hold the ohmmeter probes between the top and second lead terminals. Then, switch the probes so they touch the second and third lead terminals. If the ohmmeter shows high resistance or infinity in either instance, replace the stator.

To check the diode trio of a Delcotron, you need an ohmmeter that is powered by a 1½-volt battery. With this meter set on its lowest scale, hold one meter probe to one of the three bottom connectors of the diode trio and the other probe to the single connector that shoots off the side (Fig. 4). Then, reverse the probes.

You should get a high reading when probes are held one way and a low reading when probes are held the other way. If you don't, replace the diode trio.

Repeat this test on each of the other two bottom connectors. Then connect the ohmmeter to each pair of the bottom connectors. If any reading is zero, replace the diode trio.

To test the rectifier bridge, hold one ohmmeter probe against the grounded heat sink (Fig. 2). Hold the other probe against the flat part of one of the three terminals in the middle of the rectifier bridge. Then, reverse the probes. If ohmmeter readings are the same with probes held both ways, replace the rectifier bridge. Repeat this test for each of the other two terminals. Then, do the same test by holding the ohmmeter probes to the insulated heat sink and to the three terminals, in turn.

You can test the Delcotron rotor field winding for grounds and continuity in the same way as the Motorcraft rotor is tested (see section below). The one exception is that, when testing for continuity, you should get a reading of 2.0 to 3.5 ohms on the Delcotron.

The only other repair you might want to try is replacing the brushes. In some alternators (other than the Delcotron) the brush holder lies behind the stator and rectifier assembly. If the tests below suggest that brushes may be worn, melt solder from the brush leads and remove the brushes and brush springs. Install new springs and brushes, then solder leads securely.

With the Delcotron, a holder containing brushes is attached to the end frame alongside the voltage regulator.

In addition to electrical problems, an alternator can suffer mechanical failure in the form of a defective bearing, damaged rotor shaft, loose or bent pulley and fan assembly, and cracked housing. If the alternator makes noise, remove it from the car. Examine the housing for cracks and determine if the fan or pulley is bent or loose.

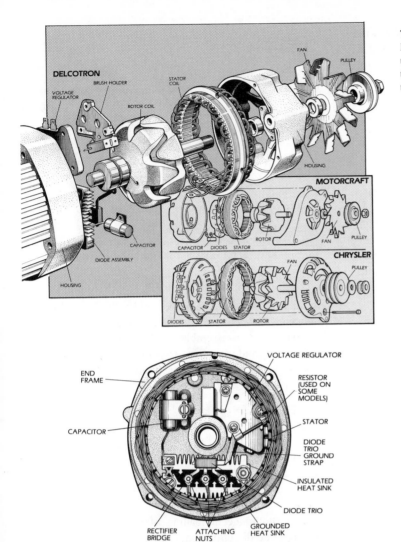

To replace the voltage regulator in a General Motors Delcotron, you must disassemble the unit. Ford Motorcraft and Chrysler alternators have externally mounted voltage regulators (see figure 7).

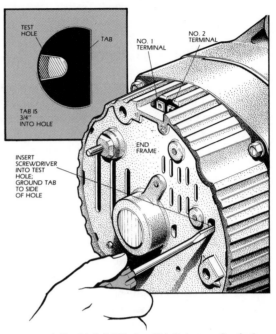

1 To "full-field" the GM Delcotron for further testing, simply insert a screwdriver into the D-shaped hole on the end frame and ground the tab inside to the end frame with the screwdriver. Then do tests described in the text.

2 If tests indicate that voltage regulator (or any other internal part) of the Delcotron is defective, disconnect the battery cables, remove alternator and disassemble it. The parts we're concerned with are in rear half of the alternator housing.

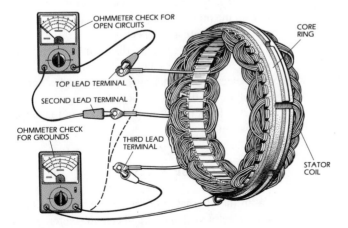

3 To test for grounding, touch ohmmeter probes to metal core ring and to each terminal. To test for open circuits, touch probes to pairs of terminals.

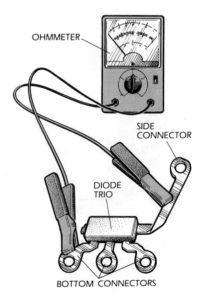

4 To test the diode trio, you need an ohmmeter with a 1½-v. battery. Set the ohmmeter to its lowest scale and perform the tests that are outlined in the text.

Now, turn the fan and pulley assembly slowly by hand. Listen for noise and feel for roughness. If there's an indication of damage, examine the rotor shaft. If it's not smooth, replace the rotor. If the shaft is okay, replace the front and/or rear bearings, or replace the whole alternator.

Testing other alternators

If a problem shows up with an alternator other than the Delcotron when you test a charging system (see the previous chapter) you can test the alternator on a workbench to isolate the weak component.

Procedures differ from alternator to alternator, and you should check a service manual for specific instructions.

Motorcraft test No. 1

With the alternator still assembled, set the ohmmeter selector switch on 10 and zero the meter (Fig. 5). Touch one probe to the battery terminal (B) and the other to the stator terminal (S). Then, reverse the probes. You should get a reading of approximately 60 ohms with the probes touching one way and no needle movement (infinity) with the probes the other way.

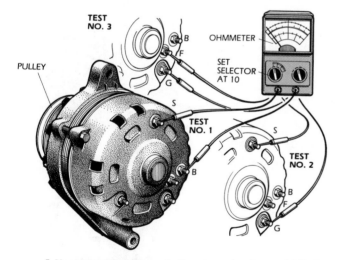

5 You can test the Motorcraft alternator used on late-model Fords without disassembling it. For test No. 1 (see text), set ohmmeter scale on 10 and touch probes to terminals S and B. For test No. 2, touch terminals S and G. For test No. 3, set ohmmeter scale on 1 and touch probes to F and G.

You might get a reading of 60 ohms or less with probes held both ways. This indicates a defective positive diode, a grounded positive diode plate or a grounded battery terminal. You could also get an

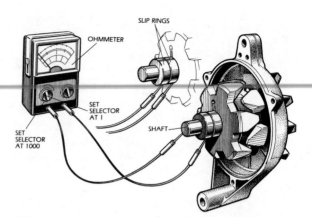

6 Disassemble Motorcraft alternator for final two tests. Set ohmmeter at 1,000 and touch probes first to shaft, then to each slip ring. Next, set the meter on 1 and touch probes to both slip rings.

infinity reading with the probes held both ways. This indicates an open stator terminal connection.

To repair it, disassemble the alternator and replace the stator and rectifier assembly. The rectifier assembly of the Motorcraft alternator contains the diode plate.

Motorcraft test No. 2

With the alternator still assembled, touch one probe to the stator terminal (S) and touch the other probe to the ground terminal (G). Then reverse the probes.

You should get a reading of approximately 60 ohms in one direction and no needle movement (infinity) in the other direction.

You might get a reading of approximately 60 ohms or less with probes held both ways. This indicates a defective negative diode, grounded positive diode plate, grounded battery or stator terminals, or grounded stator. You could also get an infinity reading with the probes held both ways. This indicates an open stator terminal connection.

To repair these problems, disassemble the alternator and replace the stator and rectifier assembly. Some electronic soldering expertise and a service manual are needed for this job. Exchange the whole alternator for a rebuilt unit if you are not equipped for this job.

Motorcraft test No. 3

With the alternator still assembled, set the ohmmeter selector switch on 1 and zero the meter. Touch one probe to the field terminal (F) and the other to the ground terminal (G). Read the ohmmeter as you spin the pulley (rotor).

You should get a reading that fluctuates between 2.4 and 100 ohms for most Motorcraft alternators. Check a service manual for specific values.

You might get a reading less than 2.4 ohms, which indicates a grounded brush assembly, a grounded field terminal (F) or a bad rotor. You could also get a reading much higher than 400 ohms. If you do, test the rotor before checking for an open brush lead, worn or stuck brushes, or a bad rotor.

Motorcraft ground test

Scribe a line across the two housings and disassemble the alternator to separate the front (rotor) housing from the rear (stator-rectifier) housing. Set the ohmmeter switch on 1,000 and zero the meter. Touch one probe to the rotor shaft and touch the other probe to one slip ring and then to the other (Fig. 6).

7 To replace externally mounted voltage regulators, unbolt them from firewall or fender housing, bolt on replacement, then transfer wiring from old unit to new one. When replacing Chrysler unit (right), replace field relay, also.

You should get no needle movement. If the needle moves when touching one or both slip rings, inspect the slip ring's soldered terminals to be sure they are not bent and touching the rotor shaft. Also make sure that excess solder is not grounding the rotor coil connections to the shaft. If everything looks okay and the rotor still fails the test, replace it.

Motorcraft rotor continuity test

Set the ohmmeter selector switch on 1 and zero the meter. Hold one probe to one slip ring, and the other probe to the other slip ring. You should get a reading between 2 and 3.5 ohms for most late-model Motorcraft alternators. Check a service manual for the exact specs on your alternator.

If you get a reading below 2 ohms or above 3.5 ohms, replace the rotor.

Notice that I've not described how to test the stator, rectifier or diodes individually. It's possible to do this, but with Motorcraft alternators, you first have to break down the stator and rectifier assembly into parts, which requires unsoldering wire leads and then resoldering them after tests are made. It's a lot less trouble to replace the entire assembly.

Troubleshooting Starting System Problems

PAUL STENQUIST

■ IT USUALLY HAPPENS WHEN you're in a hurry. You've got a lot on your mind, maybe an important business meeting or a long-awaited social event. You move quickly to your car, slide in behind the wheel and turn the key. Nothing happens. The starter motor, that basic device, won't run.

The cranking circuit consists of these major components: the battery, battery cables and terminals, switch, neutral safety switch or clutch switch, solenoid switch or starter relay, cranking motor, the pinion and its drive, and the flywheel. The battery cables, starter and solenoid are wired together in a low-resistance circuit that carries large amounts of current. The key switch, neutral safety switch and solenoid switch are wired into a comparatively high-resistance circuit that carries much less current.

Most GM products and some Fords and Chryslers use a solenoid switch unit that is mounted on the outside of the starter motor. Other Fords have a relay switch somewhere in the engine compartment and an integral engagement mechanism within the starter motor. Most Chrysler starters have the solenoid built into the end of the starter motor.

The engine won't spin when you turn the key unless a number of things happen. The battery has to provide sufficient energy (voltage) in an adequate amount (amperage). The key switch must close a circuit between the battery and the solenoid switch. The neutral safety switch must close the same circuit.

The current that flows through this circuit must then energize the winding within the solenoid switch or relay. This produces magnetic energy which moves a disc across two contacts, closing the low-resistance, high-amperage circuit that connects the starter to the battery. The solenoid also pushes the pinion gear into the bell housing, where it engages the flywheel ring gear. On cars that have a relay rather than a solenoid, there is a magnetic device within the starter that engages the pinion before the circuit to the motor is completed.

If one of those components fails, you'll be left holding the key.

Dead silence

If absolutely nothing happens when you turn the key, there may be a problem in the high-resistance circuit that links the battery, key switch, neutral switch and solenoid switch. The battery may be completely dead or, in cases where the high-resistance circuit does not begin at the battery, there may be no voltage available at the point where it begins.

You can rule out a completely dead battery by simply switching on the lights. If the lights glow brightly, try starting the car again with them on. If they remain bright with the key in the start position, wiggle the gearshift selector or clutch pedal (on manual transmission cars) while you try again. If this makes the engine crank, the problem is a defective neutral safety switch or clutch switch. If wiggling doesn't help, use a test lamp or voltmeter to check for current at the neutral safety switch or the clutch start switch. In most cases, it will be found on the steering column, transmission or clutch pedal. Chrysler usually has a neutral relay mounted under the hood on the driver's side of the firewall. Connect the negative lead of your test instrument to a good ground and touch the positive lead to each side of the switch or relay with the car in PARK or with its clutch pedal depressed. Hold the key in the START position. Current should be available on both sides.

If current is available on only one side of the switch, it should be replaced. If current isn't available on either side of the switch, you probably have a defective key switch. If the dash indicators light with the switch in the ON position, you can rule out the last possibility.

If voltage is available on both sides of the neutral switch, check the terminal where the small wire of the high-resistance circuit is attached to the starter relay or solenoid switch. Most relays or solenoids will have two small wires. One is the trigger voltage from the switch. The other usually joins the coil to the starting circuit and provides a high-voltage charge to the ignition primary circuit to help start the car. With the key in the START position, voltage should be available at the terminal that is connected to the key switch circuit. If you're using a voltmeter, you should find more than 7 volts. If voltage is not reaching the solenoid or relay, there's a problem in the wire joining the safety switch and solenoid, or in the bulkhead connector where the underhood wiring loom plugs into the passenger compartment wiring.

You should also check for loose or corroded connections at the neutral switch or relay.

If voltage is available at the solenoid switch of a GM or Ford with starter-mounted solenoid, but the solenoid won't even click when the key is turned, the solenoid is defective and must be replaced. Most Chrysler products have a solenoid that is built into the starter motor. If this solenoid fails, the starter must be disassembled for repair or replaced with a new or rebuilt unit.

If you found voltage at the switch terminal of a Ford relay, check to see if a charge of at least 9.6 volts is available at the larger terminal of the relay with the key in the START position. If this is so, there is an open circuit between this point and the starter terminal or the starter is defective. If no voltage is available, replace the relay.

Click, click

If you heard a good solid click when you first tried to start the car, try it again with the headlights on. If the headlights remain bright, the starter motor itself is probably defective, but the solenoid is okay.

If you heard a series of clicks, a weak click, or a click and a slow growling noise, try again with the lights on. If the lights go out completely or dim considerably, the battery may be dead, there may be excessive resistance in the circuit, the starter motor may be difficult to turn due to internal resistance, or the engine itself may be hard to turn due to internal damage. However, you can be certain that the principal problem is not in the switch circuit.

The best place to start with this type of starter problem is at the battery and its connections and cables. Check the battery for cracks or other obvious damage. Remove the terminals and check for corrosion or looseness. Replace any cables with terminals that have eroded or won't tighten. Don't replace the terminals (the kind that clamp the cable under a bolt-on strap), check the connection for corrosion. Even a little bit of corrosion at the point where the cable contacts the terminal can result in a no-start. Check the other end of the cables for proper connection also.

When the key switch is turned to START and the gearshift is in NEUTRAL, the circuit between the battery and the solenoid switch is complete. Once energized, the solenoid switch causes engagement of the pinion gear and flywheel, closing the circuit between battery and cranking motor.

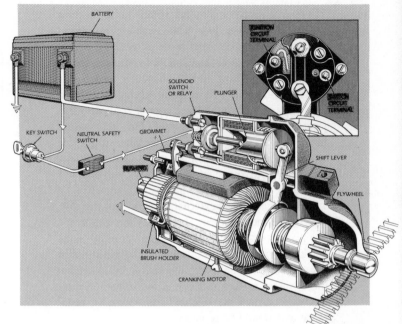

This Chrysler Corp. cranking motor has a reduction gear that's set between the motor's armature shaft and pinion gear shaft. This reduces the rotational speed at the pinion, but provides substantially increased cranking torque. The increased torque helps to eliminate the hot-start problems on high-compression engines. The solenoid assembly is built into the end of the gear reduction starter. Consequently, the motor must be disassembled in order to repair the solenoid.

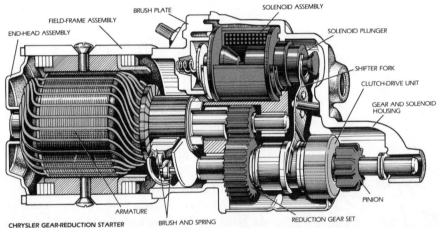

CHRYSLER GEAR-REDUCTION STARTER

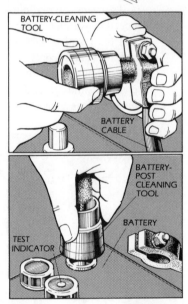

Many batteries have been replaced needlessly when a cleaning of terminals and posts would have solved the problem.

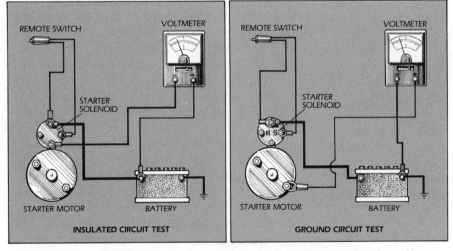

INSULATED CIRCUIT TEST   GROUND CIRCUIT TEST

To test system for too much resistance in the positive (insulated) circuit, connect the voltmeter's positive lead to the positive battery post, negative lead to the starter's positive terminal (left). To check ground circuit resistance, connect the negative voltmeter lead to the negative battery post and the positive lead to the starter housing (right). Both are done by cranking the engine with meter attached. Meter should read less than .05 v. on the insulated circuit test, less than .2 v. on the ground circuit test.

You can make a precise voltage-drop test for excessive resistance in the battery cables and connections with a voltmeter that reads in tenths of a volt. Connect the positive lead of the voltmeter to the positive battery post and the negative lead to the starter. On starters with external solenoids, connect the negative lead to the large copper connector that joins the solenoid to the starter. On other starter motors, connect it to the terminal where the cable attaches. Attempt to crank the engine with the meter attached. The voltmeter should show less than 0.5 volt if the connections are good.

If a vehicle with an external solenoid fails this test, repeat the measurement, but this time attach the negative probe of the voltmeter to the terminal on the solenoid where the cable attaches. If there is less than 0.5 volt to this point with the engine cranking but there was more than 0.5 volt at the solenoid/starter connection, then the solenoid has excessive resistance and should be replaced.

To check ground-circuit resistance, connect the negative voltmeter lead to the negative battery post and the positive lead to the starter housing. Make sure it makes contact with the bare metal of the starter housing. With the key switch in the START position, the ground-circuit voltage drop should measure less than 0.2 volt.

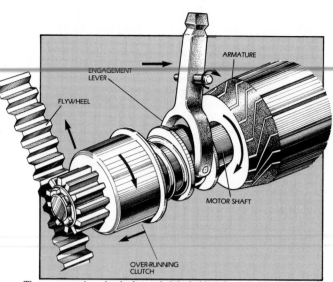

The over-running clutch, located right behind the starter's pinion, locks the pinion to starter motor shaft when drive pressure is applied in one direction, but allows the pinion to freewheel if pressure is applied in other direction.

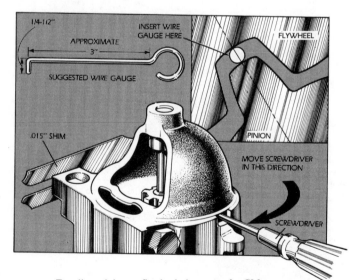

To adjust pinion-to-flywheel clearance of a GM starter, use a screwdriver to push pinion into engagement with the flywheel. Then, using a .020-in. wire gauge, measure clearance between pinion teeth and flywheel as shown.

If either ground or positive circuits fail the resistance test, clean and tighten connections and repeat. If the problem persists, you can make the same measurements progressively closer to the battery until you find the problem area.

Once you've determined that the cables and connections are okay, check the battery's specific gravity.

Measure the battery's specific gravity following the instructions on the hydrometer. If specific gravity is low, charge the battery with a trickle charger. If the battery refuses to take a charge, it's no good.

Some of the recently produced maintenance-free batteries have built-in hydrometers that indicate state of charge by changing colors. Usually a green eye indicates a full charge, while a dark eye means the battery is discharged. A clear or yellow eye means that the battery is defective and should be replaced.

Once the battery is fully charged, connect the leads of a voltmeter to the positive and negative terminals of the battery. You should find roughly 12.5 to 14 volts. Turn the ignition to the START position. If voltage remains at or above 9.6 and the starter just clicks or turns slowly, the starter is defective. If the voltage drops below 9.6, the starter is defective, the battery is defective or the engine is hard to turn.

That last cause is very unlikely, but you can check quickly by attempting to turn the engine by hand. Disconnect the negative terminal from the battery and try to turn the engine, using a socket and breaker bar on the front hub bolt. Some engines can be cranked on the front hub of one of the accessories. If the engine turns with only medium difficulty (60 to 90 pounds breakaway torque with a wrench), it's probably okay. If you have to pop sinews just to budge it, check internal engine condition.

As for the other two causes, a defective battery or bad starter, you can attempt a common sense judgement call. If your battery took a charge, has no discolored electrolyte and is in good physical condition, the starter is most likely the problem. Attempting to jump-start the car can help confirm this. If the battery is the cause of your problems, the jump start should make it crank faster. You might also turn on the lights, windshield wipers and heater motor and then attempt to blow the horn. If your battery can handle that much of a load, it is probably not the source of your difficulty.

If you have access to a volt/amp. meter with a built-in load device, you can test the battery capacity and compare it to specifications. This is the only way you can tell for sure that the battery is not at fault.

Most starter motors are equipped with an over-running clutch of some type. This device is right behind the pinion and prevents the starter from being spun and possibly damaged by the engine once it has started. It locks the pinion to the starter motor shaft when pressure is applied in one direction. The over-running clutch, in combination with the pinion and compression spring, is sometimes called the starter drive or "Bendix."

If the over-running clutch fails to engage, the starter will spin, but it will not engage the engine. An over-running clutch that is on the verge of failure will engage briefly each time you attempt to start the car, but will soon disengage and freewheel. Once the starter has been removed from the car, you can detect a faulty clutch by attempting to turn the pinion in both directions. It should turn freely in one direction, but not move at all in the other. The starter drive assembly can be replaced without replacing the rest of the starter, but the starter must be disassembled in order to do this.

Repair or replace

Once you've determined that the starter is the source of your problem, remove the negative ground cable from the battery before attempting to remove the starter. Support the front of the car on jackstands. The rear wheels must be blocked, the emergency brake applied and the transmission in PARK. Determine how the starter can be maneuvered past other components before loosening the bolts.

Sometimes the wiring connections are easier to remove from above. On some applications with in-line engines, the starter is also removed from above. On GM applications, check for shims under the starter mount. These shims determine pinion-to-flywheel clearance. If there are any, shims should be reinstalled with the new or rebuilt starter.

If you replace the starter motor on a GM car, you may have to adjust pinion-to-flywheel clearance. A sign of incorrect pinion clearance is a high-pitched whine after the engine fires. To check pinion clearance, disconnect the negative battery cable, then insert a screwdriver in the small hole in the bottom of the starter's case at the pinion end. Use this screwdriver to push the starter pinion into engagement with the flywheel. Then, using a hooked wire gauge of 0.020-inch thickness, measure clearance between the peak of the pinion gear's tooth and the space between teeth on the flywheel gear. If clearance is less than 0.020, the starter should be shimmed away from the flywheel. The GM part number for 0.015-inch shims is 9785608.

If the clearance is more than the specified 0.020 inch, check again with an 0.080-inch gauge. If clearance exceeds 0.080 inch, the starter should be shimmed toward the flywheel by installing a shim, GM part No. 1246249, on the outboard starter mounting pad.

Before you ever lay a wrench to a cranking system, remember that a great number of problems will produce the same type of poor cranking performance. Don't be too quick to condemn expensive parts. Make all appropriate measurements and evaluate them based on what you've observed.

Troubleshooting Electronic Ignitions

PAUL STENQUIST

■ THE NEARLY UNIVERSAL USE of electronic ignition systems has totally changed the traditional tuneup. Gone forever are the days when a knowledgeable home mechanic could solve almost any ignition problem with a test light and a feeler gauge. Gone, too, is the periodic parts-replacement ignition tuneup. In their place are some regular maintenance checks and the sometimes complex fault-finding procedures that are used only when performance or driveability problems appear or when a vehicle fails to start.

Ignition maintenance

Electronic ignition maintenance should be part of your 15,000-mile checkup. Start with an inspection of the coil on vehicles equipped with an external ignition coil. (Most GM engines mount the coil within the distributor cap.) Look for evidence of external current leaks or oil leaks. Check the tower (where the coil cable plugs in) for signs of carbon tracking, arcing or burn-through. Now examine the coil cable itself for split or cracked insulation, corrosion or any other signs of damage.

Replace both the coil and cable if the coil tower shows any evidence of electrical leakage. A slightly defective cable connection can quickly ruin a new coil. Replace just the cable if it is beginning to deteriorate but has not yet caused leakage at the coil.

Once you've completed your inspection of the coil, remove the distributor cap. The cap is retained by screws or spring clips.

Before attempting to remove a GM HEI cap with an integral coil, disconnect the wiring connectors from the terminals marked BAT and TACH (Fig. 1). HEI caps are retained by four screw latches; some late-model HEI caps have four conventional screws.

Carefully examine the inside of the distributor cap. Use a flashlight or drop light, so that you won't miss the more subtle signs of failure. Look for the carbon tracks that indicate current jumps. Check for cracks in the carbon button that joins the center of the distributor's rotor to the central cable terminal in the cap. Examine the entire inner surface of the cap carefully to make sure the plastic is not cracked. Replace the cap if it is even slightly damaged.

Check the metal terminals within the cap. If they are only slightly corroded, attempt to clean them by scraping with a sharp knife (Fig. 2). If they don't clean up easily, replace the cap.

Note the condition of the distributor rotor. It should be free of cracks, signs of arcing or burn-through, and serious corrosion. Again, a small amount of corrosion can usually be removed from the rotor's outer contact with a knife, but deep erosion or corrosion on the rotor's inner contact is reason for replacement.

While the rotor is off, check to see if the distributor is equipped with centrifugal timing weights that are mounted directly under the rotor. These spring-loaded weights swing away from the center of the distributor as engine speed increases, changing the position of the rotor and, consequently, advancing the spark.

If the weights are corroded, clean them and apply a very small amount of white lithium grease to pivot points and other wear areas. If the weights stick in the advanced position, hard starting and spark knock can result.

When reinstalling the rotor, make sure it is fully seated on the distributor shaft. All rotors are keyed so that they can be installed only one way.

The tips of some rotors are coated with a special silicone grease. If you found this substance on your old rotor, make sure you apply it to the new one. You should be able to purchase the right compound at a good auto parts store or from the parts department of your dealership.

Next, examine the terminal connections on the top of the distributor cap. On GM HEI caps, you'll have to release the latches that hold the cable retaining ring in place. Each cable should fit tightly on or in its terminal, and the connection should be free of corrosion. Check for signs of burn-through, arcing or current leakage around each terminal, but don't remove the cables from the cap unless signs of damage are present. (On HEI caps, the wires disengage from the cap when the retainer is removed.) Plug cables on late-model Chrysler Corp. caps are retained by locking terminals and must be released from inside the cap (Fig. 3).

Clean the sparkplug cables with nonflammable solvent on a soft rag. Do not, however, remove any insulating lubricants from the wire terminals. Examine the wires for brittleness, cracking, insulation cuts or other signs of damage. If cable condition is generally deteriorated, replace the whole set. If one cable seems to have suffered isolated damage, replace just that cable.

Voltage leak tests

Chrysler Corp. ignitions operate at relatively low voltage levels, so cables can be tested for voltage leaks while the engine is running if misfire has been a problem or if the cables are suspect. *Do not* attempt this test on late-model GM or Ford cars, as serious electrical shock and ignition system damage can occur.

To test for cable leaks on Chrysler products, connect the blade of a screwdriver to a ground with an alligator-clip jumper wire. The screwdriver must have a plastic or wooden handle so you'll be insulated from the current. Disconnect the suspect plug cable from the plug before starting the car and position it so that it cannot arc to ground. (Any metal part of the car is a ground.) Start the engine and move the blade of the grounded screwdriver along the length of the disconnected cable, watching for the telltale arc of a voltage leak. Don't touch the cable end or the screwdriver blade. Shut off the engine

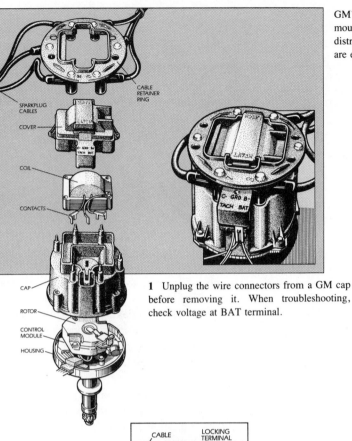

GM's High Energy Ignition (HEI) system mounts the control module and coil inside the distributor. On most other makes, these items are elsewhere in the engine compartment.

1 Unplug the wire connectors from a GM cap before removing it. When troubleshooting, check voltage at BAT terminal.

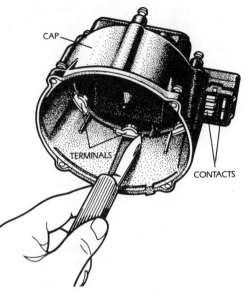

2 Clean corroded terminals inside the cap with knife blade, if possible. If not, replace cap.

3 Plug cables on late-model Chrysler cars are released from inside the cap by squeezing ends of terminals.

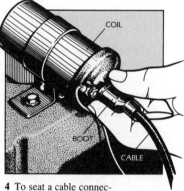

4 To seat a cable connector properly, squeeze the boot to release trapped air.

after each test, reconnect the cable and remove another for testing.

You can test the coil cable in the same manner if you disconnect one plug cable. Total test time must not exceed 10 minutes or catalytic converter damage can occur.

Ford suggests testing plug wire and cap terminal condition with an ohmmeter. With the distributor cap off and cables in place on the cap, connect the ohmmeter to a terminal within the cap and to the sparkplug end of the cable joined to that terminal. Resistance should measure less than 5,000 ohms per inch of cable length. If it does, the distributor cap and cables are okay, providing they are free of cracks or any other visual damage.

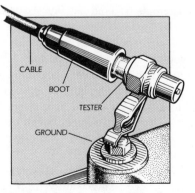

5 Use a tester to check for spark on high-voltage late-model Ford and GM systems.

If the resistance of the cable and cap terminal combined exceeds 5,000 ohms per inch, check the cable alone after removing it from the cap. If resistance still exceeds 5,000 ohms per inch, the cable is defective and must be replaced. If resistance is now okay, the distributor cap is the source of the problem and must be replaced. Check all cables, one at a time.

If you find that you have to replace the ignition cables, purchase a high-quality brand-name set that is designed specifically for your car.

If the terminals of the original wire set were coated with some type of silicone grease or other lube, make certain that the same coating is applied to the new wires.

Route the wires in exactly the same way as the original equipment, using all the original looms, separators and supports. When inserting wires with nipples into the cap terminals, push in the cable slightly, squeeze the sides of the nipple to release trapped air, then push the cable the rest of the way in (Fig. 4). It should snap into place. Make certain that the plug end of the new cable seats fully on the plug terminal. A poor connection at either end can result in damage to other ignition components.

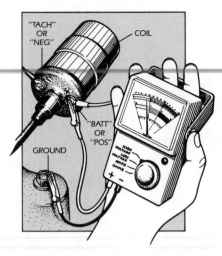

6 If the car won't start, make sure sufficient voltage is reaching the positive coil terminal (or the BAT terminal on GM HEI).

Fault-finding diagnosis

The troubleshooting of specific ignition problems—such as misfire, no-start and intermittent die-outs—can be rather complicated.

Most procedures begin with a simple spark test. This test will at least tell you if a no-start condition is the result of an ignition fault, because it can verify that current is being supplied to the sparkplugs. The test is a simple one, but the procedure differs for cars equipped with high-output systems.

To test for spark on Chrysler products and other cars with low-output ignition systems, remove the large secondary cable from the center tower of the distributor cap. Wearing a leather glove or using a pair of insulated pliers, hold the exposed terminal end of the wire $3/16$ to $3/8$ inch away from a good engine ground (any exposed steel or aluminum on the engine). If you can't find a bare metal spot, scrape a bit of paint off a bolt head. Have a helper crank the engine while you watch for the ignition spark to jump from cable to ground. It should be a bright blue, constant spark. If it's intermittent, weak or completely lacking, the ignition system is the cause of the no-start problem.

While the wire is arcing and the engine cranking, begin moving the wire farther away from ground while watching for a spark at the coil tower. If a

spark occurs at the coil, replace it and the coil cable.

To check for spark on high-voltage late-model GM and Ford systems, you'll need a spark-test device. This tool resembles a sparkplug with a spring clamp attached to its base. It allows you to test for spark without holding the dangerous high-voltage cable. You can purchase this tool at a good auto parts store.

To test, connect the ignition coil cable (or, on GM cars with integral coil, one of the sparkplug cables) to the end of the tester and clamp it to a ground (Fig. 5). Then, crank the engine while watching for spark between the center electrode of the tester and the grounded shell that surrounds it. If you don't get a bright blue spark, the ignition system is not functioning properly and further diagnosis will be necessary.

To perform further diagnosis of an electronic ignition system, you should have a factory service manual for your vehicle. The manual contains specific troubleshooting directions for determining the cause of no-start, misfire and intermittent die-out problems. In most electronic systems, possible failures include the pick-up, which determines the sparking intervals; the control module, which triggers the coil; the coil; primary wiring; and in many cases, an engine control computer that determines spark advance. Some manufacturers use different names for these devices.

The second step in diagnosing most systems is a check to see that voltage is reaching the positive (+) side of the coil (the BAT terminal on GM HEI systems). This check is made while the engine is cranking (Fig. 6). Specifications for the amount of voltage necessary vary, but in most cases the figure is 6 or 7 volts.

If the amount of voltage available is less than that specified, there is a problem that is preventing voltage from reaching the coil. It could be a broken wire, a rundown battery, a failed ignition-system resistor or resistor wire, a starter motor that draws too much current, an ignition-switch problem or a fault in any other device that is part of the circuit between the battery and ignition coil.

From this point the procedures vary significantly, even among the different models produced by one manufacturer. As an example of what's involved, we'll present the rest of the procedure for late-model GM vehicles with integral ignition coils but without electronic spark timing (those with centrifugal advance weights and a vacuum advance mechanism on the distributor).

If you found less than 7 volts at the BAT terminal of the distributor with the engine cranking, repair the primary circuit between the terminal and switch. If you found 7 volts or more, check for voltage at the distributor's TACH terminal.

If 1 to 10 volts are present at the TACH terminal, replace the module and check for spark from the HEI coil, using the test setup illustrated in Fig. 7. (When installing a new module, coat its metal base and the mounting surface in the distributor with the silicone grease that is packaged with the new replacement module.)

Testing the coil

To perform this test, you have to cut the small end off an old sparkplug boot. The boot is then used to attach your spark tester to the center terminal inside the HEI distributor cap. A voltmeter is connected between the TACH terminal and ground. The rotor is removed from the distributor, the module leads are disconnected and a test light, with its lead connected to the battery's positive post, is touched to one module terminal.

On a four-terminal module, connect the test light to terminal G. On a five-terminal module, connect the test light to terminal D. On a seven-terminal module, connect the test light to terminal P. Make sure you don't leave the test light connected to the module for more than five seconds.

As the test light is removed from the module terminal, you should get a spark at the spark tester. If you do, the module was the source of the difficulty and the system should be okay. If you don't, the coil is also defective and should be replaced.

If you found 10 volts or more when you checked "TACH" terminal voltage, check for spark at the coil output terminal by connecting your spark tester to the center terminal of the distributor cap, using the boot. Ground the tester and crank the engine while you watch for a spark.

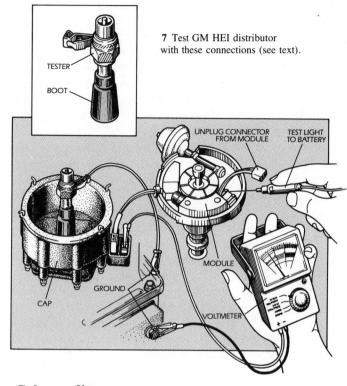

7 Test GM HEI distributor with these connections (see text).

Color coding

If you get a spark, check the color coding and routing of the wiring to the control module and coil. If these parts have been replaced, the wrong ones may have been installed, or the wires may be misrouted.

If the module connector is yellow, the wires from it to the pickup coil should be green and white and the coil wires in the cap should be yellow and red. They should not be crossed.

If the module connector is clear, black or blue, its pickup wires should be green and white. The coil wires should be red and white. Both pairs of wires should be crossed. If the wiring checks out, the rotor or cap is the source of the problem.

If you don't get a spark, hook up the coil spark test as described above. With the ignition on, keep your eyes on the voltmeter as the test light is connected momentarily to the appropriate module terminal.

If there is no drop in voltage, check the module ground and check for an open circuit in the wires from the cap to the distributor. If both the ground and wires are okay, replace the module and again check for spark at the coil. (A GM dealer would test the module on an expensive module tester before he'd consider replacing it. This is where the do-it-yourselfer may run into trouble. If you buy a new module and it does not solve the problem, you're stuck with the new module just the same because electronic parts cannot be returned.)

Check ignition coil ground

If a new module does not solve the no-spark problem, check the ignition coil's ground. If it and the module are okay, the coil itself is the cause of the problem.

If voltage dropped when you connected the test light to the module terminal, check for spark from the coil as the test light is removed from the module terminal.

If spark is present, the pickup coil or its wiring is the source of the no-start problem. In this case, the distributor must be removed from the car and disassembled in order to replace the pickup coil.

If spark is not present when the test light is removed from the module terminal, check the ignition coil ground circuit.

If it's okay, replace the ignition coil and repeat the coil spark test. If a spark is now present, the coil was the source of the problem.

If it is not, your original coil was okay, and the module is the source of the no-start problem.

D-I-Y dilemmas

As you can see, the do-it-yourselfer who attempts to troubleshoot the system may end up spending more money than he needs to in order to perform the two substitution tests. The module tester that eliminates the need for this type of testing is very expensive. This will be the basic problem you'll run into over and over again when you are trying to troubleshoot advanced electronic ignition systems.

If you don't mind stocking an expensive spare module or coil, do the job yourself; after all, you may wind up using the spare some day. And, the savings in labor may outweigh the cost of the part.

But make sure the procedure you follow is the right one for your car, and don't even begin if you don't understand the instructions fully. A misconnected test instrument can damage a lot of expensive parts in just a few seconds.

Part V:

DRIVETRAIN AND CHASSIS

Servicing CV Joints

BRAD SEARS

■ CONSTANT-VELOCITY JOINTS ARE taking the place of universal joints that Saturday mechanics know so well. In a rear-drive car, U-joints connect the driveshaft to the transmission and rear axle, allowing the axle to move up and down on its suspension. In a front-drive car, CV joints connect the drive axles to the transaxle and front wheels.

Four CV joints are used—one at each end of each axle—to allow the front wheels to move up and down with the suspension, and to steer through angles of about 20°.

The old type of universal joint from rear-wheel-drive cars would not take the abuse of the front-drive system. Furthermore, a shaft driven by a conventional U-joint will not maintain a constant velocity unless it is perfectly aligned with the driving shaft. If the conventional U-joint is flexed, the driven shaft speeds up and slows down as it rotates.

So, for fwd cars, a joint is needed that will not only deliver power at sharp angles, but also will not cause serious vibration and make driving unpleasant.

There are two types of joint that fit the bill. One, the Rzeppa joint, achieves these goals by joining the two shafts with a ball and groove arrangement. The second, called a tripode or tri-pot joint, joins the shafts with grooves and roller bearings. Tripode joints are usually found at the inboard ends of most fwd driveshafts, while Rzeppa joints are generally used at the outboard ends.

Both types are quite durable, but there are certain precautions that must be taken with these units to ensure long life.

Because the CV joint flexes farther than the older U-joints, it requires a softer seal to protect the innards from grime, dirt and salt that splash up from the road. The easiest method of protecting the unit is

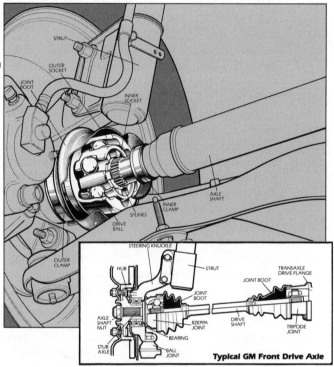

Front-wheel-drive automobiles require special constant-velocity joints at both axle ends (inset) for up/down and left/right suspension travel. Rzeppa detail is above.

to cover it with a boot similar to the old U-joint covers used on Chrysler cars from the 1930s through the '60s.

As with the old Chryslers, if this boot should rupture, all of the abrasive junk on the road collects on the lubricant in the joint and begins to act more like a grinding compound than a lubricant.

Taking care of a front-wheel-drive car, then, begins with getting the car on a lift or being able to get under it safely a few times a year to check the CV joint boots for damage. You should do this before winter sets in, then once during the winter and again in the spring. If you do an oil change and lube at 3,000-mile intervals, check the boots as part of this service.

Cold temperatures and accumulated ice and snow can tear a perfectly good boot to shreds in a matter of minutes.

CV joint inspection

During the inspection, the wheels must be free to rotate so that you can see all the way around the boot. The clamps on each end of the boot should be checked to be sure that they are tight and not rusted through or broken (see Fig. 1). The boot material, a rubbery substance, should be flexible to the touch. A boot that's hard and brittle is likely to rupture soon and should be replaced. Grease spray around the joint is a sure sign of a damaged boot.

There should be no signs of tears or holes in the boot, since any hole will allow water and dirt to enter the joint. A damaged boot must be replaced immediately.

If the boot is torn, check the lube inside for grit or particles by rubbing a bit of it between clean fingers. If grit is present or if the car has developed symptoms of joint failure, the shafts will have to be removed for joint service. A boot that has become soft and mushy should also be replaced.

Serious joint damage can usually be detected when driving. A clicking noise when turning indicates a worn or damaged outboard joint. A clunk during acceleration indicates a worn or damaged inboard joint. And shudder or vibration during acceleration usually indicates a damaged or sticking inboard joint.

On the other hand, if a boot is only slightly damaged or worn and there's no indication of further problems, the boot alone can be replaced. There's more than one way to do the job. You can install a factory original boot or one of the new aftermarket quick-fit boots.

Quick-fit boots

With the quick-fit boots the job can be done without removing the axle because the boots come with a lengthwise split in them. You simply cut the clamps that hold on the old boot and use a knife to cut the old boot off the car. In the package of the new boot you will find a container of lubricant to be used on the joint once you've cleaned it. The new boot is slipped in place and the end clamps are loosely attached to position the boot.

A special bonding solvent supplied in the kit is applied to the edges of the split (Fig. 2). The edges are tied together and in 40 to 60 minutes the solvent will cure, permanently sealing the seam. Simply finish tightening the end clamps and you're on your way. The quick-fit boot is available from most parts stores.

If your inspection revealed that the joints are damaged or contaminated with grit, or if you decide to replace the boots with conventional factory units, you'll have to remove the driveshaft and joint assembly.

You may decide that you don't want to attempt this job yourself. On some cars, you will need a two- or three-leg hub puller to push the shaft out of the steering knuckle. On other cars, particularly GM models, it may be difficult to pry the inner CV joint away from the transaxle without a special tool. If you do decide to have a professional do the job, find one you know, or one who's NIASE certified in front end and suspension work.

If you decide to do it yourself, you must obtain a factory service manual or general auto repair manual that includes specific, detailed instructions for performing this service on your particular vehicle.

Removing the axle

The procedure begins with the removal of the large axle shaft retaining nuts that are found where the front wheel bearing nuts would be on a rear-wheel-drive car. This is best done by loosening the nuts while the car is still on the ground. These nuts are usually torqued to between 180 and 225 lb.-ft. and require a good heavy socket and a long breaker bar.

Chock the wheels, apply the emergency brake and put the car in gear or an automatic transmission in PARK.

There are three methods of locking the axle nut to the shaft—with a cotter pin (just like the front-wheel retaining nut on a rear-drive car), a staked nut or a self-locking nut.

The staked nut looks much like a castle nut—one that could be used with a cotter pin—except that it doesn't have the cotter-pin grooves. The threaded portion of the shaft has a groove cut into it and, once the nut is tightened, the neck of the nut is staked in place.

When removing this type of nut, make no attempt to relieve the staked portion, just unscrew it as found. You can make a tool from a small cold chisel to stake the nut on reassembly. Grind the sharp edge from the chisel, leaving a rounded edge. The recommended radius is $1/16$ in. Place the tool directly over the groove in the shaft and, wearing safety glasses, use a couple of solid hammer blows to complete the staking (Fig. 3).

The third type of self-locking nut uses a nylon insert to keep it from backing off the shaft once it's tight.

You should replace a staked nut as well as a self-locking nut each time they are removed.

Once the axle nuts have been loosened, jack the car up by the frame and place stands under the frame in the locations shown in a shop manual, letting the wheels hang free. Remove the wheels and finish removing the hub nut and washer.

Chryslers and Fords

On Chrysler and Ford vehicles, remove the nut that connects the tie rod to the steering knuckle, then separate the rod end from the knuckle. Take care not to tear the rubber seal on the tie-rod end.

Remove the pinch bolt that holds the ball joint to the steering knuckle and use a pry bar to separate the lower control arm and ball joint from the steering knuckle. If the car is equipped with a front sway bar, unbolt it before you try to separate the ball joint from the knuckle. Don't use a pickle fork on the ball joints or tie-rod ends unless you plan to replace them, as the fork will tear the seals.

Attempt to move the knuckle assembly and strut away from the driveshaft, allowing the shaft to drop out of the hub. If the shaft won't release from the hub, get a puller that can be attached to the wheel studs on the hub. Use the puller's screw jack to push the shaft out of the hub.

Determine the method used to hold the inner ends of the shafts to the differential. There are three common methods: a flange to which the half-shaft is bolted, a stub shaft that enters the differential and is held in place with a circlip, or just stub shafts that enter the differential. The latter are held in place with thrust bearings in the hub assembly. Stub shafts are common on General Motors and Ford vehicles.

On all Chryslers, except those equipped with the A-412 transaxle, the speedometer drive gear must be detached from the transaxle before the right-side driveshaft can be removed.

If the inner axle end is held in place by a bolted flange (Fig. 4), as on some Chrysler and Volkswagen cars, mark the flanges with a scribe to ensure their proper relationship when you reassemble them. The attaching bolts on this type are socket-head (Allen) capscrews. Use a good ³/₈-in.-drive socket-head wrench with a ratchet to remove the screws and a torque wrench to reinstall them. The socket-head screws may be hidden behind protective plastic caps on some Chrysler models. Apply 33 lb.-ft. of torque to the screws during reassembly.

When there are no flanges on the inner ends of the drive axles, the differential cover may have to be removed to relieve the pressure on the circlip that retains each shaft. This arrangement is used on early Omni/Horizon models.

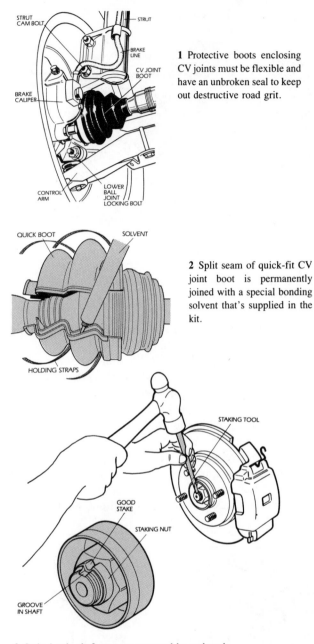

1 Protective boots enclosing CV joints must be flexible and have an unbroken seal to keep out destructive road grit.

2 Split seam of quick-fit CV joint boot is permanently joined with a special bonding solvent that's supplied in the kit.

3 Staked axle shaft nuts are removed by unthreading. Restake them as shown with a rounded chisel edge.

Omni/Horizon axles

To begin with, the procedure is the same: Loosen the hub nut; jack up the car and support it on stands with the wheels and suspension hanging free; then remove the hub nut, washer and wheel. Next, place a drain pan under the differential cover. Loosen the bolts and remove the cover. Rotate the driveshaft until the circlips' ends are visible (Fig. 5). Squeeze the tangs of each circlip with a pair of needle-nose pliers and push the stub shaft into the side gear by

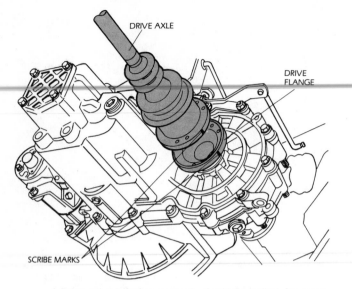

4 Drive axles bolted to transaxle should be scribed for proper alignment on reassembly.

prying with a screwdriver inserted between the stub shaft and the differential pinion shaft.

Release the ball joint and tie-rod end as described below. Separate the splined end of the shaft from the knuckle by pushing the knuckle away from the CV joint. Remove the driveshaft assembly from the vehicle by pulling outward on the inboard CV joint. Don't pull on the shaft.

When reinstalling the differential cover, Chrysler recommends that you use the silicone RTV gasket material in a tube. After all traces of the old gasket material have been removed from both mating

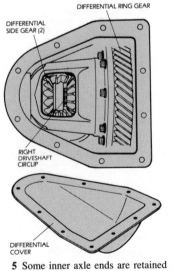

5 Some inner axle ends are retained by circlips. Release the clips after the differential cover has been removed.

6 CV joints may be serviced individually after the axle has been removed. Disassemble the CV joints by removing circlips.

surfaces, draw a bead of the RTV material on the cover, going completely around the cover and making a circle around each bolt hole.

Allow the material to skin over—about five minutes—and install the cover loosely. Just snug the bolts up a bit more than finger tight and allow the material to set for about five more minutes. Then finish the job by torquing the bolts to 12-15 lb.-ft. for Chrysler-built cars.

Removing the third type of axle shaft requires the use of a couple of O-ring pullers. Some auto parts jobbers who carry rebuilt axle shafts or a stock of CV joints will either lend or rent the tools to you. You still must remove the axle hub nut and washer as before, as well as the wheel.

GM joints

When removing CV joints on GM cars, you should disengage the steering knuckle from the strut rather than from the control arm (see lead illustration). Before the strut can be disengaged, the brake line must be disconnected from the strut and the caliper must be detached and supported.

You must also mark the cam bolt on the strut mount so it can be reinstalled in the same position to retain wheel alignment (Fig. 1).

A special adapter is used with a slide hammer to remove the stub shaft end (inner end) from the differential of a GM fwd car. You should have a drain pan handy because fluid will leak from the differential.

The next step requires a puller that resembles a steering wheel or harmonic balancer puller. It is used to force the axle shaft out of the front wheel hub. Don't use a hammer here since the blows would probably ruin the front wheel bearings, which cost over $100 each.

Once the shafts are on the bench, you must determine whether to replace them with rebuilt units or to disassemble them and replace only the CV joints and boots. (The CV joints would be making noises if they are defective or worn out—noises like snapping on turns or grinding and backlash when applying the throttle or letting the car coast.)

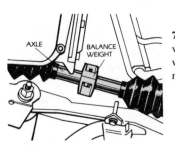

7 To prevent unwanted vibrations, axle balance weights should not be removed.

CV joints that need replacement can also cause a shimmy in the steering system. If you've managed to get the shafts out of the car and know that the joints will need to be replaced, you should consider replacing the entire axle shaft assemblies with rebuilt units. (A rebuilt shaft assembly for the right side of an Omni, for example, carries a list price of $240, while the parts needed to rebuild the shaft in the shop carry a list price of $195.) Then the procedure boils down to bolting in the rebuilt shaft, which is already assembled and lubricated.

Replacing CV joints

However, if you are adventurous, you can remove the CV joints and install new ones on the axle. To perform the job, you must have a service manual with specific instructions for your car.

Most CV joints are held together by a series of circlips which, when removed, allow the joint to be disassembled (Fig. 6). Before disassembling the joint, make sure your work area is really clean. Cover the entire work surface with a piece of towel. The thickness of the towel will stop any pieces that drop from bouncing and becoming lost.

Some axles have balance weights (Fig. 7) which should not be removed.

Without a doubt, servicing front-wheel-drive components is a more involved job than many home mechanics are willing to take on. In some cases it may require special tools to torque the axle shaft nuts (which must be tightened to 225 lb.-ft.), pullers to remove the driveshafts or equipment to realign the front end after unbolting and reinstalling front strut components. But regular inspection and maintenance of the CV joint boots, coupled with the knowledge of how these parts function, will go a long way toward making life with front-wheel-drive cars easier and less costly.

Checking fluid level regularly and replenishing when necessary is vital for long automatic transmission life.

lutely,'' say transmission repair shops.

Since the early 1970s, carmakers have dismissed regular A/T maintenance as a waste of time and money for cars that are driven under normal conditions. For example, Chrysler and Ford contend that it never has to be done. GM says to do it once every 100,000 miles.

''Our durability tests prove that given the quality of present-day transmission fluids, maintenance beyond what is recommended in GM maintenance schedules will not prolong the life of a transmission,'' an official at GM Service Research said.

Those who run transmission repair shops don't agree. Jerry Lowen, owner of the AAMCO transmission facility in Bridgewater, N.J., contends that servicing every 20,000 miles helps extend transmission life in several ways. First, you are able to determine if a problem has developed that could, if not treated,

Servicing Automatic Transmissions

MORT SCHULTZ

■ DOES AUTOMATIC transmission maintenance pay? ''Not usually,'' say the automakers. ''Abso-

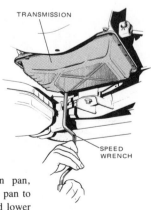

1 To drain transmission pan, loosen bolts that hold the pan to the transmission body and lower one corner of the pan.

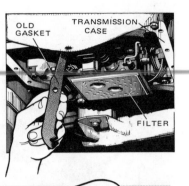

2. Strip all of the old gasket from the transmission body and pan. Use a scraper if necessary.

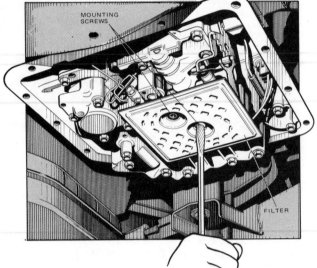

3. Transmission filter is held by one or two screws. Replace the filter if it's paper. Wash metal filters in solvent and reuse.

4. Metal particles on the back of this filter could have circulated through the transmission, causing unnecessary wear.

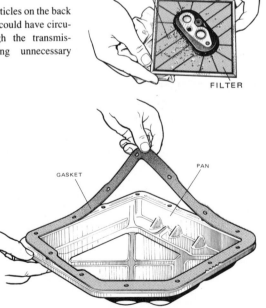

5. Lay new gasket carefully in place, making sure that the holes in the gasket align with those in the pan. Do not crack or wrinkle the gasket—if you do, fluid will leak.

lead to extensive damage. Second, as fluid is drained small particles that can slip through the filter and enter the heart of the transmission to hasten wear are also drained. Third, some of the new compact transmission filters eventually clog and need replacement. Finally, owners may not be aware that the way they use their cars is considered "severe" by automakers. Scheduled maintenance will provide the needed protection.

"Severe" versus "normal"

There is no disagreement that high temperature brought about by severe usage causes A/T fluid to oxidize and its additives to break down, and car manufacturers encourage transmission maintenance under these conditions. Chrysler and GM, for example, recommend service every 15,000 miles—Ford every 20,000 to 22,500 miles—in vehicles that are subjected to severe usage. They define severe usage as follows:
■ Vehicles used more than half the time in city traffic when the temperature is 90° F. or more.
■ Vehicles that tow trailers.
■ Vehicles operated in dusty areas.
■ Vehicles driven frequently on hills and mountains.
■ Vehicles that are used for taxi, police, limousine or commercial operation.

Early detection

By performing regular A/T service, you may detect a developing transmission problem early enough to save a lot of money. When you drop the transmission pan to drain fluid, you can see if brass or white metal particles are present, then you can replace the affected part before the damage progresses past the danger point.

Lowen's AAMCO shop charges $650 to $850 to overhaul the transmission of a rear-wheel-drive car; $850 to $1,050 if the car has front-wheel drive. To replace a single planetary gear that is breaking down and depositing metal particles in the fluid, Lowen charges about $350.

It's important to remember that there will always be some clutch material in the bottom of a transmission pan and that this does not necessarily indicate excessive wear. With some cars, a small amount of powdered brass may even be considered normal.

More than one car owner has been talked into unnecessary repairs after being shown a transmission pan that contained only normal wear material.

Here are the steps to follow for periodic A/T service:

1. Warm the transmission to operating temperature, shut off the engine and raise the car. If you've put a drain plug in the pan (see below), place stands under the front wheels and chocks behind the rear wheels. This way, the pan is pitched toward the rear so the fluid will drain freely. Drain plug or not; you'll be working under the car, so make sure it's securely supported.

2. Place a drain pan under the transmission and loosen bolts holding the pan in place. If you don't have a drain plug, drop one corner of the pan lower than the others and allow it to drain (see Fig. 1). Once the flow stops, remove the remaining bolts, being careful not to spill the fluid still in the pan. *Caution:* Be careful not to get fluid in your eyes. Wear eye protection.

3. When the pan is down, examine the fluid left in it. It should be red. If it's dirty and smells like varnish, the fluid is worn out and has oxidized. If the fluid oxidation is accompanied by large deposits of clutch material, it may be the result of slipping clutches. Any condition that causes excessive fluid temperature can cause oxidation. Remember, some clutch wear is normal.

Severe usage can cause fluid oxidation. The installation of an auxiliary transmission oil cooler can help prevent overheating that occurs due to trailer towing, mountain driving or other severe use.

If the fluid looks milky, the transmission oil cooler has sprung a leak and coolant is mixing with A/T fluid. Drain coolant as well as A/T fluid. Remove the radiator and have a radiator repair shop replace the cooler.

Continue fluid inspection by holding the pan to sunlight or shining a light over it. See if you can spot white metal or brass particles. If you find them, you can have the transmission disassembled and the deteriorating part replaced before it leads to more extensive damage, or you can gamble that greater damage won't occur—it may not.

4. Strip the old gasket from the transmission and pan (Fig. 2). Then wash the pan in a nonflammable solvent.

5. Remove the filter (Figs. 3 and 4). Discard and replace a paper or felt filter. Clean a metal filter in solvent and reuse it. When you install the filter, make screws snug without overtightening them.

6. Place a new gasket on the transmission pan (Fig. 5) and carefully lay the pan against the transmission case so the gasket doesn't crimp or tear. Install bolts finger-tight. Then, using a wrench, tighten bolts snugly in an alternating pattern. Do not overtighten. You may crush the gasket and cause a leak.

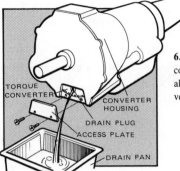

6. Most Fords have torque converter drain plugs, which allow you to empty the converter for a complete change.

7. Remove the A/T fluid dipstick and place a clean funnel in the dipstick tube. Add fluid, a quart or two at a time. Reinstall the dipstick each time to get a reading until the fluid level shows FULL. Start the engine and let it get warm. Move the transmission shift lever slowly through the shifting pattern, stopping for a few seconds at each gear. Check fluid level again and, if necessary, add fluid to bring the level back to FULL.

There are two important facts you should be aware of. First, dirt is an A/T's worst enemy. Take steps to see that none is introduced into the transmission through the dipstick tube. Second, don't overfill the transmission. Excess fluid can cause the transmission to slip.

To make sure you haven't botched up and caused a fluid leak, keep an eye on the fluid level for a few days. If it drops below the FULL mark on the dipstick or you see signs of fluid on the ground, find the leak and fix it. Transmission fluid doesn't evaporate. If the level ever drops, look for a leak.

Transmission drain plugs

When you drop the transmission pan to drain fluid, only some of the fluid pours out. A considerable amount remains in the torque converter. Most torque converters don't have drain plugs. To drain all of the fluid remaining in the torque converter, the transmission and torque converter have to be removed from the car and the converter has to be power-flushed on a special machine. Generally, many Ford-built cars have a torque converter drain plug. GM models don't, and neither do most Chrysler-built cars from 1977 on.

There is a way around this problem, but first find out if there is a drain plug in your torque converter. Look for an access plate on the converter housing. Unscrew the attachment bolts and remove the plate. Then, have someone in the car click the starter motor in short bursts to see if a drain plug comes into view.

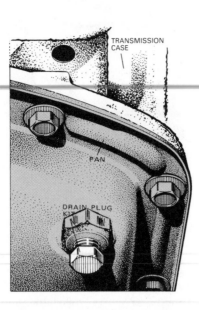

7 Installing a drain plug on the pan will let you dilute and drain most of the dirty fluid from the torque converter.

(Keep the engine from starting by disconnecting the ignition coil.) If the torque converter has a drain plug, remove it to drain all the fluid (Fig. 6).

Even if your car doesn't have a drain plug in the torque converter you can still do a good job of removing dirty fluid and replenishing additives with two or three successive pan drainings and refills. Installing a plug in the pan will allow you to do this easily. To install a universal drain plug, drop the pan, pour off fluid and wash the pan in solvent. Drill a ½-inch hole near a rear corner of the pan.

Clean off all burrs and bolt the fitting through the ½-inch hole. Screw the drain plug into the fitting (Fig. 7) and reinstall the pan. Make the plug secure, but don't overtighten it or you'll damage the plug or fitting. (B&M Automotive Products, 9152 Independence Ave., Chatsworth, Calif. 91311, sells a drain plug kit through auto parts stores.)

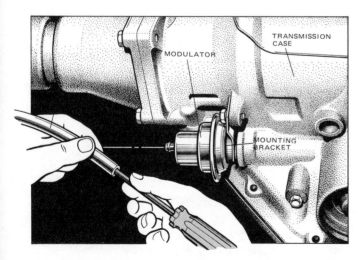

8 To test a vacuum modulator for leaks, remove the vacuum hose and look for fluid inside. The hose should be dry. If it's wet, unscrew or unbolt modulator and replace it.

Pour in enough fresh A/T fluid to fill the transmission. Drive the car for a day or two, so fresh fluid mixes with the old fluid that was trapped in the torque converter. Then unscrew the new transmission drain plug and allow the fluid to drain. Refill the transmission and repeat this filling-driving-draining procedure two or three times to replace most of the old fluid with new fluid. Of course, you will still have to remove the pan to inspect or replace the filter.

Band adjustment

Should transmission bands be adjusted as part of a servicing program? That depends. Most GM transmissions are nonadjustable—bands are adjusted automatically. Manufacturers of transmissions that have adjustable bands stipulate that an adjustment is not necessary unless the transmission is used under severe conditions. Ford, for example, calls for an adjustment on some vehicles every 7,500 miles when severe usage is evident. However, if you follow a periodic maintenance program with a transmission that's used under normal conditions, it's usually not necessary to adjust bands.

Transmissions that call for a band adjustment usually have an adjustment mechanism on the outside of the transmission housing that tightens the front bands. The rear band adjustment mechanism is usually inside the transmission, and in many cases you have to remove the valve body to reach it. Bands should be adjusted to manufacturer's specification, which is normally given in inch-pounds. A torque wrench and a shop manual are needed.

Vacuum modulators

In some cars—those made by Chrysler, for example—the linkage or cable between the carburetor and transmission allows the car to respond to driving demands. This linkage usually needs no adjustment unless the transmission is removed from the car.

The other control, used primarily by GM and Ford, is a vacuum modulator. If there is a sudden change in the way the transmission shifts, pull the vacuum line from the vacuum modulator, which is on the side of the transmission (Fig. 8). If A/T fluid drips out, you've uncovered the trouble and, luckily, can make an inexpensive repair. The modulator diaphragm has failed, so replace the modulator. Other signs that the modulator has gone bad are a drop in fluid level and white or gray engine exhaust smoke. Also, make certain that the vacuum line is not leaking at the end where it connects to the carburetor.

Choosing fluid

It's important to follow the manufacturer's recommendation for the type of A/T fluid, since improper fluid may cause malfunctions. Ford calls for Type H fluid to be used in its C5 transmission. Otherwise, manufacturers recommend either Dexron II or Type F. Check your owner's manual before you add or replace fluid. If you can't find the information in your owner's manual, look it up in a shop manual or ask a mechanic at a dealership or transmission shop. Be sure you know the transmission model and year of manufacture. Some carmakers (like Ford) use Type F fluid in older models and Dexron II in new ones.

If you service your automatic transmission periodically, it should never let you down. You are less likely to be victimized by an unscrupulous transmission shop if you can shop around, rather than having to settle for the most convenient shop after a breakdown.

Adjusting Cable-Operated Shifters

BRAD SEARS

■ WITH THE ADVENT OF transverse-mounted engines in front-wheel-drive cars, many things have changed. However, some mechanical systems which were long ago abandoned by automakers have been reclaimed because they happen to be suited to this new type of drivetrain.

One such item is the cable-operated gearshifter. The cable shifter that we knew many years ago was a cantankerous device connecting a pair of shift levers on the bottom of the shift column to the transmission. It rarely stayed in adjustment and gave a rubbery feel to shifts. Later, we saw the cables emerge again in automatic transmission selectors including some of the Chrysler pushbutton units of the '50s and '60s.

But certain designs tend to resurface in the car business because old mechanisms can sometimes solve new problems. So, today many carmakers have adapted cable mechanisms to their front-wheel-drive designs.

There is an up side to the story. The cable shifter allows flexibility of design in new cars. Due to the placement of the engine and transaxle in a front-wheel-drive car, linkage shifting devices on the manual units can present unusual problems. Because of the torque reaction movement of the engine and transaxle, a solid linkage shifter must move with the engine and trans or the trans will jump out of gear. Some automakers, like Ford and Honda, tie the shifter to the transaxle and use a solid linkage. This leaves you with a shaking shifter but, under normal conditions, no adjustment is necessary.

GM and Chrysler have evidently decided that a shaky shifter is unacceptable. GM has two cable-type shifters—one for the four-speed and one for the five. Chrysler uses rod shifters (with pivot points that allow engine movement) on some transaxles and a cable shifter on others. While these shifters do present some compromises, they can function well if they're properly lubricated and adjusted.

In the following paragraphs, you'll learn how you can keep your GM or Chrysler manual transmission shifter shifting slickly.

General Motors

General Motors uses cable shifters on its front-wheel-drive X- and J-body cars. Two different shifters are used—one for the four-speed and one for the five-speed. The shifter is mounted to the floorboard of the car and all the workings of the shifter are located inside the passenger compartment. There is little danger of affecting the shifter end of the cables.

Two cables extend from the shifter itself to the transmission. One cable is called the trans-selector cable, while the other is described as the trans-shifter cable. For service procedure information, they are simply referred to as cables A and B (see lead illustration). Cable B is closest to the driver where it attaches to the shift lever, and it passes through the firewall to the left of cable A. On the four-speed transaxle, cable B is attached to a vertical "select" lever and is toward the front of the vehicle. Cable A is behind it and is attached to a horizontal "shift" lever.

On the five-speed transaxle, cable A is connected to a shift lever that GM calls lever F. It's a vertical lever that hangs down alongside the transaxle case. Cable B is connected to an odd-shaped lever G that moves horizontally.

In order to shift correctly, the shift cables must be properly adjusted. If the adjustment is okay and there is still a hang-up in the 1-2 shift, it may be necessary to replace the shifter shaft selective washer with one of a different thickness. This washer helps position the shifter shaft for minimum shift effort.

Adjustment of the shifter and cables can be done quite simply on most GM cars, but the procedure is different for the two manual transaxles in use. The first step for both transaxles is the removal of the negative battery cable.

Four-speed adjustment

Cable adjustments are made at the transaxle end of the cable, but you will need access to both ends of the cables. The shifter cables are attached to the studs in the transmission shifter levers by a couple of clips. The studs are inserted through slotted holes in the shifter levers and are secured with nuts. If the nuts are loosened, the studs will slide back and forth in their mounting slots. This movement is the means of adjustment. From under the hood, loosen the nuts so the studs will slide in the slots (Fig. 1).

Next, remove the center console or boot that covers the shifter. This may involve removing the console cover or trim plate, peeling back the shifter boot toward the top of the shifter, locating the screws that hold the console in place and removing them. The console slides out easier if the shifter is in FIRST.

On the side of the gearshift lever, down near the base, you will probably find a $5/32$-in. alignment hole (Fig. 2). The hole goes through the base of the shifter that mounts to the floor. With the gears in FIRST or LOW, slide a $5/32$-in. drill bit through the holes. This aligns the shifter in a known position. Next, have a helper hold the shift handle to the left toward the driver. Some late models may not have alignment holes. In this case, have your helper simply hold the shift lever in FIRST and apply pressure so that it is as close to the driver as possible.

With the shifter locked in position, locate the shifter select lever and remove lash by pushing it toward the driver's side of the car. With the lever held in position, tighten up the nuts on the cable-mounting stud. A bit of caution here: Don't loosen the nut any more than needed to allow the stud to slide and, when tightening the nut, take care not to lose the adjustment you have just made.

Adjust the shift lever in a similar manner. Push against the lever in such a way that all of the slack in the cable and its connections is taken up before retightening the nut.

The idea behind this is that you'll end up with a tight cable, shifter and lever assembly. When the shifter is moved to change gears, you'll get an immediate reaction at the transaxle.

Once the adjustment is made, remove the drill bit from the alignment hole (if used). Work the shifter through all of the gears and check its operation. If it does not feel right, run through the adjustment procedure again. If the shift still doesn't feel right, you will have to check the cables for binding. To do this, remove them from the transmission end and the shifter. Work the cable by hand and replace the cable if there are rough spots.

If you find that the shifter hangs up between FIRST and SECOND even after the adjustment is okay, a change may be needed in the size of the spacer washer at the base of the gearshift stick. This is fairly complicated and you really need a depth micrometer and tension gauge to do it correctly. If you have these tools and a shop manual, you may want to attempt it. If not, ask your dealer to check for proper shift selective washer size as described in section 7B1 of most GM manuals.

Five-speed adjustment

As with the four-speed, begin by disconnecting the negative battery cable. Then, shift the transaxle to THIRD gear. On the transaxle, directly in front of the two shift levers, you'll find a locking pin consisting of a stud and a set screw that are threaded into the trans case (Fig. 3). Remove this locking pin and reinsert it with the tapered end down. This will lock the trans in THIRD.

Loosen the shift-cable attaching nuts at shift levers G and F (on the transaxle). After removing the console or shifter boot, install a $5/32$-in. or No. 22 drill bit into the alignment hole at the side of the shifter handle (Fig. 4).

There's another hole in the shifter assembly close to where cable B attaches to the shift mechanism. Align the hole in the shift lever with the hole in the bracket and insert a $3/16$-in. drill bit.

Now, with both drill bits holding the shifter in the correct position, tighten the nuts on levers G and F. Remove the lockpin and reinstall it with the tapered end up. Reinstall the console and battery cable and road test the vehicle. If the shifter doesn't have a good neutral gate feel, that is, if you can't move the stick back and forth laterally while it's in NEUTRAL, readjust the shifter mechanism and test it again.

Once the adjustment is completed, lubricate the moving parts of the shift mechanism with white lithium grease. Use a stiff-bristled, small brush to apply the grease to the parts. (This should be applied to both four- and five-speed shifters.)

If the transmission still does not shift right after all of the adjustments have been made, the shifter has been lubed and (on four-speeds) the size of the selective washer is correct, the transmission will have to come out of the car for further service.

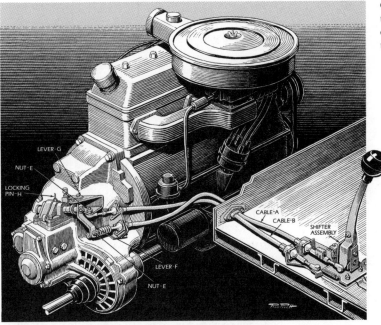

Gearshifting cables used on front-wheel-drive transaxles may require occasional adjustment to cure rough shifting problems. Typical setup uses trans-shifter cable and trans-selector cable.

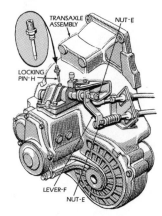

3 On the GM five-speed transmission, locking pin H must be reinstalled tapered end down to lock the trans in THIRD gear.

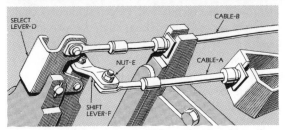

1 Nut E, on the threaded stud which attaches the cable to the transaxle lever, must be loosened to make adjustments. Lever holes are slotted so stud will slide.

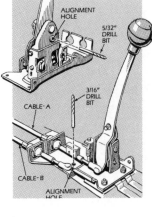

4 Drill bits inserted in both alignment holes permit five-speed shifter adjustment.

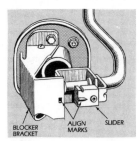

5. The hole in the blocker bracket and the U-shaped slot on the slider must be aligned.

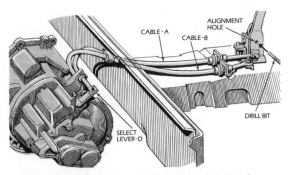

2 A ⁵/₃₂-inch drill bit inserted into the alignment hole at the shifter base (shown) will lock the gearshift lever in FIRST, allowing the cables to be adjusted as required.

Chrysler

There are three transmissions used in Chrysler front-wheel-drive cars—the A-412 four-speed, the A-460 four-speed and the A-465 five-speed. The A-412 unit is linkage-operated while the A-460 and the A-465 could be either linkage or cable.

Identification of the three transmissions is easy.

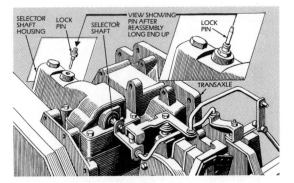

6 On the Chrysler A-460/465 transaxle, the locking pin must be removed and reinstalled with long tapered end down to lock the gearbox in NEUTRAL and allow shift rod alignment.

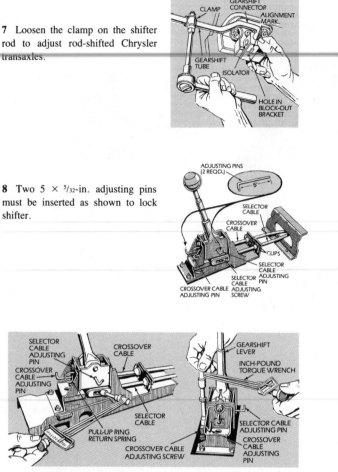

7 Loosen the clamp on the shifter rod to adjust rod-shifted Chrysler transaxles.

8 Two 5 × $^5/_{32}$-in. adjusting pins must be inserted as shown to lock shifter.

9 After adjusting pins have been inserted, torque the crossover and the selector adjusting screws to 60 in.-lb. with a torque wrench and remove the adjusting pins.

The A-412 has a two-piece case while the A-460 and A-465 have a one-piece case.

A-412 adjustment

To adjust the rod-type linkage on an A-412 transaxle, position the gear shift lever in NEUTRAL on the 3-4 side of the shifter gate. Find and loosen the clamp on the shifter rod that looks like an adjustment clamp on a tie rod.

Then, on the lower part of the shifter, find the two alignment marks (Fig. 5). One is on the blocker bracket—a hole—while the other—a U-shaped slot—is on the slider bracket. Align the tab or slot on the slider with the hole on the blocker bracket.

Make a $^3/_4$-in. spacer block and place it between the slider and the blocker bracket. Tighten the clamp on the shift tube while pushing the slider toward the blocker, with the spacer sandwiched between them.

If the bushings are okay, the pins in place and the shift tube not bent, this should result in a smooth shifting linkage.

Rod-operated A-460 and A-465

To adjust a rod-type shifter on either the A-460 manual four-speed or the A-465 five-speed, position the shifter on the 1-2 side of the neutral gate. Then, while leaning over the left front fender, find the selector-shaft housing on the transmission. On top of it, there is a 10-mm hex head locking pin that looks like a pointer screwed into the transaxle (Fig. 6). Remove this pin with a 10-mm wrench and reinstall it with the tapered end down. This will lock the selector shaft in the 1-2 NEUTRAL position.

Jack up the car and support it on jackstands with the rear wheels securely blocked and the emergency brake applied. From under the car, loosen the clamp bolt that secures the gearshift tube to the gearshift connector. Make certain that the gearshift connector moves and slides freely. Then, align the hole in the blockout bracket with the rib on the isolator attached to the base of the gearshift (Fig. 7). The isolator should be contacting the upstanding flange.

Hold the connector isolator in this position while tightening the clamp bolt on the gearshift tube to 170 in.-lb. Don't exert any force on any part of the linkage while tightening the clamp bolt.

Lower the vehicle and remove the lock pin from the selector shaft housing. Reinstall it with the long tapered end up and torque it to 105 in.-lb. Check to make sure the trans shifts well into FIRST and REVERSE and that it blocks out going into REVERSE.

A-460 and A-465 cable shifter

Before beginning this adjustment, make two adjusting pins as illustrated (Fig. 8). Each should be 5 × $^5/_{32}$-in., and each should be bent into an L-shape to facilitate removal. (If you just use 5 × $^5/_{32}$-in. drill bits, you may have trouble removing them.) Once you've made the adjustment pins, remove and reverse the lock pin that is screwed into the selector shaft housing in the same manner as described above for rod-type shifter adjustment. The shifter should be in the 1-2 side of the neutral gate.

Then, remove the gearshift lever knob and the pull-up ring under it. Remove the console assembly and shifter boot.

Loosen the crossover cable adjusting screw and the selector cable adjusting screw, and insert the adjusting pins into the shifter mechanism in the places indicated (Fig. 9). With the pins in place, the shifter will be in NEUTRAL on the 1-2 side of the gate.

Leave the pins in place and retighten the selector cable-adjusting screw and the crossover cable-adjusting screw to 60 in.-lb.

Remove the lock pin from the selector shaft housing and reinstall it with the long tapered end up. Tighten the lock pin to 105 in.-lb. Check the shift into FIRST and REVERSE and the REVERSE blockout.

Smooth shifting

Shift cable adjustments should restore the alignment of moving parts so that the lever glides smoothly between the gears and will make the crossover between 1-2 and 3-4 gates without hang-up. In addition to making sure that the cable sheaths are routed in smooth arcs and the cables themselves are properly lubricated, you should look after the condition of any grommets or bushings where the cable attaches to the transaxle and shifter assembly. If they are worn or distorted, replace with new, lubricated parts.

A little time spent on the shifter, if it is not working smoothly, could make all the difference between enjoying your car or complaining about it.

Troubleshooting Your Brake System

PAUL STENQUIST

■ BRAKE-SYSTEM MAINTENANCE is probably the most critical part of vehicle care. While the car that won't go may frustrate you, the car that won't stop can kill you. To avoid the complications that can occur when pads or shoes wear beyond limits, check brake condition at regular intervals.

Of course, brakes should always be inspected when their application results in noise or when the vehicle pulls to one side during braking. Some late-model GM and Ford products have brake-wear warning devices. But in most cases, the only way to

determine pad or shoe condition is to remove the disc caliper or the drum and inspect the friction material.

If the brake pedal pulsates when stopping, a rotor or drum is probably bent. If brakes don't perform as well as they should, if the pedal sinks or if the master cylinder loses fluid, the hydraulic system is probably at fault.

Before removing anything, inspect the entire brake system, including master cylinder, lines, valves, hoses and brake assemblies, for leaking hydraulic fluid. If you find leaks, see a professional.

Caliper removal

To remove the pin-slider–type disc brake calipers found on most GM cars you'll need a 7-inch or larger C-clamp and a ⅜-inch hex key wrench. After lifting and securing the vehicle, remove the front wheels. Siphon two-thirds of the fluid from the master cylinder. Then place the C-clamp over the disc brake caliper so that the pad on the top of the clamp rests against the back of the caliper, and the clamp's jack screw rests against the back of the outboard brake pad, which is accessible through an opening in the caliper. Then turn the jack screw, tightening it against the brake pad. As you tighten, the caliper should move away from the pad. This indicates that the caliper piston is being pushed back into its bore. If the piston won't retract, it may be frozen: See a mechanic.

Once the piston has been bottomed gently, the caliper guide bolts can be removed with the ⅜-inch hex key wrench or an open-end wrench. Don't let the caliper hang from the rubber brake hose.

The procedure for removing non-GM calipers varies somewhat. In general, you should remove one caliper at a time, leaving the other side as a reference.

Most late-model Ford calipers are mounted similar to GM's. While the C-clamp is not necessary for caliper removal, you'll need a 4-inch clamp and a 2¾ × 1 × ¾-inch block of wood to retract the piston once the caliper is off. Many Ford calipers slide on a machined surface and are held in place by a key. A locking screw holds the key in place. Late Chryslers use a caliper that slides on machined guides. These can be removed by disengaging the retaining clips that hold it in place. Other Chryslers use a pin-slider caliper that retains the pins with clips.

Inspection and diagnosis

Once the caliper has been disengaged from its anchor and lifted off the rotor, inspect the friction material. Nonmetallic pads should have more than $\frac{1}{16}$ inch of material above the rivets. Semimetallic friction material should be at least $\frac{1}{32}$ inch above the rivets. If the friction material is bonded to the pad without rivets, the thinnest section of material should be at least as thick as the backing plate to which it is bonded. If you still have a lot of friction material on the pads, bolt everything back together. If the rotors are discolored or heat-cracked, replace them. If you encountered the previously mentioned pulsating pedal, send the rotors to a machine-shop–equipped auto parts store for resurfacing. Rotors should likewise be resurfaced if they're scored more than a slight amount. If your rotors are too thin or warped for remachining, the machinist will tell you that they must be replaced.

Once the disc pads have been removed from the calipers, wipe all caliper surfaces clean and check around the dust boot and bleeder screw for fluid leakage. Inspect caliper bushings for excessive wear or deterioration. Some mechanics renew the bushings every time they remove a caliper. If the caliper is leaking it will have to be rebuilt or replaced. If the caliper's okay, hang it from a suspension arm with a piece of coat hanger until you're ready to reinstall it.

Most professional mechanics don't rebuild the caliper at every pad replacement. They contend that a road test following reassembly reveals any hydraulic malfunctions.

Reassembly

When buying new pads, get the right type of friction material. Although inexpensive organic pads are available for some vehicles originally equipped with semimetallic pads, they shouldn't be used. Brake life may be cut in half.

While you're at the parts store, pick up a tube of brake silencing paste. Before installing the pads in the calipers, coat the back of the outboard pad with the paste and apply a strip of it to the back of the inboard pad. If there was an antirattle spring on the back of the old inboard pad, install it on the new pad. You can buy new antirattle springs if the old ones have been eaten up by corrosion.

Make sure the pads are retained in the caliper in the same manner as the old ones. On GM cars, you have to clinch the ears on the pad so that they fit tightly over the caliper. Squeeze them around the caliper with 12-inch sliding-jaw (slip-joint) pliers. Other pads may have pins in the back that fit into recesses in the caliper, or antirattle clips that hook into the caliper. The pads may differ from one side of

the vehicle to the other. Check for left- or right-side designation.

When you reinstall the caliper, you may have to tap it into place on its mount, but don't use excessive force. If it won't go, the piston may not be retracted.

With pin-slider–type calipers, lubricate the pins before installing them, if the calipers have steel bushings. If they have plastic bushings, install the pins dry, but make sure they're clean. If they're slightly corroded, you can polish them with No. 400 emery paper. Some mechanics lubricate all pins, but other experts contend that this can cause excessive dirt accumulation. If the pins look bad, replace them.

Hold the caliper and pads in place while you install the pins. Tighten bolt-style pins to the recommended figure with a torque wrench.

After you've renewed or inspected all disc brakes, refill the master cylinder with DOT 3 brake fluid.

Drum-brake basics

Drum-brake service is more time consuming than disc service. Again, it is extremely important that you disassemble the brake mechanisms one at a time, so that you have the other side for reference.

Before the front drums of rear-drive cars or the rear drums of front-drive cars can be pulled, you'll have to remove the wheel bearings. These must be cleaned, inspected and repacked with grease before reassembly.

The drums usually can't be removed until the brake shoes have been retracted. To retract the shoes on most vehicles with self-adjusting brakes, locate the adjusting slots, which are probably plugged with rubber inserts. Some adjusting slots may be blocked with metal slugs. In that case, knock out the slug with a hammer and chisel. Remove the insert, reach in with a very small screwdriver and push the self-adjusting lever away from the star wheel.

Hold the lever away from the wheel and insert a brake adjusting tool into the slot. Engage the end of the tool in the star wheel and turn the star wheel to back off the brake adjustment, using the edge of the slot as a fulcrum.

On most cars, the brake-tool handle should be moved upward to retract the brake shoes. Some Chryslers have a self-adjuster lever mounted behind the star wheel. For these cars you'll have to bend an old screwdriver or a piece of metal in order to reach the adjuster lever.

Before pulling the drums off the brake shoes, cover your mouth and nose with a breather mask, available where automotive paint is sold. This will prevent you from inhaling asbestos fibers.

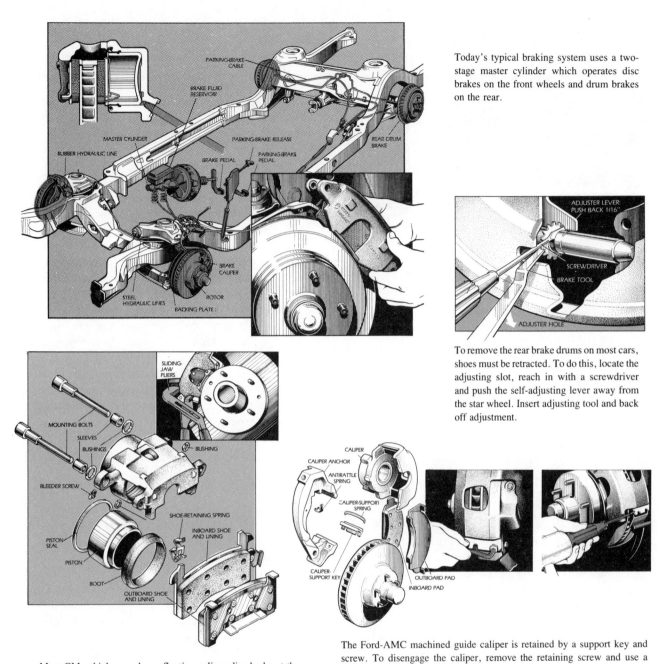

Today's typical braking system uses a two-stage master cylinder which operates disc brakes on the front wheels and drum brakes on the rear.

To remove the rear brake drums on most cars, shoes must be retracted. To do this, locate the adjusting slot, reach in with a screwdriver and push the self-adjusting lever away from the star wheel. Insert adjusting tool and back off adjustment.

The Ford-AMC machined guide caliper is retained by a support key and screw. To disengage the caliper, remove the retaining screw and use a hammer and drift to drive the retaining key out of the anchor.

Most GM vehicles employ a floating-caliper disc brake at the front wheels. Piston and seals aren't removed from the caliper unless it must be rebuilt. Upon reassembly, clinch outboard pad ears over the caliper with sliding-jaw pliers as shown (inset).

Inspect the friction surface for scoring or other damage. If the drums are discolored or heat-cracked, replace them. If they are scored, take them to your parts store/machine shop for machining. Inspect the lining for wear. Bonded linings without rivets should be replaced when they wear down to $\frac{1}{16}$-inch thickness. Replace riveted linings when they wear to within $\frac{1}{32}$ inch of the rivets. If the shoes are worn unevenly from side to side, have a machine shop check the drums.

Disassembly

At the top of each shoe you'll probably find a return spring that secures it to an anchor above the wheel cylinder. This is best removed by inserting a brake tool between the spring and anchor. Turning the tool lifts the spring off the anchor. Some mechanics remove these springs by gripping them with a side-cutter and stretching them over the anchor. This is okay if the springs are going to be

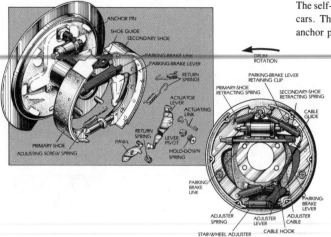

The self-adjusting mechanism at left is typical of GM cars. The actuating link joins the actuator level to anchor pin.

Cable-type self adjuster on the right is typical of Ford, Chrysler and AMC vehicles. Cable is hooked over the anchor pin at top and connected to the lever at the bottom. The adjuster is actuated when brakes are applied while the vehicle is backing up.

replaced, but not if the springs will be reused. Note the color and location of all springs, so they can be reinstalled correctly. You might want to color-code the old brake shoes with little dabs of paint to help in reassembly. Any springs that have been subjected to unusually high temperature or that have obviously stretched should be replaced. Some manufacturers recommend you replace the springs whenever the brakes are serviced. Once the springs have been disengaged, remove the shoe guide plate from the anchor pin.

Most drum brakes are equipped with a self-adjusting mechanism that turns the star wheel when lining wear creates excessive clearance. Some of these mechanisms consist of a cable, a cable guide, a lever and a spring. Others use a heavy-gauge wire link, a pawl, a pawl return spring, a lever and an adjuster spring. To disassemble the cable type, the cable is detached from the lever once the spring has been stretched slightly by moving the lever away from the star wheel. Make a note of the hole in which the cable guide is inserted before removing the adjuster assembly.

Most brake shoes are attached to the backing plate by means of springs and retainers that lock on anchor pins. To remove, grasp the retainer between the jaws of a pliers, push down, and turn it until the slot in the retainer aligns with the locking tabs on the end of the anchor pin.

On many vehicles, you can remove the shoes with the lower adjuster connecting spring and star wheel adjuster in place. Most rear brake mechanisms have a parking brake lever attached to a shoe that must be removed.

Before installing the new shoes, inspect the wheel

cylinders by lifting the rubber dust shields on each end of the cylinder and looking for signs of brake fluid that may have leaked past the pistons and seals. If you find fluid, the cylinders should be rebuilt or replaced.

Once the cylinders have been replaced and the brakes have been reassembled, the system will have to be bled. Make sure no one depresses the brake pedal while the drums are off the car or the pistons will pop out of the wheel cylinders.

Clean the brake backing plate using brake-cleaning fluid and a rag. Be sure to use a protective face mask and don't blow brake dust off with compressed air.

Then compare your new brake shoes to the old ones to make sure they're the same. Look for shiny spots on the backing plate where the shoes make contact and lubricate these with a small amount of white lithium grease. If the shoes have ridges worn into the contact pads, file them smooth before lubricating. Lubricate the star wheel adjuster with the same grease.

Reassembly

Reassembly varies with different brake configurations. If you've left the other side intact for reference, you'll be able to determine the order for component installation.

To reassemble the common GM self-adjusting brakes install the adjuster connecting spring on the primary and secondary shoes along with the star adjuster. The wheel should be on the side with the secondary shoe. The secondary shoe is the one with more lining than the primary, and is installed toward the rear of the vehicle. The primary shoe, the one with less lining material, is installed toward the front of the vehicle.

Position the shoes on the backing plate, making sure the shoes engage the wheel cylinder push rods and that the parking brake lever, on rear-wheel applications, engages the secondary shoe.

Position the adjuster lever and its spring on the secondary shoe, and install the shoe hold-down springs and retainers. On rear-wheel applications, position the parking brake link and its antirattle spring between the primary shoe and the parking brake lever. Place the shoe-guide plate in position over the anchor pin. Install the self-adjuster pawl and actuating link. Next, insert the hooked ends of the brake return springs into their respective holes in the shoes.

Then, using a large Phillips screwdriver or a brake tool, stretch the springs until they slip over the anchor pin. Install the adjuster lever return spring on the adjuster and stretch it until you're able to hook it to the adjuster pawl.

Once you've reinstalled the brake drum and wheel, use a brake adjusting tool to expand the lining against the drum. Hold the self-adjuster lever away from the star wheel, as you did before. Turn the adjuster until you feel a heavy drag while turning the wheel. Then turn the adjuster 16 clicks in the opposite direction.

Road test the car. If the pedal pumps up, air has entered the system and you'll have to bleed it out. Make a number of stops in reverse to equalize adjustment on self-adjusting brakes. If the car doesn't brake satisfactorily after you've made 20 to 30 stops to seat the lining material, go to a professional for assistance.

Solving Five Tough Brake Problems

PAUL STENQUIST

■ AS AN EXPERIENCED SATURDAY mechanic, you've probably become proficient at normal brake system maintenance chores. A complete inspection and overhaul at 30,000-mile intervals is often recommended. This includes replacement of linings and pads, resurfacing of drums and rotors if needed, and inspection of all hydraulic components.

Mastery of these regular maintenance procedures is the first level of mechanical expertise. Problem solving is the next level, and it's more difficult than maintenance service because it requires a broad background in theory along with years of experience.

The skilled Saturday mechanic, however, can learn to recognize and solve certain common problems. Here are the potential causes of five tough brake problems—problems that occur with some frequency. Also following are some general guide-

lines for the repair of these brake malfunctions.

Before attempting any repair, you should be equipped with the factory service manual for your car. At the very least, you should have a general auto repair manual that includes a section for your car.

Car pulls to one side

A violent tug of the steering wheel to one side or the other that occurs when the brakes are applied could be the result of a brake-system malfunction. Most often this is caused by the brake on one side of the car becoming less effective than the one on the other side.

It's sometimes tough to determine whether a pulling problem is caused by the front or rear brakes. Of course, unequal effectiveness of the front brakes causes a more violent pull than the same problem in the rear. As a general guideline, we can say that a pull which moves the car violently and yanks against the steering wheel is probably due to a front brake problem. A pull that is more of a drift, and does not tug on the steering wheel, is probably the result of a rear brake problem.

If you suspect that a pull is being caused by a disc brake, chock the rear wheels, jack up the car and support it on sturdy stands. Remove both front wheels and examine the calipers and discs for obvious signs of trouble. Look for a brake fluid leak or a loose caliper or caliper mounting bracket. Most disc brake calipers are designed to slide in and out on pins or machined guides. However a caliper should not be free to wobble in any other direction.

If everything appears to be in order, you'll have to remove the caliper to check the pads and caliper itself. Many calipers are retained by threaded pins on which they slide (Fig. 1). Others are retained on machined guides by a key and setscrew. Refer to your repair manual for specific removal directions if you're not already familiar with your vehicle's brakes.

Examine the pads. If they're contaminated with grease or brake fluid, their effectiveness is reduced and you've found the immediate cause. It will also be necessary to repair the grease seal or caliper leak that caused the contamination before you replace the pads on both sides of the car.

Replace a leaking caliper with a new or rebuilt unit, or rebuild the old caliper yourself. If the caliper piston and bore are not scored or otherwise damaged, the caliper can be restored to working order by replacing its seal and dust boot. Check your manual for specific step-by-step instructions.

If you find that the caliper piston is stuck in its

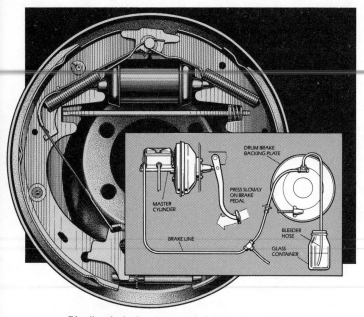

Bleeding the brakes to purge air from the hydraulic system must be done with the bleeder hose submerged in brake fluid.

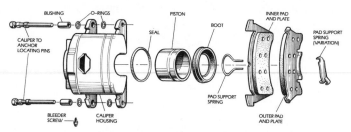

1 Disc brake calipers generally are allowed to "float" freely in and out on the locating pins, but in no other direction.

2 To back off star wheel, move adjuster lever with screwdriver (top) or hook.

3 Fluid leaking from around the edge of a wheel cylinder dust boot indicates failure.

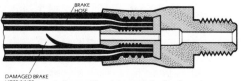

4 Internally damaged brake hose can restrict pressure to one brake, cause pulling.

bore, the caliper should be replaced, as the contaminants that caused it to stick have most likely damaged the piston and caliper bore.

If you have to replace the pads on one side of the vehicle, do the same on the other side so braking will be equal.

If a drum brake problem seems to be the cause of the problem, back off the adjusting screw star wheel. Use a brake adjusting tool inserted in the adjuster access slot, which is located either in the drum itself or in the backing plate (Fig. 2). On vehicles with the adjuster slot in the backing plate, you may have to hold the adjuster lever away from the star wheel with a screwdriver while you turn the wheel with the adjusting tool. If the access hole is in the drum, use a small hook to pull the adjuster away from the wheel. For cars equipped with other types of adjusting mechanisms, check your manual.

Once the adjusters have been backed off, remove the drums and check for incorrect or distorted shoes, damaged lining, grease or brake fluid on the lining, or a loose or damaged brake backing plate.

If shoes, lining and backing plates look okay, check the wheel cylinders for leaks (Fig. 3). Then, examine the drums. Look for hard spots or an out-of-round condition that prevents full shoe contact. Hard spots will show up as spotty wear. An out-of-round condition may cause wear on one side of the drum only. But in less serious cases, remachining of the drum may be the only way to confirm whether an out-of-round condition exists.

If the drums have hard spots, they must be replaced. Drums that are slightly out of round can sometimes be remachined, but you might wind up with an imbalanced condition. Replacement is your best bet.

Again, if you replace the lining on one side of the car, you must do the same on the other side, or you may end up with a more severe pull than you had in the first place.

If a brake pull problem defies solution, try replacing the brake hoses. A brake hose that is damaged internally can delay hydraulic pressure buildup at one wheel cylinder or caliper (Fig. 4).

Once you've replaced the hose it will be necessary to bleed air from the brake hydraulic system. See the *Pedal Pump Up* section of this article.

Pulsating brake pedal

A brake pedal that pulsates when applied indicates a brake rotor, brake drum or wheel bearing problem. Steering-wheel vibration at highway speeds may also be a symptom of this type of problem.

On cars with drum brakes, the problem can be due to a bent rear axle, a distorted drum or a bad wheel bearing.

To eliminate the possibility of a bent axle on rear-drum, rear-drive cars, have someone observe the wheels while you drive the car. If a rear wheel wobbles, the axle is probably bent.

A rear wheel bearing that is bad enough to cause pulsation of the pedal would also be abnormally noisy.

If both bearings and axles appear to be okay, back off the adjusters as described above and remove the drums. Have the drums resurfaced at an auto parts store or machine shop that is equipped with a brake lathe. If one drum or the other is distorted seriously, the machinist won't be able to resurface it and it will have to be replaced.

Check front wheel bearings by tugging on the top and bottom of the freely hanging wheel before you remove it. Noticeable looseness indicates either a wheel-bearing problem or ball-joint trouble. Loose ball joints will not cause a pedal pulsation. If the bearings are okay, have the drums resurfaced or, if necessary, replace them.

Pedal pulsations are even more common on cars with disc brakes. Remove the wheels and check the discs for lateral runout by mounting a dial indicator perpendicular to the disc. A magnetic base offers the easiest method of mounting. Measure runout 1 in. from the edge of the disc and on both sides of the disc (Fig. 5).

Specs vary somewhat, but for most discs, runout should not exceed 0.005 in. when the disc is rotated one full revolution. If it does exceed manufacturer's specs, mark the position of the disc, remove it and check hub runout (on cars where the hub and disc are separate units). Generally, hub runout should be less than 0.002 in. If hub runout is in excess of the manufacturer's tolerance, replace the hub.

If hub runout is within spec, but disc runout is not, try installing the disc with your index mark positioned 180° from its previous location. Check disc runout again. If it's not within specs, replace or refinish the disc as necessary.

If lateral runout is okay, check the disc for thickness variation by taking micrometer readings at 12 equidistant points, 1 in. from the edge (Fig. 6). Compare your figures to the manufacturer's specs. In most cases, thickness variation must be less than 0.0005 in. (one-half thousandth of an inch). If a disc is not within specs, it must be refinished or replaced.

Some manufacturers, most notably Honda, insist that rotors must be refinished on the car, using special equipment designed for the job. If this procedure is recommended for your car, you'll have

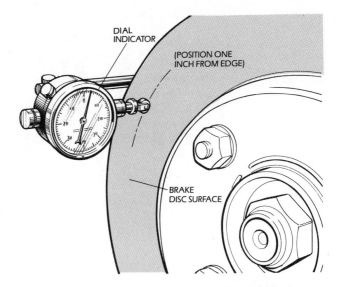

5 Check for disc runout with a dial indicator mounted 1 in. from rotor edge.

to get professional help from a shop equipped with the proper on-car rotor refinishing tool.

Brake squeal

Disc brake pad vibration is the most common cause of brake squeal—a shrieking noise that occurs when the brakes are applied.

The noise can also be due to excessive pad wear if your brakes haven't been overhauled in a while.

An application of antisqueal compound is the simplest and most effective remedy for problems on cars with new or relatively low-mileage pads. The compound, a paste-like substance, is available through auto parts stores.

To apply the compound, disengage the calipers from their mounts as you would when replacing pads. Then apply a thin strip of the product across the center of the inboard pad backing plate and a round patch on each end of the outboard pad backing plate. Do not apply the material to the front of the pads. Clean the rotors with brake cleaner and reassemble the caliper mount, taking care to attach any antirattle clips or springs properly (Fig. 7).

If squeal is a problem on drum brakes, back off the self-adjusters and remove the drums. Then sand each lining with medium-grit sandpaper until any glazing has been removed. Clean the drums with brake cleaner and reinstall. If this does not solve the problem, replace the lining with a premium-grade, name-brand shoe and lining and have the drums refinished.

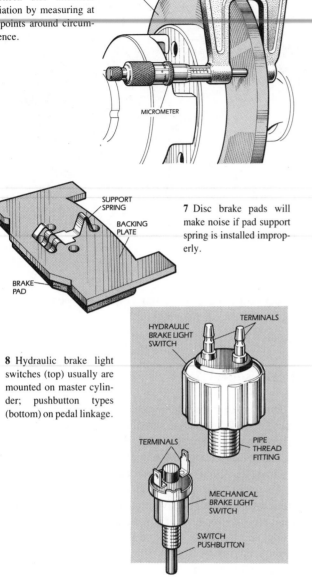

6 Check disc thickness variation by measuring at 12 points around circumference.

7 Disc brake pads will make noise if pad support spring is installed improperly.

8 Hydraulic brake light switches (top) usually are mounted on master cylinder; pushbutton types (bottom) on pedal linkage.

loosen the bleeder screw with a 6-point socket or box wrench. Don't try to loosen a bleeder screw with an open end wrench or crescent wrench. The wrench will probably slip and ruin the screw, necessitating caliper or wheel cylinder replacement.

Once you've loosened the bleeder screw, close it and attach a neoprene hose to its nipple (see lead illustration). The hose must fit snugly over the screw's nipple. Insert the other end of the hose in a glass bottle that is half full of clean brake fluid. Make sure the hose is submerged in fluid.

Have a helper pump up the brake pedal and continue to apply firm pressure. Then open the bleeder screw and let the fluid run through the hose and into the jar until the brake pedal hits the floor. Fluid flow will stop at this point. Tighten the bleeder screw and have your helper release the pedal slowly. Check the master cylinder, top it off if necessary and repeat the procedure. Continue until the expelled fluid is free of air bubbles. Do not return expelled fluid to the master cylinder.

Bleeding all the air from the hydraulic system is a time-consuming process, but be patient because it's the only way to end up with a firm brake pedal when the job is finished. It may take several pump-up-and-release cycles to get a flow of pure brake fluid. When the line still has air in it, there will be a gurgling, spitting sound as you crack open the bleeder valve. When there's a smooth flow of brake fluid, with no air bubbling into the catch bottle, you'll know that the air is out of the system.

Once the wheel cylinder or caliper that is farthest from the master cylinder is free of air, repeat the procedure at each of the other wheels. On some vehicles, particularly those with multiple-piston disc brakes, you may not be able to bleed all of the air from the system using this method. If this proves to be the case, have a professional do the job using a pressure bleeder.

Pedal pump up

If your brake pedal goes to the floor or almost to the floor the first time you hit it, but then "pumps up" to a normal height and firmness after repeated applications, there are air bubbles in the hydraulic system. These bubbles must be bled out to restore the system to proper working order. Brake bleeding must also follow the replacement of a caliper or any other job that allows air to enter the hydraulic system.

Begin by filling the master cylinder to within 1/2 in. of the top. Then, starting with the wheel cylinder or caliper that is most distant from the master cylinder (or the one recommended in your service manual),

No brake lights

A car without brake lights is an accident waiting to happen.

Some motorists make it a habit to check their brake lights by depressing the brake pedal when the car is parked directly in front of another car or a wall. If the brake lights are working, you'll see the reflected red glow.

If only one light fails, it's usually just a bad bulb. But if both lights fail, the culprit is probably a fuse or brake light switch. Check for a bad fuse first.

Two basic types of brake light switches have been used by automakers (Fig. 8). Hydraulically operated switches, most often found on older cars, are closed by hydraulic pressure when the brake pedal is depressed. Mechanical brake light switches are conventional pushbutton-type switches that are operated by the brake pedal or by a bracket on the pedal. If your car has a hydraulic switch, it's probably right on the end of the master cylinder, or nearby. If it has a mechanical switch, look for it under the dash and behind the brake pedal assembly.

To test either type of switch, remove the wiring connector from the switch terminals. Then, with the engine running, connect the two contacts in the connector using a jumper lead. If the switch is the cause of the problem, this should cause the brake lights to turn on.

If the lights still don't work, you'll have to look for an electrical circuit problem. Check for voltage into the switch with a test light or voltmeter. If voltage is available, check for an open circuit between the switch and brake lights using an ohmmeter.

When doing any kind of brake work, seek professional help if you run into problems. Don't take any chances.

Repairing Power Steering Systems

MORT SCHULTZ

■ THERE ARE SOME SATURDAY mechanics who want nothing to do with troubleshooting and repairing power steering systems. If you're one of them, consider two factors before deciding to wash your hands of the matter.

1. You can do a lot of troubleshooting using only your eyes. If you decide to buy a test gauge that reveals whether the system is developing and holding ample pressure, there isn't a power steering problem that you can't track down for yourself. The test gauge, described later, costs about $75.

2. Replacing two of the three key elements of a power steering system is not difficult. Changing the high-pressure (delivery) and low-pressure (return) hoses can be done in less than 30 minutes. Installing a power steering pump takes less than two hours. However, replacing the power steering gear should probably be left to a professional. Fortunately, it fails much less frequently than a hose or pump.

Replacement vs. overhaul

Replacing a pump with a used or reconditioned unit is less expensive than overhauling it. To give you an idea of costs, compare the following price quotes for a 1982 Grand Prix:

■ The service department of a Pontiac dealership quoted $200 to overhaul it. (A new pump is $450, installed.)

■ An independent mechanic wanted $150 to replace the defective pump with a junkyard unit.

■ By comparison, it would cost only $50 if you went to a junkyard to buy the pump, then installed it yourself. Even if you purchased a remanufactured pump for an '82 Grand Prix and installed it yourself, it would cost $95.

As for do-it-yourself overhaul of a power steering pump, you may need special tools. The repair kit costs about $20 and it takes longer to do than simply replacing the pump. Do-it-yourself overhauling doesn't seem like a practical approach.

Finding trouble

The first step is to isolate the cause of a problem if, indeed, the cause is confined to the power steering system. A steering problem could also be the result of faulty wheel alignment, a defective steering linkage or faulty suspension component.

Problems normally associated with a malfunction in the power steering system are a jerky feeling in the steering wheel while moving at a slow speed or when turning the wheel with the car standing still; noise (groan, grind, squeal); a momentary loss of steering assist; and hard steering.

There are two kinds of power steering systems: integral and linkage. The integral system (see lead illustration) has the power cylinder built into the steering gear. The linkage system (Fig. 1) has the power cylinder mounted externally on the steering linkage.

The integral system, now in widest use, is the one we concentrate on here. For a linkage system, troubleshooting is done the same way, except you also must inspect the power cylinder.

Drive belt

If the problem you're having is a jerky feeling in the steering wheel or hard steering, first check tires for proper inflation. Then, inspect the belt that drives

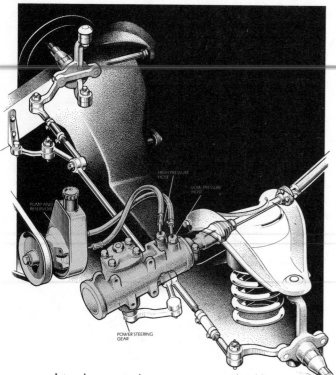

Integral power steering system uses an engine-driven pressure pump to operate a built-in power cylinder.

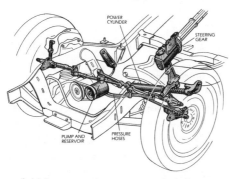

1 Linkage-type systems are an early design used into the 1960s. The power cylinder provides power assist to an otherwise standard steering linkage.

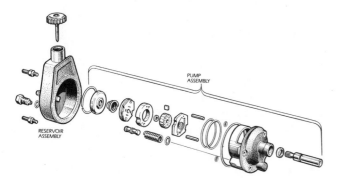

2 Pressurized fluid to operate the steering is provided by the pump assembly, while the fluid itself is stored in the reservoir, a stamped metal housing.

the power steering pump. If the drive belt is frayed or split, it must be replaced.

To determine if a power steering pump drive belt is too loose, check it with a belt tension gauge or press down on the belt with your finger. A properly adjusted belt should deflect $1/4$ to $1/2$ inch—no greater.

Tighten a belt by loosening the adjustment bolts and pulling the pump toward you. Use a pry bar, if necessary, but don't press against the reservoir. You may bend or distort it. Place the bar against the pump housing, which is solid. The pump and reservoir actually are separate components (Fig. 2).

Tracing a fluid leak

Next, check the fluid level. Power steering fluid doesn't evaporate, so a low level indicates a leak. Often, a low oil level will cause the steering pump to make a groaning noise.

However, there is the possibility that in checking fluid level on a previous occasion someone left the cap loose and fluid was lost out the neck of the reservoir. Therefore, refill the reservoir, tighten the cap and keep an eye on the level for a few days.

If the level drops again, check for leaks by wiping high and low pressure hoses clean. These hoses extend from the power steering pump to the steering gear. Examine them for cracks and splits and for fluid seeping from around fittings (Fig. 3).

A leak may not show up then and there, especially a small leak. If there's doubt, spread chalk dust or talcum powder on the hoses. Start the engine and move the steering wheel from stop to stop three or four times. Shut off the engine and check to see if the chalk dust or talcum powder reveals a leak.

Replacing hoses

If the leak seems to be coming from a metal fitting where the hose connects to the power steering pump or gear, tighten the fitting and test again. Notice that in order to replace a hose you often have to disconnect it at these fittings and not where the rubber part of the hose connects to the pipe. On many pumps, the hoses and pipes are one-piece units at both ends. On some pumps, low-pressure hoses and pipes can be separated where they are joined together with clamps.

The new hose you buy must be one designed for power steering systems. Make certain that the metal parts of the new hose are the same as the old hose. If they aren't, make sure they can't make contact with any electrical connections. After installing the hose bleed the system to expel air.

Bleeding the system

Fill the reservoir, start the engine and turn the steering wheel all the way from one stop to the other. Do this five times in each direction, pausing a second or two at each stop—*but no longer*. Keeping the steering jammed against a stop can damage the pump.

Now, with the steering wheel in a straight ahead position, run the engine at idle for three minutes. At the end of this time, siphon some power steering fluid from the reservoir into a glass container and examine it.

If fluid is light tan or a milky color, there may still be air in the system or the fluid may have been contaminated with water. Repeat bleeding. If the color doesn't clear up, siphon fluid from the reservoir, add new fluid and repeat the bleeding procedure.

Inspecting pump and gear

If hoses aren't leaking, inspect the power steering pump and steering gear for leaks. Start with the pump. Clean it with a rag, using a cleaning solvent if necessary. Then, spread chalk dust or talcum powder, concentrating it in areas pointed out in Fig. 4.

Start the engine and turn the steering wheel slowly from stop to stop two or three times. Remember—don't put force or hold the wheel against the stop.

Turn off the engine and examine the pump. If there's a leak, fluid will show up on the chalk dust or talcum powder.

Some leaks are easy to repair. A leak from the reservoir cap usually can be fixed by replacing the cap. On GM power steering pumps, a leaking shaft seal can be replaced without disassembling the pump; even the reservoir seal is fairly easy to replace. Leaks from the area where a hose connects can frequently be repaired by simply replacing an O-ring seal. Before replacing a pump with a junkyard or rebuilt unit, check your service manual to see what's involved. Leaks caused by damage to the pump reservoir are grounds for replacement.

While checking the pump, try rocking the pulley back and forth. This test establishes whether the shaft is worn. If you find that it is, replace the pump and bleed the system.

Check the steering gear for leaks the same way, concentrating on those areas that are pointed out in

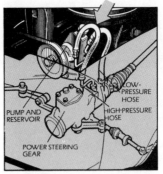

3 High-pressure hose is the weak link in the system, and most likely to leak.

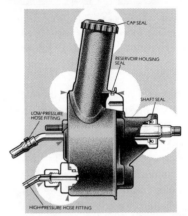

4 Power steering pumps are mostly likely to leak at pressure hose fittings, cap seal, shaft seal and housing flanges.

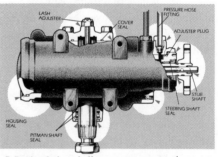

5 Recirculating ball-type power steering gears can drip fluid from housing flange, shaft seal or pressure fitting.

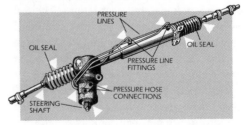

6 Rack-and-pinion power steering gears carry additional pressure lines and oil seals prone to leakage.

Figs. 5 and 6.

If the steering gear leaks, should you have it replaced or overhauled? There is no simple answer.

There's a good chance that a steering gear leak is the result of seals having been chewed up, because the steering shaft has corroded or pitted. New seals

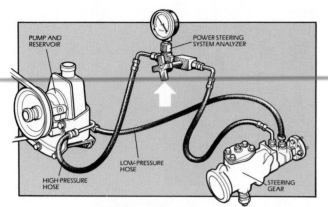

7 Power steering system analyzer is tapped into the high-pressure hose to troubleshoot pump failures. Use control valve (arrow) in order to take pressure readings.

will only suffer the same fate. If that's the case, overhauling the unit would be a waste of time and money.

Make the decision whether to repair the leak or replace the unit after consulting with a mechanic and/or your service manual.

One potential problem with junkyard parts is that they may be in no better condition than the parts you're replacing. The junkyard will probably permit you to return defective parts, but you lose out on the labor involved. Don't attempt to replace a steering box or rack without a service manual.

Pressure testing

After checking the drive belt and looking for leaks, the final step in troubleshooting a power steering system is a pressure test. A power steering system analyzer is needed for this.

A pressure test can determine if a problem is caused by a pump or steering gear failure. The test should be performed when any of these symptoms are noted: an increase in effort required when turning the wheel fast, jerking action in the wheel when turning that is not cured by V-belt replacement, or generally hard steering and lack of assist.

Disconnect the high-pressure hose at the steering gear and pump. Attach the analyzer between the two (Fig. 7). Identify the high-pressure hose by starting the engine and holding your finger on each hose as someone moves the steering wheel from stop to stop. The hose that you feel a surge from is the high-pressure hose.

Another way to identify high and low pressure hoses is by the fittings that secure hoses to pipes. Generally, crimped fittings are used on a high pressure hose while a clamp is used on a low pressure hose.

Warm the fluid

With the analyzer connected and its control valve open, start the engine and let it run until the power steering fluid gets warm. For accurate test results, fluid temperature should be between 150° and 170° F. Help raise the temperature quickly by turning the steering wheel from stop to stop a few times.

Now, with the steering wheel in the straight-ahead position, make a note of the reading on the analyzer gauge. Check this reading against the *at standstill* specification given by the car manufacturer in the service manual.

If the reading is higher than this and hoses are not kinked, replace both of them. One or both have restrictions.

Close and open the analyzer valve three times. Record the pressure reading each time it is closed. *Caution:* Don't keep the valve closed longer than five seconds at a time. You may damage the power steering pump.

Again, check readings against the specifications. Notice the difference in pressure between the three readings. It should vary no more than 50 psi.

Interpreting readings

A lower-than-specified pressure reading or pressure readings not within 50 psi of each other could indicate a malfunctioning flow control valve or pressure relief valve, which is in the power steering pump of most non-GM cars. In a GM car, the pressure relief valve is in the power steering gear. It may be possible to restore these parts by removing and cleaning them. If the pressures are constant but below specs, the rotor and vanes are damaged and the pump must be replaced.

To test the steering gear, open the analyzer valve. Turn the steering wheel all the way to the left. Record the reading. Then, turn the steering wheel all the way to the right and record.

Compare both readings to the *maximum* reading you got when you closed the analyzer valve during the last test. If the two readings are lower, there is an internal leak in the power steering gear. Overhaul or replace the unit.

Tips on replacing a pump

1. Replace a power steering pump when the engine is cold to avoid burning yourself.

2. Remove battery negative cable.

3. If possible, remove hoses from the pump after removing the pump from the engine to keep from spilling power steering fluid.

4. When you've disconnected hoses, place caps or tape over their ends to keep dirt out of them.

5. If the drive belt pulley is in front of the bracket holding the pump to the engine, you may have to remove the pulley before you can detach the pump. If the pulley is pressed on the shaft, you'll need a puller. You may also need a puller to remove the pulley from a pump after taking it off the engine, so you can transfer the pulley to the replacement pump.

6. In some cars, the power steering pump and bracket are two separate parts. Remove the pump by unbolting it from the bracket. In other cars, the pump and bracket are removed from the engine as an assembly.

7. After installing the new pump, tighten the drive belt until it deflects 1/4 to 1/2 inch—no more, no less. If you make the drive belt too tight, the pump bushing may wear.

8. Fill the reservoir with power steering fluid—not automatic transmission fluid. The two are not the same. *Note:* This precaution does not apply to cars made by Ford Motor Co. According to Ford, you may use Type F automatic transmission fluid (but not Dexron or any other type) in a Ford, Lincoln or Mercury power steering system.

9. Bleed the system to purge air.

Servicing Ball Joints

PAUL STENQUIST

Front suspension rebuilds include servicing tie rod ends, ball joints and the idler arm for a complete steering-system renewal.

■ A LOT OF SATURDAY MECHANICS are afraid to attempt steering linkage and chassis component repairs, thinking that these are jobs better left to a professional mechanic. Actually, they're among the easier jobs that the driveway technician might attempt.

On the following pages, you'll learn how to diagnose and replace faulty ball joints, tie rod ends, idler arms and sway bar components. Since steering angles can change significantly when new components are installed, a professional front end alignment will be a necessary procedure after ball joint or tie rod end replacement.

Diagnosing front end problems

You should suspect front end problems if your front tires wear abnormally, if your mechanic says he can't align your front wheels because steering linkage parts or ball joints are too loose, if you hear clunks when you turn the wheels or corner, if there seems to be excessive free play in the steering mechanism or if you experience wheel shimmy and/or vibration.

To confirm a suspected chassis part problem, you're going to have to spend some time under the greasy side. Before raising the car with your hydraulic floor jack or scissors jack, chock the rear wheels and apply the parking brake. Raise the car and locate jack stands in the recommended positions on the frame or frame/body structure. Lower the car until it is resting on the stands, leaving the floor jack in place for additional security.

Examine your steering linkage and front suspension. Most rear-wheel-drive cars use parallelogram linkage—a center link, two tie rods, an idler arm and a Pitman arm (see Fig. 1). This steering linkage is usually used with a coil spring mounted on the lower or upper control arm. Some cars with upper and lower arms have torsion bars in place of coil springs. Most front-drive and some rear-drive cars are equipped with rack and pinion steering. The steering arms on the wheel spindles are joined directly to the steering rack by a pair of tie rods. The idler arm and Pitman arm are not used. Most front-wheel-drive cars and a few rear-drivers have only lower control arms. A MacPherson strut replaces the spring, shock absorber and upper arm.

Checking ball joints

While cars with MacPherson struts have only one ball joint at each wheel, those with parallelogram steering linkage usually have both upper and lower ball joints. But the two joints don't wear out at the same rate, since only one ball joint carries the full load. If the coil spring is mounted on the lower control arm, the lower ball joint is the load carrier (Fig. 2). If the spring is mounted on the upper arm, the upper joint is the load carrier. When checking joints for wear, check the load carrier first. If it's okay and has never been replaced, you'll probably find that the unloaded joint is okay as well.

Before you check for wear, inspect the rubber seal of each ball joint. If it's torn, the joint must be replaced.

If your car has wear-indicator ball joints—as many produced after 1973 do—checking them is a simple matter. Before checking the joints, the car must be lowered to the ground or its wheels must be resting on ramps.

Most wear-indicator joints have a collar that protrudes from the lower surface of the joint and encircles the grease fitting (Fig. 3). As the joint wears, this collar sinks below the surface of the joint, indicating that replacement is necessary.

A second type of wear-indicator joint is used on some vehicles, including late-model Chryslers. On this type joint, you merely attempt to wiggle the grease fitting (Fig. 4). If you can move it with your hand, the joint is worn out.

If your car does not have wear-indicator ball joints, you'll have to measure free play with a dial indicator or check it by feel.

The ball joints of most front-wheel-drive cars that are equipped with MacPherson struts should be checked with the wheels off the ground and the car supported on jack stands. Grab each wheel at the top and bottom and shake it in and out while watching for movement of the steering knuckle relative to the ball joint. Any noticeable movement is grounds for replacement.

To induce movement in a loaded joint, relieve the load. If your car has loaded lower joints (spring on lower arm), lift the car and relocate the jack stands under the lower control arms, as close to the ball joints as possible.

If your car has loaded upper joints, wedge a block of wood between each upper control arm and the frame, with the wheels resting on ramps or with jack stands under the lower control arms. Then lift the car, locate the jack stands under the frame and lower the car to rest on them.

Ball joints are excessively worn if they permit too much sideways movement (radial play) or up and down movement (axial play). To measure axial movement, mount a dial indicator so that its stem rests against the bottom surface of the spindle assembly (knuckle). The stem should be parallel to an imaginary line that runs through the center of both ball joints. Insert a pry bar between the bottom of the tire and the floor and lift the wheel. Watch the indicator to see how much movement the joint

permits. The figure should be less than the tolerance listed in your service manual.

To check radial movement, mount the indicator so that its stem is in contact with the edge of the wheel and perpendicular to the wheel. When checking an upper joint, the indicator should be located at the top of the wheel. For a lower joint, locate it at the bottom of the wheel. Push the wheel in and out and watch the indicator. (Make sure that any motion is not the result of incorrect wheel bearing adjustment.) Radial movement maximum is 0.25-inch, at the edge of the wheel.

Checking rod ends, idler arms

For most cars, there are no specific procedures for checking tie rod ends and idler arms, but a little common sense is all that's needed. For the driveway technician, the most practical way to check the four tie rod ends of a car with parallelogram steering or the two outer rod ends of a rack and pinion system is simply to grab the tie rods and shake them vigorously. The tie rod ends should not be sloppy or loose. Rod ends must be preloaded, but even a brand new one allows some horizontal movement. A good joint should show little or no vertical movement. Missing or torn dust boots are also grounds for replacement.

To check an idler arm, push the end of the arm that is attached to the center link up and down. It should show little or no vertical movement.

Examine the bellows boots that cover the inner tie rod ends of rack and pinion cars for cracks, splits or other physical damage. If they're not in good condition, replace them. On cars with power rack and pinion, fluid in the boot can be a sign of leaking seals. Manual racks with lubricant in the boot are normal.

To check the inner tie rod end, squeeze the bellows boot and feel around for the rod end. With one hand on the rod end, push and pull on the tire. If the rod end seems to be loose, it should be replaced.

Checking sway bar components

A loose sway bar will make a clunking noise every time you turn or hit a bump. Check the bushings and links that join it to the control arm and the bushings that secure it to the frame. If any are worn, broken, deteriorated or missing, they must be replaced.

Ball joint replacement

You'll need a ball joint separator—a wide-slot pickle fork—to replace ball joints on any car. For cars that have press-in–type joints, you'll need a ball-joint press as well. This tool can usually be rented from the parts store when you purchase the new ball joints. Some Chrysler and Ford models have joints that are secured by rivets, so you'll need a good chisel to service these cars. The ball joints used on front-wheel-drive Fords and many Japanese imports cannot be removed. If joints are worn, replace lower control arms.

If you're not sure how the ball joints in your car are attached to the control arm, consult your service manual before attempting the job.

To replace load-carrying lower ball joints on most cars, loosen the lug nuts on both front wheels, and lift the vehicle with your floor jack. Place a set of jack stands under the frame and remove the wheels. Lift the car, remove the stands from under the frame and relocate them under the lower control arms, as close to the ball joints as possible. Lower the car until it is resting on the stands.

Disengage the tie rod ends from the steering arm using a tie rod end separator or narrow pickle fork (Fig. 5). Insert the pickle fork between the rod end and its rubber boot so that you won't tear the boot when you knock the rod end off the steering arm. If you tear the boot, replace the rod end. A more expensive jackscrew-type separator is used for releasing rod ends that will be reused. This tool won't tear the boot.

Make sure that the lower control arm is firmly supported by the jack stand, then remove the cotter pin from the ball-joint retaining nut and unscrew the nut. Reinstall the nut approximately three turns, then insert your ball-joint separator between the steering knuckle and ball joint, and hammer it in until the joint is disengaged from the knuckle. Unscrew the nut. If you can't unscrew it by hand, the jack stand is not supporting the control arm. Once the joint is completely disengaged from the knuckle, lift the knuckle and upper control arm assembly clear of the ball joint and support them.

If you're working on a car with pressed-in joints, install the ball-joint press on the joint and control arm, following the directions included with the press (Fig. 6). Then, tighten the jackscrew on the press until the ball joint drops out of the control arm. Inspect the tapered hole in the steering knuckle and remove any dirt. If the hole is out of round, the steering knuckle assembly must be replaced.

Once you're sure the knuckle is okay, reverse the press, and, using the appropriate adapters, install the new joint. Torque the nut to spec and install the cotter pin. Don't back off the nut to insert the pin; tighten it a bit more.

On cars with riveted joints, simply chisel the rivet heads off after disengaging the ball joint from the steering knuckle. Be careful not to damage the

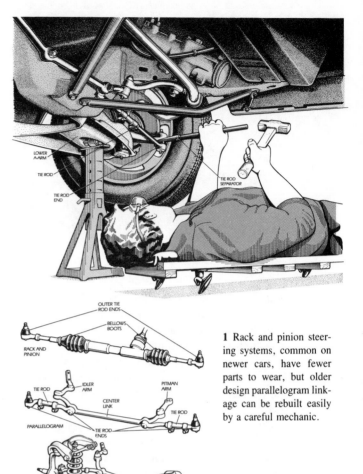

1 Rack and pinion steering systems, common on newer cars, have fewer parts to wear, but older design parallelogram linkage can be rebuilt easily by a careful mechanic.

2 When springs are on the lower A-arm, weight is carried by lower ball joint. Upper A-arm mounted springs put load on upper ball joints.

3 Wear-indicator ball joints show condition by position of grease fitting shoulder.

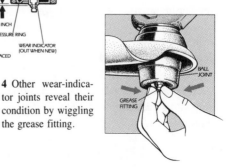

4 Other wear-indicator joints reveal their condition by wiggling the grease fitting.

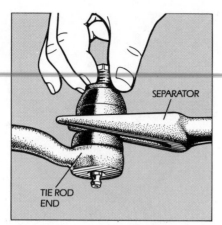

5 To prevent boot tearing, insert separator carefully between rod end and dust boot.

control arm with your chisel. Inspect the steering knuckle as described above. Then install a new joint, using the bolts that came with it.

A third type of joint, much less common than the other two, has a threaded body and screws into the control arm. It can be removed with a large socket and breaker bar. The new joint must be torqued to spec.

The replacement of load-carrying upper joints is similar. A block of wood is wedged between the upper control arm and frame to relieve the load on the joint so it can be removed. If you're unable to support your upper control arm in this manner, check the service manual for specific instructions.

The replacement procedure for non-load-carrying upper joints is approximately the same as that for lower joints. Because the rivets used to hold many upper joints are on top of the control arm, you may not be able to reach them with a hammer and chisel. If this is the case, drill them out from below, using a ⅛-in. drill bit. Drill right in the center of each rivet to a depth of about ¼-in., then drive the rivets out with a punch or drift.

To replace joints on most front-wheel-drive cars with removable joints, unscrew the clamp bolt that secures the ball-joint stud in the steering knuckle and disengage the joint from the knuckle (Fig. 7). You might have to tap it out with a mallet. Then, chisel off the rivets that secure the joint to the control arm or, on cars with pressed-in joints, remove and replace them with a ball-joint press.

Replacing tie rod ends

A separator is needed for tie rod end service. Make sure you get a pickle fork with a narrow slot between the tangs.

To replace any of the four tie rod ends on a car with parallelogram steering linkage or an outer end on a car with rack and pinion steering, remove the nut that secures the rod end to the steering arm or center link.

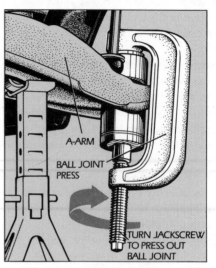

6 A screw-type ball joint press is required for servicing many GM and Chrysler cars.

In most cases, you'll have to pull a cotter pin from the nut before you can loosen it. In some cases, you may find that the rod end is secured with a locking nut. Locking nuts cannot be reused.

Separate the rod end from the center link or steering arm by driving the pickle fork in between the rod end and its mount. On cars with parallelogram steering, measure from the center of the tie rod's other end to the center of the rod end you plan to replace and record this figure (Fig. 8). Then, loosen the locking bolt on the tie rod collar and unscrew the faulty rod end.

On cars with rack and pinion steering, measure from the center of the outer rod end to the boot-

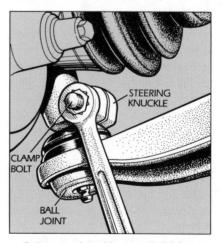

7 On many front-drive cars, ball joints are retained in the knuckle by a clamp bolt.

retaining groove on the inner rod end, then unscrew the rod end.

Install the new tie rod end and screw it in until the rod length is equal to the measurement you recorded earlier. This will give you an approximate toe setting that will allow you to drive the car to an alignment shop.

Several types of inner tie rod ends are used on cars with rack and pinion steering. Procedures vary significantly, so consult your service manual.

Replacing an idler arm

To replace a worn idler arm, remove the cotter pin and nut or the locking nut that secures it to the center link. Then, use your tie rod end separator to disengage it from the center link. Unbolt the bracket that joins the idler arm to the frame. On some cars, you'll have to access the nuts through holes in the frame. Install the new arm, tightening the retaining bolts to 35 lb. or the spec provided in your manual. Check the taper on the center link for damage before reattaching it to the arm.

Replacing sway bar bushings

To remove a typical sway bar link, hold the bolt head on one end of the link and remove the nut from the other end. Once the nut is off, remove the link and worn bushings and install the new parts. On most applications, the bushings are installed above and below the sway bar and the control arm. A washer backs up each bushing.

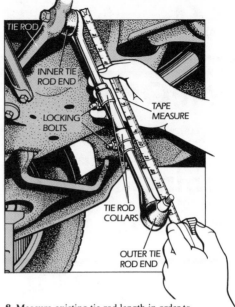

8 Measure existing tie rod length in order to get an approximate alignment setting.

Repeat the procedure on the other side, then remove each frame-mount bracket and replace the rubber bushings that surround the sway bar. If you don't find any bushings when you remove the brackets, the old ones probably deteriorated and fell out. If this is the case, you've located the source of an annoying clunk.

Don't forget that an alignment check is essential following the replacement of tie rod ends or ball joints. Also, chassis parts are only part of the handling and steering equation. Equally important are the vehicle's ride height, springs and shocks, tires and steering box.

Part VI:

COMFORT AND APPEARANCE

Cleaning Your Car Like a Pro

PAUL STENQUIST

■ THEY CALL THEMSELVES "DETAILERS," and they clean cars inside and out for very demanding customers—auto-show exhibitors, car dealers and fussy owners of expensive luxury and sports cars. Their methods are as far removed from a quick spritz at the corner carwash as their prices—$100 and up per car! When they're finished, the car looks immaculate.

In general, the procedure includes washing, surface restoration and polishing. With cars that haven't been neglected, the last two steps can usually be combined. If a finish has become severely oxidized and sun-faded, however, more extensive measures are called for. Some important tips on washing and polishing your car follow. The restoration of faded and chipped paint will be covered in another article.

Frequent washing is a critical part of exterior car care. Industrial fallout and pollution, road salt, acid rain, tree sap, dead insects and bird droppings are constantly assaulting the finish of your car. Removal of all that accumulated crud once a week is not excessive.

Taking care of the shining exterior won't do much to extend the car's life if you ignore the greasy side. Most corrosion begins somewhere on the underside of the car and works its way through to the top. You can help prevent this by cleaning road salt and other foreign material from the underside panels and inspecting to make sure the undercoating is in good condition.

The easiest way to wash the underside is to use the pressure washer wand at a self-service carwash. But you can do the job at home with a brush, soap and a garden hose if a self-service facility isn't available.

Using a soft brush, scrub the inside of the wheel wells, the inside of the door-mounting areas, the underside of the front and rear bumpers, and as much of the chassis as you can reach. Rinse off all of the soap with the pressure washer or with your garden hose.

Make sure you don't knock off any undercoating while you're scrubbing. After the wash job, inspect the bottom for missing undercoating or corrosion. If you find bare spots, get rid of any rust and apply an aerosol rustproofer. Undercoating (a thick sound-deadener) is less critical—restore it if you like.

Soap it up

Once you've cleaned and inspected the nasty parts, you can trade in your coveralls for a swimsuit for the rest of the job.

Don't use laundry or dish detergent for washing your car since their grease-cutting formulas can remove wax. A general household cleaner, recommended for use on painted walls, is okay, but the best choice is one of the carwash soaps sold in auto parts stores. Make sure you get a product that is meant to be mixed with water and rinsed off. The flushing action of a good rinse is an important part of the wash job. Use a garden hose for rinsing—a bucket of water isn't enough. It's best not to use a high-pressure spray wand on the exterior but, if you must, keep it well away from the car and use cold or lukewarm water, not hot.

If you're using a household cleaner, mix a solution somewhat weaker than what is recommended for painted walls. If you're using a commercial carwash product, mix according to directions on the label. Unless otherwise indicated, use warm water, not hot.

Never attempt to wash or wax a car in the sun—a cloudy day or well-shaded area is best.

Before you begin washing, have the garden hose standing by, ready to rinse. You can't allow soap to dry on the car or it can cause streaks and spotting in the wax (if any) remaining on the car.

Begin by washing the roof. Use a sponge or soft cloth and rinse immediately. Then move on to the hood or deck lid and finally the doors, fenders and quarter panels. Work in areas that are small enough to allow complete rinsing before the soap dries. After a thorough rinsing, dry the car with a chamois that has been water-saturated and wrung out. Keep wringing the chamois as it collects water.

Wash tires and whitewalls with one of the cleaners sold specifically for this purpose. Use a stiff brush and follow the directions on the product's label. Use clean, soft rags and a liquid glass cleaner to wash the windows. To remove the film that accumulates on the inside surface of the windows, use an ammonia cleaner.

Surface spots

Check the vehicle's painted surface. If there are bug or tar spots, use a commercially available paint-cleaning solvent to remove them. Follow the directions on the label—not all solvents are fully compatible with every type of paint. Test in an inconspicuous place, such as the door-mounting area, before applying solvent to the exterior.

If the finish is lightly scratched or spotted with material that cannot be removed with solvent, you can probably. clean it up with a little polishing compound. Apply fine polishing (not rubbing) compound to a small area with a damp cloth. Rub only until the foreign matter has been removed or the scratch has disappeared. Don't overdo it and don't rub on an edge or you'll end up with a bare spot. Don't try to compound areas larger than a couple of inches across in this manner.

Beautify with polish

The polishing operation is next. This is important because it beautifies and protects the finish. While two- and three-step polish systems are available, there are many single-step products that give excellent results. In fact, there are a tremendous number of products available and a couple of different ways to do the job. For our purposes, we'll use the term ''polish'' to describe all the types of paint-beautifying products that are intended for use as a final operation.

The newest category of polish products includes compounds called *polymer glaze* or *protectant*. This is the type of coating the new car dealer tries to sell you for upwards of $100. They are now available in kit form from auto parts stores for $6 to $30. The higher-priced kits include preparatory cleaning compounds.

Use a soft rag or sponge with plenty of water to wash painted surfaces. Use a car or household soap made for these surfaces.

Rinse each area of the car immediately after it is washed. Wash a small area at a time and do not allow the soap to dry, or it will leave marks on the paint.

Special cleaners are available for tires and for cast aluminum wheels. Use a stiff brush to remove brake dust and grime.

Remove stubborn stains and light scratches with fine polishing compound (not rubbing compound). Rub lightly with a damp cloth.

Polymers are shiny by nature, so buffing is not required. The products reportedly screen ultraviolet rays, which cause paint to fade, and they last for six months to a year. A restorative is packaged with some of the more expensive kits that will preserve the shine over an extended period of time if applied at six-month intervals.

Protection vs. sheen

Most detailers feel that polymers offer long-term protection and a certain amount of gloss, but that they can't produce the type of deep, lustrous sheen that some other products can, particularly those that are applied with an electric or air-powered polisher.

Most polishes contain wax, silicone, abrasives, and/or chemical solvents. The abrasives or solvents are for removing dirt and faded paint, while the silicone and wax produce the glaze. These products are available as one- or two-component systems. Some are intended only for hand application, while others are designed to be applied with a power polisher.

Products containing a high percentage of wax produce the best initial luster, but wax breaks down faster than most other polishing products. Silicone polishes form a more durable barrier than waxes—they don't oxidize—but initial gloss is not quite as good. You can tell which type of glaze is predomi-

nant in the formula by reading the label and list of ingredients. One-component products clean and polish in one step, while two-component compounds require separate operations.

Many of the one-component products—particularly those sold for metallic paint finishes—do not contain abrasives. These usually contain a cleaning solvent of some type to remove dirt that washing can't dislodge. Use this nonabrasive type of polish if your car does not have surface scratches.

Remove stains and scratches

If the car has surface scratches or a moderate amount of faded paint and oxidation, use a two-component polish or a one-component type that contains abrasives. (Heavily faded, oxidized or stained paint calls for machine compounding of the entire car.) If a product's label doesn't tell you whether abrasives are included, you can tell by rubbing some between your thumb and finger. If it's abrasive, you'll feel a slight grit.

You also have liquid and paste products to choose from. In general, liquid products are not as prone to rub through the paint. This is particularly important if you're going to apply the product with a machine.

If you want to use a wax and/or silicone polish and you don't mind polishing at fairly frequent intervals—like once a month—you can do a reasonably good job by hand. But, if you'd like to produce an ultrahigh-gloss shine that will last for six months or more, you should rent an automotive polishing machine.

Machine polishing

Auto parts stores that specialize in supplying body shops sell polishes of all types that are intended for use with a polishing machine. The counterman should be able to tell you what type of pad to use and how fast the machine should run with the product you choose. Polishing machines can be rented from tool-rental stores.

It's very important that you get a machine that runs at the right speed so the surface glaze will harden. Too fast and you'll burn through the paint. Too slow and the glaze won't last as long as it should.

A third alternative is a polishing pad mounted on an electric drill. Available through a variety of consumer-oriented outlets, these are generally okay for use with polishes intended for application by hand because they run at relatively low speed and

Polishing pads can be fitted to an electric drill for buffing. A power polisher, used with a product formulated for power buffing, will give a longer-lasting shine.

will stall if a significant amount of pressure is applied.

There are some general guidelines to follow, although you should always follow label directions. Work in the shade or on a cloudy day whether you're using a machine or applying by hand. Apply the polish to a small area—about 2 feet square.

If you're using a polishing machine, begin by rubbing a small amount of polish evenly into the pad. Work it in well, coating the entire surface. This will condition the pad so it won't soak up the polish you'll be applying to the vehicle.

Apply the polish directly to the vehicle, using only the amount specified in the instructions to avoid clogging the pad. Then, spread the polish around the 2-sq.-ft. work area before turning on the machine. Experts suggest four full passes with the polishing machine to produce a perfect gloss—if the machine is used at the right speed, with the correct amount of polish, and if the pad is not gummed up and dirty. Keep the pad flat against the paint surface and don't bear down.

You might not be able to reach some areas with the machine, so polish these sections by hand.

If you use a carpet-type pad and it starts to block up, you should clean it by loosening the accumulated polish with a dull screwdriver or similar tool. If you're using a lamb's wool- or sponge-type pad, it shouldn't block up unless you've been applying too much polish. When you've finished the polishing operation, clean the pad in your washing machine and save it for future use.

Finally, wash the car with lukewarm water and a soft rag to remove any polish residue. Make sure to remove any polish that is caught in crevices. If you leave it there, it will attract moisture that will eventually lead to corrosion. Dry the car with a chamois.

If you used abrasive polish on the painted surfaces, don't use it on chrome, aluminum or anodized aluminum (black chrome) trim. Instead, use a non-abrasive polish sold specifically for use on these surfaces. There are even some that are specifically formulated for anodized aluminum and for plastic.

Some detailers and body shop mechanics use engine oil to protect the chrome-plated steel parts of their vehicles. Believe it or not, this offers terrific rust protection and a fairly good shine. The drawback is that it collects dirt. But, if you adhere to once-a-week washing and reapplication of the oil, dirt shouldn't be a big problem. When cleaning oiled chrome, don't use the rags that you use on the rest of the car.

Before applying oil, cover the driveway under the bumpers with a dropcloth or newspapers. Liberally apply the oil with a rag and allow it to soak for several minutes before wiping off the excess with a clean rag.

Tricks of the trade

Detailers use a few other tricks to make cars look new. The application of black rubber dressing on the tires, for example, will make them look very nice. If you don't take a good look at the tread, the tires might pass for new. The dressing may also help preserve the rubber. Applied with a paintbrush, the coating leaves the tire sidewalls shiny black. Check the instructions on the can to make sure it's compatible with all types of tires before using it.

Engine cleanup is a part of the detailing job as well. Engine-cleaning compounds are available from auto parts stores for this purpose. They are sprayed on, allowed to soak in for a while, then hosed off. Make sure you cover all electronic components with plastic bags before attempting to clean an engine. Avoid spraying water directly on these components.

Once the engine is clean, the pros will sometimes

Rubber dressing, applied to the sidewalls, will make your tires look dark, shiny and new. It also helps preserve the rubber.

spray the entire engine compartment (except the exhaust manifolds) with a clear high-temperature paint. This paint will make hoses look like new and will brighten up what is left of the engine's original paint job.

The inside story

There are special products made for cleaning vinyl upholstery. Harsh detergents, abrasives or cleaning fluids just won't do—instead, they'll damage the surface. Vinyl repair kits are available from specialty mail-order houses.

For cloth upholstery, use a whiskbroom or a vacuum cleaner to remove ordinary dirt. Car upholstery is unlike home-furniture upholstery in that it is chemically treated with a flame retardant, and sometimes with other products that make it stain resistant. Work on any stain immediately or blot up or scrape off as much of the stain as you can, and treat it as soon as possible.

Leather upholstery should be cleaned only with saddle soap and treated with preservatives made especially for leather.

Detailing is more work than a pass through the carwash, but it can literally make an old car look like new.

Repairing Minor Body Damage

PAUL STENQUIST

Time-ravaged paint jobs and small nicks, scratches and dents can be fixed in your driveway with basic bodywork techniques and a little patience.

■ YOUR FAMILY WAGON ISN'T quite the glamorous machine that it once was. The effects of use, road salt, pollution, parking lot mishaps and a variety of other hazards have taken their toll.

Where it was once bright and shiny, it is now dull

and fading. The paint is chipped behind the front and rear fenderwells, and a couple of long scratches cross the door panels. A professional bodyshop repair job would be a very expensive proposition. Can you do it yourself?

Unlike mechanical work, success in body work can be measured in degrees. With a mechanical job, you either can do it or you can't. When it comes to bodywork, however, even a feeble effort may make the car look better than it does right now, and if you can't afford a pro job, you have little to lose.

In the following sections, we'll outline some simple exterior repairs.

Restoring faded paint

A paint surface that is extremely faded and scratched may not respond to the normal cleaning and polishing techniques described in the previous chapter. In these cases, machine or hand compounding is necessary. But remember, whether you do the job with a machine or by hand, there are no guarantees. You may rub through the old paint before you have removed the oxidized surface. Rubbing through, however, is less likely if the job is done by hand.

Hand compounding is hard work. You can do only a small area at a time and a considerable amount of elbow grease is needed. Use a rubbing compound that is intended for hand rubbing and some 600-grit sandpaper.

Begin by lightly wet-sanding an area of about 2 sq. ft. with the 600-grit paper, which should be folded into quarters. After uniform sanding, polish the area with a fine grade of hand rubbing compound. Apply the compound with a soft damp rag that has been wrung out and folded into a pad. Use medium pressure and straight back-and-forth strokes. Following directions on the label, remove the compound with a dry rag. If the surface isn't glossy, you haven't removed enough of the faded paint. Do it again.

Avoid rubbing hard on edges or raised parts of a panel, since these areas will rub through first. If you do rub all the way through the paint, refinishing is the only completely satisfactory fix.

Machine compounding

Machine compounding is faster and removes more paint, but, of course, the danger of rub-through is increased. To do the job, you'll need a power polishing machine which runs at 1,400 rpm or higher under load, and some rubbing compound designed for machine compounding.

A carpet-type pad is usually used for compounding, rather than the lamb's-wool–type pad, which is generally used for waxing. An auto parts store that specializes in body shop repairs can help you with both the pad and the compound, and a tool rental store can supply the machine.

Rub-through precautions

Before polishing, apply a thin strip of masking tape to creases, raised edges and sharp corners of the body that will be passed over by the polisher to minimize the chance of rub-through. Mix the compound with water if the instructions so indicate. Wear old clothes. The compound will fly all over when you turn on the machine.

When using a power polisher, wear safety goggles and a dust-type respirator. Make sure you grip the polisher firmly at all times, and keep the electric cord out of the way. (Air-powered polishers are considerably safer.)

Apply compound to a 2 by 2-ft. area of the car with a 2- to 4-in. brush. Don't apply compound to the polishing wheel. Use only as much as needed for uniform distribution. Spread the compound over the area with the pad before turning on the machine.

Turn on the polisher and stroke the area to be compounded left to right and right to left. Don't push. Let the weight of the machine do the work.

When moving to the right, lift the right half of the pad a bit (see Fig. 1). Lift the left edge of the pad when moving to the left. Overlap the stroke directly above or below by about half its width. Once you've compounded the area moving in a horizontal direction, do the same thing moving up and down. Again, slightly lift the edge of the pad that is toward the direction of the stroke. Overlap as before.

Four passes over the area, two horizontally and two vertically, should be sufficient. If the compound is all used up before you're done, you didn't use enough. If there's a bunch left over, you used too much.

Pad cleaning

As you're compounding, clean the pad from time to time. Lay the machine on the ground and turn it on. Hold it firmly and scrape compound buildup from the pad by applying a dull screwdriver blade to it as it spins. Move the screwdriver from the outer edge of the pad toward its center.

Dull paint can sometimes be refurbished with a compounding treatment, either by hand or machine.

1 When compounding with a polishing machine, tilt the pad at a 10° angle from the surface, with the lifted side in the direction of travel.

2 Use a sanding block and 80-grit paper for the first sanding of a nicked area. Follow that with the 240-grit, and then wet-sand with 400-grit.

After you've done all areas that can be reached with the polisher, remove masking tape from raised edges and corners and compound these spots by hand, as well as any other areas that cannot be reached easily with the machine.

Repairing chips and nicks

Perhaps the toughest part of repairing chips and nicks is deciding how you want to do it. Small nicks can be repaired "temporarily" in just a few minutes (more on that later). But if you want to restore the area to like-new condition, complex techniques are recommended for the various types of finishes used by carmakers today.

If you don't have a spray gun and compressor and don't want to rent one, you'll have to have a body shop finish up the job once you have repaired the nick. However, you can still save a lot of money by doing the body repair yourself.

Don't try to refinish part of a panel with touch-up spray cans. You won't get a good match. On a small panel that is not particularly visible, such as the lower half of a rear quarter that is split by a trim line, you may decide to have a go at refinishing with touch-up spray. The results may not please you, however.

To produce a professional-looking nick repair you'll need a sanding block, 80-, 240- and 400-grit sandpaper, zinc chromate primer, finishing primer, wax-removing solvent, a tack cloth, glazing putty and a rubber contour squeegee. You should be able to purchase all of these products at any well-stocked auto parts store. If you can't find them there, you can try a parts store that specializes in body shop supplies. You'll also find a knowledgeable body work oriented counterman at most such establishments who will usually be willing to help you with problems.

Before you begin the repair of a nick, clean the panel with a wax-removing solvent. Wipe it dry.

Using 80-grit sandpaper on a hand sanding block, sand the area until the edges of the nick or chip have been smoothed out and the surface is totally free of rust (Fig. 2). Hold the sanding block flat against the panel and apply moderate pressure. Work with a back-and-forth motion over an area that is sufficiently large to allow complete feathering of surrounding paint.

Continue working until you can't feel the edges of the nick. Insert a piece of 240-grit paper and sand until the surface is free of deep sanding scratches, then wet-sand lightly with 400-grit paper until the surface is satin smooth. Wash with water, dry with a cloth rag and then wipe the entire panel with a tack cloth.

Next, mask any trim near the repair area or the edges of any adjoining panels that are close enough to be threatened by overspray (Fig. 3). Then coat the bare metal and the sanded paint with zinc chromate primer. Hold the spray can parallel to the surface and at a distance of about 10 in. Move the can back and forth, keeping it the same distance from the surface at all times.

Once the primer has dried, put a lump of glazing putty on the edge of the contour squeegee and apply it to the prime-coated repair area (Fig. 4). Apply with moderate pressure, move quickly, and in one direction only. Don't attempt a second pass with the squeegee. If you don't like the results of your first attempt, remove all the glazing putty and try it again with a fresh lump of putty.

Finishing putty repairs

Let the putty dry overnight, or as specified on the product label, then sand with 240-grit paper in a sanding block until the repair area is completely level with the surrounding area. Feel for any high spots and sand some more if necessary. Inspect the puttied area carefully for pits, low spots or rough areas, and apply glazing putty again if necessary, resanding as above.

Finally, insert a piece of 400-grit paper in the sanding block and wet-sand the area until it is satin smooth. Flush the area with lots of water as you sand to avoid leaving scratches.

Wash the panel with water, dry it and wipe it with the tack cloth. Then apply a final finish primer that is compatible with the color coat that will be applied.

Temporary touch-up

If your car is nicked and chipped but you don't want to get involved in a repair that will necessitate the refinishing of a panel, you can do a temporary touch-up.

Buy a can of touch-up paint that is an exact match for the color of your car (vehicle type and year as well as the name of the color are listed on the can of paint). The best type is the brush-applied touch-up paint, but this is sometimes hard to find. You'll probably have to settle for a spray can.

Remove all rust from the nick area, but don't attempt to feather the edges. A pocket knife used as a scraper works well for this.

Once all the rust has been removed, spray some of the paint into the cover of the spray can and let it sit for about five minutes until it thickens a bit. (If you have bottled brush-type paint, use it as it comes.) Use a matchstick to apply the paint. Dip the end of the match that is not coated with sulphur in the paint and dab it onto the chipped area. Try to apply a heavy coat on the first attempt to completely fill the nick. Make sure that you have covered all of the bare metal.

In conspicuous places, this type of repair won't produce very satisfactory results, but it is far better than simply spraying touch-up paint over an unrepaired chip. In less conspicuous places, it will serve quite well to protect the metal until a more extensive repair can be completed.

Repairing scratches

Deep scratches can be repaired following the same procedures recommended for repair of chips and nicks. And, of course, surface scratches that have no depth to speak of can usually be removed with rubbing compound. Scratches that fall in between— not deep enough to have reached bare metal but too deep to be removed with rubbing compound—can be repaired with glazing putty.

You'll need glazing putty, finishing primer, a tack cloth, a squeegee, masking paper and tape, 240- and 400-grit sandpaper, rags and wax-remover solvent.

Clean the scratched area with the solvent, then lightly sand the scratch with the 240-grit paper. Fold the paper into quarters or smaller, and sand only enough to slightly roughen the area directly around the scratch. Sand evenly along the length of the scratch. Don't concentrate on one area.

Wash the area with a wet rag, dry it and then wipe it with the tack cloth. Apply a dab of the putty to the edge of your squeegee and smoothly wipe it across the scratch, making one pass next to the other, all along the length of the scratch. As before, don't attempt a second pass. If you're not satisfied with your first attempt, remove the putty and try again.

Allow the putty to dry overnight or as specified, then sand the area with 240-grit paper on a sanding block. Sand evenly to avoid creating low spots. Wash the area with water, dry it and wipe with the tack cloth.

Don't be alarmed if there are low spots or if parts of the scratch are not completely filled with putty. Simply reapply another coat of the putty as before. Repeat the application of putty as many times as necessary to effect a smooth repair.

Once you're satisfied that the repair is perfect, sand with 400-grit paper in a sanding block, wetting the paper and the repair area with water (Fig. 5). Keep splashing water on as you sand to flush away sanding residue. Use long strokes and sand until the

3 After the nick has been sanded smooth, mask adjoining areas. Then coat nick with a rust-inhibiting primer.

4 After applying a rust-inhibiting primer, coat the area with glazing putty, using a flexible squeegee. Apply the putty with a single stroke.

area is perfectly smooth. Then rinse, dry and wipe with the tack cloth.

To complete the repair, coat the area with the right type of finishing primer, depending on what type of paint will be used to color coat (Fig. 6).

As we pointed out earlier, spot repair of automotive finishes can be complicated. To find out what type of color coat or primer must be used, you'll have to visit a bodyshop supply store. Before you do, make sure you know the color code for your vehicle. You can find this code on the body identification plate.

Each of the various carmakers has its own name for this plate. On GM cars, other than Corvette, the body number plate is under the hood on the front or upper surface of the firewall shroud. On Corvettes, it's on the dashboard brace below the glove box or on the left door hinge pillar.

On Fords the vehicle certification label is on the lock face panel of the driver's door.

On Chrysler products, the body code plate is under the hood on or near the left front fenderwell, or on the radiator support.

On some cars, it's quite obvious which of the many numbers on the body plate is the paint code. On other cars, you'll need the assistance of a factory service manual or the counterman in the body supply store. If you have to, make a sketch of the whole tag and let him pick out the correct paint code.

5 When the glazing putty has dried, wet-sand with 400-grit paper. Splash water on the area as you sand to flush away sludge and keep the paper fresh.

6 Once the surface has been sanded to a shiny smoothness, apply a finishing primer that will be compatible with the final color coat.

Primer and color coat

Once the code has been determined, the man in the body supply store can check it against the color chart for your year and model car. The chart will tell him exactly what type of finishing primer and color coat should be used. For most types of automotive finish, the final color is applied in a number of coats. The first coat is sprayed so it covers an area only as large as the spot repair. Each subsequent coat covers a slightly larger area.

For some types of paint as many as six coats are necessary. Spray gun pressure usually is altered for the final coats. This technique blends the new paint into the old.

Don't attempt to do this yourself without specific instructions for your type of finish. You might be able to get instructional literature from the auto body supply store. Various books are also available.

Remember that patience is the key to successful body and paint work.

If you apply paint haphazardly, your car won't look any better than it did before the damage was repaired. If you concentrate sanding efforts in one area in an attempt to remove an imperfection quickly, you will create a low spot. And if you sand before filler, glaze or primer has had a chance to dry properly, you'll create a real mess.

Tuning Up Your Air Conditioner

PETE WARREN

■ IT'S THE MIDDLE of summer, that brief time of year when the $600 you spent for air conditioning is justified. It's also the time when most A/C shops have long waits for appointments.

Air conditioning is not one of those "forget-it-'til-it-fails" systems. You should give it a bit of periodic maintenance. Checks whenever you feel A/C performance is below par, you may be able to avoid some problems and correct others.

Obviously, you're not anxious to do a lot of work on the A/C (or any other part of the car) during the hottest time of year. Fortunately, an inspection won't take more than 10 minutes. Much you can do is even less time-consuming.

Begin with a look at the front of the condenser (the finned, tubular part in front of the radiator). It should be clean, so air can flow freely through it and the radiator behind. If it's plugged with road film, leaves, bugs and so on, clean it with a soft brush and a solution of detergent and water. Be gentle so you don't bend the fins and reduce airflow through the unit.

Next, look at the drive belts. Inspect the A/C belt for signs of deterioration. Check belt tension by pushing down with your thumb midway between the pulleys. It should deflect no more than ¾ inch. Do the same for the water pump fan belt. If it's slipping, the engine will run hot and the coolant flowing through the radiator will be much warmer than normal. The radiator and condenser are so close that excess heat from the radiator will be transferred to the condenser and raise the temperature of the refrigerant gas inside. As a result, A/C performance will suffer. In fact, anything that reduces cooling system performance will affect A/C performance. On front-wheel-drive vehicles, make sure the electric cooling fan switches on when the A/C comes on.

Basic checks

If you feel A/C performance is below normal, make a series of simple checks. First, while a helper turns on the system, watch the compressor. You should see the magnetic clutch on its front hub lock onto the pulley with a slight, but obvious, move-ment. If it engages, run the engine at fast idle; set the blower fan on high; the A/C lever on max, high, or inside; and the temperature lever on cold. With the car parked far from any wall that might block the flow of air to the condenser, open the hood to min-imize engine compartment temperature. Close all doors and windows and allow five minutes for the system to stabilize.

Then insert a thermometer in a center air vent on the dash and take a temperature reading. There are manufacturer's specifications for air temperature, but if you don't have them, this rule of thumb will pinpoint obviously bad performance: The air should be 28°-30° F. below the outside air temperature. (If the weather is humid, the temperature differential is less.)

If the temperature of the air coming out of the register is right, your system is doing its job. If the system is blowing cool but not-cool-enough air, make a pressure check.

To check system pressures, you need a pressure gauge. Although pros have elaborate equipment, they also use inexpensive testers in the $8-$20 range for quick checks. Such testers, sold in auto parts stores, can be used on any system with Schrader (tire type) test fittings. All U.S. cars except a few Ford and AMC products have these fittings. The inexpen-sive testers resemble tire gauges and are used in the same way.

Locate the two pressure test fittings, which are usually in one of three places:

1. On many cars they're near the compressor.

2. You might also find them in the tubing that connects the condenser, compressor and evaporator. (The evaporator is a box-shaped part that is found in the dashboard ductwork or protruding from the fire-wall side of the dashboard ductwork.)

3. They might also be found on the accumulator, a cylindrical part found on some systems.

The A/C has high- and low-pressure fittings. On a few older Ford and Chrysler products, you may find three fittings, two of which are for low pressure. On these Fords, measure pressure at the fittings nearest the compressor. On Chrysler products with three fit-tings, ignore the one on the cylinder head of the compressor.

Remove the screw caps from the fittings, run the engine at fast idle, and turn on the A/C, setting the controls as you did for a temperature check. After allowing five minutes for the system to stabilize, take your pressure readings.

Compare the readings with factory specs, which can be found in a general service manual. Typically, you should get a reading of about 140 p.s.i. to 250 p.s.i. on one fitting, and 24 to 35 p.s.i. on the other

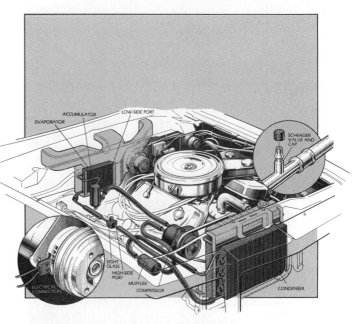

A typical A/C system. Shown in detail are a refrigerant charging port and the compressor clutch electrical connector.

fitting. On some Fords the low-side reading may be as low as 10 to 20 p.s.i. Again, to be sure, you'll have to compare your results to specs. When ambi-ent temperatures are high, expect the system pres-sure to be near the high end of the range.

If both readings are 15 percent or more below spec, a minor loss of refrigerant gas is indicated. This is quite likely with cars at least 3 years old. The minor loss is the result of normal leakage over the years. Adding some refrigerant should restore the usual performance.

Before you do this, however, double-check the sight glass. Many older systems and some current ones have a sight glass—a little window in the refrigerant tubing. The sight glass is usually on the receiver, a cylindrical can connected to the condens-er by tubing. Don't confuse the receiver with the similarly shaped part called the accumulator, which is used on many current models and is connected by tubing to the compressor. The accumulator doesn't have a sight glass.

With the system running for five minutes, look at the sight glass. If the system has a cycling compres-sor, a small amount of bubbling in the sight glass is normal during an off-to-on cycle. You can tell if your system has a cycling compressor by watching the front compressor clutch. If it's a cycling system, you'll see the clutch disengage and engage periodi-cally once the system has stabilized. After the clutch engages, however, the bubbling should stop until it cycles off again.

If the system is the type that does not cycle the clutch, you should see no bubbles. If you see con-

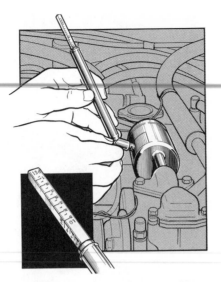

Above: A quick check of A/C system pressures can be made with this inexpensive pressure gauge. Available in most auto parts stores, the tester resembles a tire gauge. Below: A sight glass, found on some systems, checks refrigerant level and aeration.

READING A SIGHT GLASS

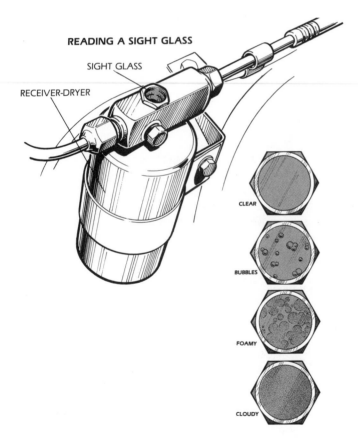

SIGHT GLASS

RECEIVER-DRYER

CLEAR

BUBBLES

FOAMY

CLOUDY

tinuous bubbling and performance is just so-so, the system is low on refrigerant gas.

If the system doesn't have a sight glass and you don't have gauges, you can check some A/C systems for refrigerant loss with your hands. Just grasp the refrigerant tubing where it disappears into the duct-

work, one hand on the thick tubing, the other on the thin tubing.

With the system running, the thick tubing should be somewhat cooler than the thin tube. If the thin tube is colder than the thick one, feel the thin tube about a foot farther away, toward the compressor. If it's warm, the system is probably low on refrigerant.

This test can't be performed on all A/C systems, but it is useful on many of the recently produced cycling-clutch systems.

Adding refrigerant

There are many do-it-yourself kits for adding refrigerant, and they come with complete instructions. Just be sure to connect the hose from the refrigerant can to the low-pressure test fitting. On most GM and Ford products, the hose in the kit will thread only onto the low-pressure fitting, so you can't make a mistake.

Hold the can upright while the system is running. Rub the can with your hands or place it in a pan of warm tap water (no hotter than 125° F.) to speed flow into the system. If the 13- to 16-ounce refrigerant can included in the typical kit raises pressures to nearly normal, you may add a bit more to the system with a second can. Check pressures as you go along and stop adding refrigerant when low-side readings are within spec and high-side pressures are over the minimum. Whenever you stop charging with refrigerant (either for a pressure test or because you're finished), shut the dispensing valve on the refrigerant can first, then disconnect the hose from the test fitting.

If the addition of refrigerant restores performance for only a brief period, you may have a bad leak in the system. Let a pro check it. Do the same if the pressures are low on a relatively new car.

Ductwork problems

If the system passes pressure and other tests, but the air from the registers is warm, perhaps the problem is in the ductwork. Operate the temperature control lever and see if there is any change. If not, turn off the A/C and turn on the heater. See if operating the temperature lever makes any difference in heat output. If not, perhaps the flap door it controls is stuck. Or the cable may have come off the flap door (which mixes heated and cooled air). On some cars, you can reach the cable connection at the flap door under the dash and check, freeing up a stuck flap or reconnecting the cable.

If there is no substantial volume of air flowing through the registers, the blower may not be working. Sometimes the problem is as simple as a blown fuse or two. Or, it could be in the fan switch, which is easy to remove for testing and replacement on many late-model cars. Even the blower motor is easy to change on most late models. Test the blower by hot-wiring it directly to the battery with jumper cables.

A/C won't come on

If the A/C won't come on at all, a common reason is that the refrigerant has leaked out and a low-pressure protection switch has opened to keep the compressor clutch circuit from activating. With the system off, pressure in a high or low fitting should be at least 60 p.s.i. If not, have a pro recharge the system. If the pressures are normal, check the fusebox for a blown fuse and the compressor for a loose electrical connection.

On many GM cars (late 1971 through 1976 except Vega and Chevette, plus 1977-78 Toronado-Eldorado), there is a compressor clutch fuse that can prevent the clutch from engaging if it fails. Pull the fuse out of its holder and connect a jumper across the B- and C-terminals of the holder. If the compressor now runs when the system is turned on, the fuse is defective and should be replaced. This fuse is supposed to blow only when system pressures are very low, but it may also fail if engine compartment temperatures get too high.

Many GM cars are equipped with a compressor clutch fuse that will prevent the clutch from engaging if it fails. Connect a jumper across the B- and C-terminal of the holder to test for a bad fuse. If the compressor runs, fuse was defective.

If both low- and high-side pressure readings are 15 percent or more below specification, the system has lost refrigerant. A minor loss of refrigerant is quite likely with cars that are at least three years old. The loss is the result of normal leakage. Adding refrigerant will improve performance.

With the engine running at fast idle, A/C system at maximum setting, and all doors and windows closed, let system stabilize for five minutes. Then take the temperature reading at the center vent. Air temperature should be about 28° to 30° below the outside temperature during normal conditions.

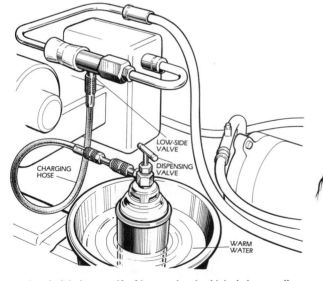

A typical do-it-yourself refrigerant charging kit includes a small can of refrigerant, a charging hose and a dispensing valve. The charging hose must be connected to system's low-side charging valve. A pan of warm water (less than 125° F.) can help move refrigerant.

Carefully clean the condenser of your A/C system with a soft brush and a solution of mild detergent and water.

Index

METRIC CONVERSION

Conversion factors can be carried so far they become impractical. In cases below where an entry is exact it is followed by an asterisk (*). Where considerable rounding off has taken place, the entry is followed by a + or a – sign.

CUSTOMARY TO METRIC

Linear Measure

inches	millimeters
1/16	1.5875*
1/8	3.2
3/16	4.8
1/4	6.35*
5/16	7.9
3/8	9.5
7/16	11.1
1/2	12.7*
9/16	14.3
5/8	15.9
11/16	17.5
3/4	19.05*
13/16	20.6
7/8	22.2
15/16	23.8
1	25.4*

inches	centimeters
1	2.54*
2	5.1
3	7.6
4	10.2
5	12.7*
6	15.2
7	17.8
8	20.3
9	22.9
10	25.4*
11	27.9
12	30.5

feet	centimeters	meters
1	30.48*	.3048*
2	61	.61
3	91	.91
4	122	1.22
5	152	1.52
6	183	1.83
7	213	2.13
8	244	2.44
9	274	2.74
10	305	3.05
50	1524*	15.24*
100	3048*	30.48*

1 yard = .9144* meters

1 rod = 5.0292* meters

1 mile = 1.6 kilometers

1 nautical mile = 1.852* kilometers

Fluid Measure

(Milliliters [ml] and cubic centimeters [cc or cu cm] are equivalent, but it is customary to use milliliters for liquids.)

1 cu in = 16.39 ml
1 fl oz = 29.6 ml
1 cup = 237 ml
1 pint = 473 ml
1 quart = 946 ml
= .946 liters
1 gallon = 3785 ml
= 3.785 liters

Formula (exact):
fluid ounces × 29.573 529 562 5*
= milliliters

Weights

ounces	grams
1	28.3
2	56.7
3	85
4	113
5	142
6	170
7	198
8	227
9	255
10	283
11	312
12	340
13	369
14	397
15	425
16	454

Formula (exact):
ounces × 28.349 523 125* = grams

pounds	kilograms
1	.45
2	.9
3	1.4
4	1.8
5	2.3
6	2.7
7	3.2
8	3.6
9	4.1
10	4.5

1 short ton (2000 lbs) = 907 kilograms (kg)

Formula (exact):
pounds × .453 592 37* = kilograms

Volume

1 cu in = 16.39 cubic centimeters (cc)
1 cu ft = 28 316.7 cc
1 bushel = 35 239.1 cc
1 peck = 8 809.8 cc

Area

1 sq in = 6.45 sq cm
1 sq ft = 929 sq cm
= .093 sq meters
1 sq yd = .84 sq meters
1 acre = 4 046.9 sq meters
= .404 7 hectares
1 sq mile = 2 589 988 sq meters
= 259 hectares
= 2.589 9 sq kilometers

Kitchen Measure

1 teaspoon = 4.93 milliliters (ml)
1 Tablespoon = 14.79 milliliters (ml)

Miscellaneous

1 British thermal unit (Btu) (mean) = 1 055.9 joules
1 calorie (mean) = 4.19 joules
1 horsepower = 745.7 watts
= .75 kilowatts
caliber (diameter of a firearm's bore in hundredths of an inch) = :254 millimeters (mm)
1 atmosphere pressure = 101 325* pascals (newtons per sq meter)
1 pound per square inch (psi) = 6 895 pascals
1 pound per square foot = 47.9 pascals
1 knot = 1.85 kilometers per hour
25 miles per hour = 40.2 kilometers per hour
50 miles per hour = 80.5 kilometers per hour
75 miles per hour = 120.7 kilometers per hour